PR99.
C76   Cooper   68-1050
La   Late harvest
1952

JUL **2000**

Date Due

		JUN 2004	
		JUL X X 2015	
	JUN 09		

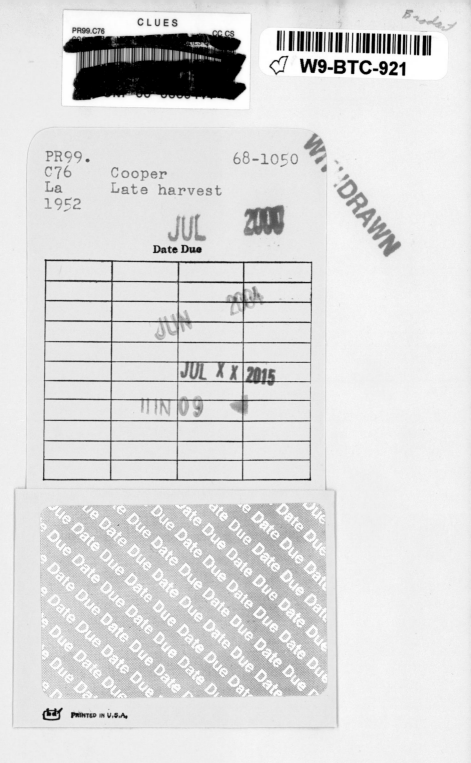

PRINTED IN U.S.A.

Late Harvest

LATE HARVEST

Sketches of Cook, Adams, and
Kleist; The College President;
with Philosophical Reviews,
and Papers on Coleridge,
Wordsworth, and Byron

By LANE COOPER

PROFESSOR EMERITUS OF THE ENGLISH LANGUAGE
AND LITERATURE AT CORNELL UNIVERSITY

And gladly wolde he lerne,
and gladly teche.

CORNELL UNIVERSITY PRESS

ITHACA, NEW YORK

PRINTED IN THE UNITED STATES OF AMERICA BY THE

VAIL-BALLOU PRESS, INC., BINGHAMTON, NEW YORK

To my Friend and Former Pupil

Dr. HARRY GOLD

Eminent Physician, Investigator, and Philanthropist

This book is dedicated for his

constant loyalty, and kindness

Preface

THIS volume appears through the generosity of my pupil and friend, John D. Hertz, Jr., who has again made possible a reissue of books of mine that otherwise would no longer enjoy the light of publication. And the volume is dedicated to another friend and pupil, Dr. Gold, whose name Mr. Hertz desired to join with his and mine in an undertaking which the Cornell University Press deems right and proper. Mr. Hertz and Dr. Gold have done more than words of mine could ever reveal to ease for me the burden of advancing years, and to delay perhaps the stealthy approach of that which the old Adam in us all is prone to dread. Of Mr. Hertz and his donation Dr. Gold has said: 'It was an act by which his name will be firmly imbedded in the hearts of generations of students to come.'

The books which Mr. Hertz has now enabled the Cornell University Press to issue or reissue are these: (1) *Theories of Style,* to appear in a new, revised and enlarged, edition, which will henceforth be known as *The Art of the Writer;* originally published in 1907 by the Macmillan Company of New York. (2) *Aristotle on the Art of Poetry, an Amplified Version with Supplementary Illustrations;* originally published in 1913 by Ginn and Company in Boston, later by Harcourt, Brace and Company of New York, more recently by the Cornell University Press in Ithaca. (3) *The Greek Genius and its Influence;* originally published in 1917 by the Yale University Press, New Haven. (4) The present volume, this *Late Harvest;* a new undertaking, though made up of materials reprinted from sources both older and more recent. (5) *An Aristotelian Theory of*

Comedy is included in the program. This book was printed about thirty years ago at Weimar, Germany, with funds supplied by me, in part with the help of a grant from the Heckscher Foundation at Cornell University; it was published in 1922 at Halle, Oxford, and New York. Since the bombing of Weimar, the record there cannot be traced. The copies that were taken in New York, or the remainder of them, came from Harcourt, Brace and Company to Ithaca, where all were finally sold off by the Cornell University Press; the book has seemingly become very rare in the United States, where latterly stray copies can be purchased only at fanciful prices. But lately, unexpectedly, we have learned of copies of the book that have survived in Germany and England, enough of them, when they are transferred to Ithaca, to make reissuing the work unnecessary in the next few months at least.

Whatever value any of these books may have, far more important is the affectionate personal motive of Mr. Hertz in his donation. And more important yet is the principle involved. In American education there is nothing at present more urgently needed in the way of money than the support of scholarly research and publication, help for the kind of books that can not, without pecuniary aid, be brought to light, to keep the life of the spirit of our nation pulsing. It is our hope that this beginning will not go unnoticed, that these words will help to bring a permanent and growing fund for the publication in years to come of scholarly works at Cornell University. The donors are likely to begin a movement that will never end.

As for the opening article in this collection, my gratitude to the great scholar I have tried once more to honor here is in a measure known to all who ever knew me well; and for the second item, my friendship with my noble colleague Adams, unbroken by his shift from Ithaca to Washington and the Folger Shakespeare Library, must be known to many others, certainly among those who have attended Cornell University. With Father Kleist, who died (on April 28, 1949) not many months after my tribute to him had been published, the case is different. We met not more than twice in all, and yet were drawn together from the first, and through frequent letters and exchanges otherwise of an affectionate scholarly sort, at length over many years, we came to be as closely knit as if we saw each other every day. Thrice in life it has so happened to me—with Father Kleist; with the illustrious Jacques Maritain, to whom I have just dared to dedicate a booklet on Rhythms in the English Bible; and with Nathaniel Micklem, Principal of Mansfield College, Oxford, author of that great contemporary poem, *The Labyrinth*. Among acquaintances of like age, these three (to me) stand out as friends too seldom met, and yet within a circle of affinities that embraces my lifelong, dear, familiar friend Charles Osgood, and many, many pupils who never have ceased to cheer me by maintaining through their letters a relation with their teacher 'nearer than that of aunt or niece'—as the poet of *Pearl* describes it. Truly the author of this Late Harvest has been blessed in one main element of happiness, a wealth of friends.

Let me also say a word or two on the care and kindness of the University Publisher, Mr. Victor Reynolds, Manager of the Cornell University Press, in particular for his solicitude in carrying out the wishes of Mr. Hertz, and my wishes too, in a multiple and exacting enterprise.

No chronological order has been attempted for the items in this present volume; one of the last in it was the first in time, and the very last, my latest speech in public; the aim has mainly been to bring together things, where possible, that are alike, or have some natural association of ideas in them, and to have a natural opening and a suitable close. In the papers on Coleridge and Wordsworth there is something of a chronological arrangement. The longish article called The Power of the Eye in Coleridge was put in when we found we had the means to print it, and because readers of it in the past have seemed to like it better than its author does. It still throws light upon the poet.

In the review that deals with Father Kleist a serious damage that arose from the good, but mistaken, intent of an interfering editor has been repaired; my statement on the method Homer followed in the Iliad and Odyssey with respect to legends of the gods did not originate with the amiable, now lamented John A. Scott, but with me; it is a view of some importance, as I think, and probably worth notice now as an interpretation new but true. Where possible, in fact, I have aimed to correct the content of the articles here reprinted, and —a difficult matter—to normalize the usage in detail. In this attempt I have had loyal help.

And so let us end our thanks to the Cornell University Press with an expression of gratitude to yet another of my pupils, Fatanitza Schmidt, for her assistance and good will in preparing copy for the printer. Now add the name of Philip Nolan, again in Ithaca to finish off his doctoral dissertation, who has given me essential help by reading all the proofs of this as well as a preceding volume, *The Art of the Writer.*

Some periodical publications and other sources from which the contents of the volume are extracted no longer survive, or were never 'copyright.' Otherwise, in every case where any question of rights could be raised, I have sought the requisite permission to reproduce each article of mine that is here reprinted, and have added words that indicate the said permission in the proper places.

LANE COOPER

Ithaca, New York,
May 15, 1952.

x

Contents

CONTENTS

Albert Stanburrough Cook[1]

(1853-1927)

PROFESSOR COOK died peacefully at his home in New Haven on the first day of September, a few hours after he had been conveyed thither from his summer home in Vermont. It had been hoped that the sea-level would decrease the cardiac strain from which he suffered; but this was not to be. The loss will be felt by the Mediæval Academy; a loss will be felt on every side, and by scholars in every land. Yet his influence will continue potent in the years to come.

Perhaps the most striking aspect of his notable scholarly life was the ever-fresh productive activity of his latter years, which saw much of his best work on Chaucerian problems, and on the background of Old-English poetry. His intellectual, his spiritual, energy was amazing to the end.

A telegram asks me to write a few words on his service to the study of the Middle Ages. First of all, that service, very great as it was, must be seen in due perspective. In literary and linguistic scholarship, in the kind of history that makes the human past move in living detail before us, his interests were all-embracing. He saw the whole. He also saw the parts precisely. From childhood a lover of the best literature, he was first trained as a mathematician; yet his earliest publication was a rendering from the German of Uhland. He took up the study of Greek by himself, and shortly acquired a knowledge, which became far-reaching, of the ancient classics. His intimate knowledge of the Bible and

[1] Published in *Speculum* 2 (1927). 498–501. Reprinted by permission.

Biblical studies can be but mentioned. His investigation of the Biblical influence in Old and Middle English, and his spirited chapter in the *Cambridge History of English Literature,* on the Authorized Version, are alike well known. The range of his publications includes work on Greek and Latin authors, on Dante, Petrarch, and Boccaccio, on Spenser, Shakespeare, Milton, Gray, Tennyson, Browning, Bacon, Arnold, De Quincey, and Ruskin. His courses in Ruskin and Dante will not be forgotten by those who attended them.

Perhaps in his middle period, and by those who did not know him well, he was often regarded as only a student of 'Anglo-Saxon.' His insistence upon the use, rather, of the term 'Old English' marks his inclusive view of our language and literature from Cædmon to Kipling. *Puck of Pook's Hill* was one of his favorite books. And those who knew him better were well aware of his philosophic tendency never to separate the particular from the general, or the one from the many. Hence the training he gave his pupils—and he was greatest as a teacher—in philosophic method as applied to the study of English. Hence also the training he gave them in the principles of poetry, from those of Plato and Aristotle down. No summary of his work should omit his address, *The Province of English Philology,* or his editions, prepared for use with classes, of Sidney, Addison, Shelley, Hunt, and Newman, or his Horatian volume entitled *The Art of Poetry.*

But he certainly laid stress upon mediæval studies, and therewith plunged his students *in medias res* as a wholesome thing for their literary perspective. For them he adapted Sievers' *Old English Grammar,* and produced *A First Book in Old English,* which is a model for an introduction into any language. Latterly he opened the treasures of Middle English to the public eye through his fascinating *Literary Middle English Reader;* since that appeared, its subject-matter never again can be dry as dust, as it was to so many in the days before.

And what could be said in narrow space of his editions of the Old English *Judith* and *The Dream of the Rood?* In that of the *Christ* he applied the method of classical scholarship to the elucidation of a native masterpiece, setting a standard of editorial workmanship which has hardly been surpassed in his own sub-sequent edition of the *Elene, Phœnix,* and *Physiologus.*

Or what can be said of his study of the mediæval crosses, or of his work on and for concordances? But where shall we end the list? The amount of valuable work he did himself can partly be gaged from the *Bibliography* of his writings (then numbering more than 300) which was privately issued in 1923; like the simi-lar bibliography for Gaston Paris, it is a document for all mediævalists. The extent of the work which he stimulated others to do, whether by correspondence or yet more through constant and intimate relations with his graduate students, can never be known; an inkling of it may be gained from the volumes—some seventy-five of them—in his series, the *Yales Studies in English.* This series, begun thirty years ago, he edited single-handed, and with meticulous care; he was reading proofs of at least two forth-coming volumes in the past summer while in the grasp of a mor-tal ailment. Many of the volumes, needless to say, are on mediæ-val subjects; editions, syntactical studies, translations from the Latin, are included.

He lavished himself on his students. His scholarly and friendly correspondence was very large. How could he find time for all he did? Certainly in latter years he almost never worked at night. But, rising betimes, he worked with extreme rapidity, with tire-less industry, and with an artistic method. For those who can understand, he doubtless bared his secret in a fine address, *The Artistic Ordering of Life.*

Professor Cook hated folly and fraud, but was sympathetic with all honest endeavor. He was unwearied in his helpfulness, resourceful for himself and others, cheerful, and, above all, cou-rageous and alert. There was a quickening power in his first sug-gestions, there was a quickening power in his final criticism. His quiet, deep-seated Christianity rendered him peculiarly sympa-thetic with the better side of the Middle Ages. He showed a prompt enthusiasm for the Mediæval Academy, and soon became a valued contributor to *Speculum.* He was elected a Fellow of the Academy on April 23, 1926.

He was born in Montville, New Jersey, on March 6, 1853; graduated from the Latin-scientific course at Rutgers College in 1872; was tutor in mathematics there for the following year; taught at Freehold, New Jersey, from 1873 until 1877; studied abroad under Wülker, Sweet, and Sievers in two periods, 1877–78 and 1881–82; and put his mark upon the teaching of English at Johns Hopkins in 1879–81. On returning from Europe, he went to the University of California, where he remained until 1889. From then on, he was active at Yale, shortly as Professor of the English Language and Literature, until his retirement in 1921. He did not retire to be idle.

On short notice, and at a distance from his books, it is difficult in limited space to write fittingly of his many and varied gifts to learning; but it is not unfitting that this tribute should proceed from Greensboro, Vermont, where for years the happiest seasons of his life were spent, and where so much of his constructive work was accomplished; and it is a faithful hand that writes these lines.

Joseph Quincy Adams[1]

(1881-1946)

HAIL and fare well, my Friend! Fare well in no pagan sense. 'Don't let them expose my body when I am gone,' said he (in effect), 'for I shall not be there.' So we hope to see each other again ere long, with all our good friends who have gone before us.

Joseph Quincy Adams was born on March 23, 1881, at Greenville, South Carolina, and died suddenly, of a chronic cardiac ailment, in the city of Washington on November 10, 1946. He was the son of the Reverend Joseph Quincy Adams and Mamie Fouchée Davis Adams, and was one of five children, three sons by this first marriage of his father, and two by the widowed father's second marriage; he had no sisters. He himself was happily married on January 29, 1931, to Helen Banks, of Ithaca, New York; she died on September 14, 1935, leaving one child, Helen. After his great bereavement, he said to me concerning himself in that loss: 'I had not known that any one could suffer so.' As evinced by his sorrows and his joys, and by his scholarly work, his two most eminent qualities were the constant strength of his affection and friendship, and the clarity of his productive mind.

As for his ease in composition, where others labored for a fine order, in this point he had no trouble at all. Once ready to write, he wrote with habitual pleasure; he did not suffer from a hardship common among teachers of 'English,' who mostly wish to

---

[1] Published in *Joseph Quincy Adams, Memorial Studies,* The Folger Shakespeare Library, Washington, 1948, pp. 5–11. Reprinted by permission.

write better than they can. He prepared himself, had the parts and the whole of his subject in his hand, then flowed with a natural (and beautiful) facility. Things came, and fell into their places as he wrote. With him revision called for no major changes.

I speak of this matter the more readily, because it was my good fortune to be in close touch with him almost from the day when he came to Cornell University, a year or so after my arrival there. With no great disparity in age, he being by five years the younger, we promptly took to each other, became close friends, and neighbors, and companions at table, until close to the end of his career in Ithaca, when he married and left in the year 1931 to direct the work of the Folger Shakespeare Library in Washington. After that, we remained in touch through the frequent exchange of letters, and jokes clipped from newspapers, and through visits, more often by his visits to Ithaca, where he had a host of friends and had relations-in-law. Among his friends I will mention Professor Horace L. Jones and his family, Professor Madison Bentley and his, Dean Robert M. Ogden, Mrs. Ogden, and their children, and the friends with whom I still live, Professor James Hutton and his mother, Mrs. Elizabeth Hutton. He liked our buckwheat cakes and maple syrup, and also greatly enjoyed the ample hospitality of the University Librarian, Dr. Otto Kinkeldey and Mrs. Kinkeldey. Adams did justice to good cooking. He enjoyed his pipe, too, and fragrant tobacco, kept alight with innumerable matches—when, for example, he invented stories, impromptu and serial as well, for young children, little girls above all.

Our long association was of the utmost value to me; without false modesty I may say that it was of value to us both. On occasion we disputed with a little heat that commonly ended in smiles. We never had a quarrel. From an early date we formed the habit of reading each other's work before publication. For years neither of us ever wrote a line (so to say) for the printer without criticism from the other before the 'copy' was sent off. As the years went on, we spent less time in preliminary compliments, but quickly got down to friendly help, pointing out what, if anything, we found amiss in evidence or style, and wherein the composition might be brought nearer to euphony, good usage,

6

and truth. We always read each other's proofs. We encouraged each other. We did not think that we could be good teachers without filling our minds beforehand, or proving our faith by works. And gladly would we learn, and gladly teach. Every scholar needs a friend of that sort, one who is not afraid to give faithful wounds, and is magnanimous enough to profit by the like.

Did Adams have the defects of his virtues (and vice versa), or any defects at all? No scholar on earth is perfect; scholars must support each other by pursuing their special interests, making the most of the talents and training they have received. But if it is seemly and right for me to say so, Adams, in spite of his good Classical training in the South, nevertheless somewhat underrated the Attic drama, and in particular, when I saw most of him, hardly perceived the excellence of Sophocles in depicting tragic character and in the subtle construction of powerful dramatic speeches. Accordingly, he did not always draw the line upon which Edmund Burke insisted, between the 'felicities' and the 'infelicities' of Shakespeare. For Adams, Shakespeare, the King, could do no wrong; and hence the hell-broth of the Witches in *Macbeth* (in lines that are hardly the work of Shakespeare, but rather in the main by Middleton!) did not need to be compared with other, superior, imitations of a well-known passage by Ovid. My friend could readily explain how the passage in *Macbeth* came to be where and what it was, and that was all we needed to know. If this trait carried a defect, what was the virtue? The virtue of his utter sympathy with Shakespeare, of his detailed knowledge of all the Elizabethan and Jacobean background of Shakespeare as an actor, dramatic author, manager, led to the best, truest, most imaginative biography we have of Shakespeare, completed by Joseph Quincy Adams, at the height of his amazing powers, in the year 1923.

Let us sketch his career. He attended school in more than one Southern state, as his father held the pastorate successively in various Baptist churches; had an early practical experience in setting types as a printer—one that later greatly helped him in his scholarly work, for example, in solving the altered order of plays in the first and subsequent impressions of the Folio edition

7

of Shakespeare—and graduated with high honors at Wake Forest College in the year 1900, where also, in 1901, he attained the degree of Master of Arts. He was Principal of Raleigh Male Academy for 1901–02. He always set a high value upon the influence he received at Wake Forest from Benjamin Sledd, professor of English, and a poet. In the years 1902–03 he studied under John M. Manly at the University of Chicago, and then accepted the fellowship in English under James Morgan Hart at Cornell University for the academic year 1903–04. Under the stimulus of Manly he gained an excellent introduction to the study of the Mediæval and Elizabethan drama in England, a fine training which he could, and did, follow with great liberty and independence under Hart at Ithaca; here he began his university career as a teacher; and here too he promptly won the right to give a notable course in Shakespeare. Other courses ere long he developed and gave with a like high success in the same and adjacent fields; such as his course in Elizabethan Non-dramatic Literature. And soon his better pupils, among them scholars now well known, came to him after undergraduate courses as graduate students.

Since scholarly apparatus for their work and his own was largely wanting in Adams' chosen field, already he had proceeded to build up his own exhaustive card-index of persons and things (with dates and hints of interrelations) in the realm of Elizabethan and Jacobean scholarship, and for the study of the course of the English drama in general; thus early he laid a solid foundation for all his varied researches in the earlier and later English drama, and the history of the playhouses. A notable asset for all his work was his intuitive, highly-developed sense of timing. He had breadth of interest, too. He did not confine himself to the age of Elizabeth and James; while a graduate student under Hart, he won the Hiram Corson prize with an essay on Browning; later he produced an admirable edition of Sheridan's comedy *The Rivals*. He advanced to the doctoral degree at Ithaca in the year 1906, having meanwhile studied in London (1904–05), and then attending the University of Berlin in the summer of 1907; Brandl was active there at the time, justly proud of the apparatus of

8

books he had gathered for his English Seminary. As a teacher Adams rose quickly. He became Instructor in English in 1905; Assistant Professor in 1909; Professor in 1919.

Honors soon began to come to him, first the recognition by scholars at home and abroad that his knowledge, and statements, and acumen, could be relied on; the best sort of recognition, that by his most competent fellows. For the students, undergraduate and graduate alike, he was a most excellent teacher, clear, ample, interesting and not tricky, full of an illuminating humor, a fine lecturer—one of the best I ever heard; immensely stimulating in private to an increasing body of special students, quietly stimulating to the best of his colleagues too, and soon recognized as a force for sound learning, and a man of sound judgment for education throughout Cornell University. He was an active and useful member of the Society of Phi Beta Kappa. Providence and his own good sense saved him from too many committees, and too much of the vain drudgery for them.

The great honor of his life was the choice that fell to him to serve in command at the Folger Library. Thereafter he became, or continued to be, a member of virtually every important society concerned with Shakespeare or the Elizabethan drama; as, The Shakespeare Association of America, The Grolier Club, The Malone Society, the Deutsche Shakespeare Gesellschaft, The Elizabethan Club of Yale University, The Tudor and Stuart Club of the Johns Hopkins University.

No sketch of him could fail to mention his achievement as a collector of books and other documents. For an ill-paid instructor, before he became better known, he had gathered a marvelous collection of his own, including rarities, in his own domain. When he felt his collection to be complete enough, and doubtless foreseeing his migration to the Folger Library, he let his treasures go to the University of Oklahoma, whither certain of his pupils had preceded it. In brief, he had a genius for collecting books at the lowest prices; in finding bargains, an order of talent unequaled, I believe, in his time. At Washington his developed skill, displayed, for example, when he obtained the Harmsworth collection from England, accomplished wonders for

9

the great Shakespearian and Elizabethan library; these specific terms do not properly indicate its wealth in related items, or its general riches. I should mention the array of Folios of Shakespeare, but am not competent to expand this topic aright. There are means and persons enough elsewhere, above all in Washington, to enable any inquirer to gage this part of Adams' work; which, save for his teaching in and out of class, and the training he gave to his associates in Washington, is likely to go down as his most weighty achievement.

At Ithaca, his course in Shakespeare lifted the subject out of the flats and shallows where the study of this poet had floundered. Accordingly, there were many groans when he left us to go to Washington. I said: 'No one can take away from Cornell University what Adams has given it.' Nor can time, or any other creature, diminish the work that he did in Washington. A God-fearing man, he knew it too. Upon the basis which he laid down, the work that he did can only grow and prosper without end.

There is a little more for me to say on my personal relations with this great man and good friend. When I went to Ithaca, a year before Adams came thither, I belonged to the class of persons who aim to work and play in a fashion that makes play and work all one. At Cornell University, however, there seemed to be two sorts of persons among the colleagues I met, those who aimed to play and not to work, and those who worked and could not play; these latter did not, like Milton, distinguish between learned pains and servile drudgery. When Adams came like a breath of vernal air, we each found a friend to work and play with. Above, I have tried to hint somewhat about our work in the stricter sense. For play in leisure hours we mostly fished and hunted. He was the better shot, though, coming from a point South of Mason and Dixon's line, sometimes a little quick on the trigger; not always too discriminating, either, about the local Yankee rules on shooting cock-birds only in the pheasant season —and once when he was tired by an extra burden he got us into trouble by asking me to carry a hen that he should never have retrieved. He paid the fine, but I had to shoulder the credit. Apart from incidents, on the march, though I was the poorer shot, I fancied (think of it!) that I knew better where to find the game. Fortunately, for some years we had in Ithaca a friend, George F. Foote, an older man and well-to-do, and a better shot even than Adams, who also knew more than either of us about the best places for game—grouse, woodcock, and later the ring-necked pheasants. Mr. Foote, moreover, had a small but handy yacht on Cayuga Lake for fishing (and hunting too), and one of the first of the few motor-cars in Ithaca then or Tompkins County. He was good to us with his motor-boat and car. Also as Steward, he brought us to his table in Sage College, a dormitory; and there, when luck had favored us afield, we feasted on fish and game of our own taking. At other times Adams and I went shooting with the help of bicycles, and a setter-dog to trot behind us; later we each had a car to take us farther. In those latter days he did not hear too well, and sometimes strayed beyond shouting-distance—and then the big Library took him away. But he came back to visit when he could, and we continued our shooting till the medical doctor warned him not to struggle up hills for grouse, and finally not to tramp our rugged fields at all. Meanwhile we had come to know every road in Tompkins County, and every field, so to speak, within some miles of Ithaca. Since I now have reached an age when men dislike the thought of killing anything to which our Creator gives life, I will say no more of shooting in itself. Let me speak instead of the wonderful sympathy that existed, and still exists, between Joseph Q. Adams and me. Afoot, we often talked but little; and in time he was often hard to reach with the voice; and yet often, when we had been walking side by side in silence for a while, it was clear that our minds had been marching together, for we would break the silence with talk about some matter, perhaps not recently mentioned, of which we had in unison been thinking. After his death last Autumn, I found myself instinctively driving much on roads to the Northeast of Ithaca where we had taken the air most often together. And there we seemed to be, we were, in communion as of old.

Shall I end with words about Adams, the scholarly sleuth, God's spy, about the amazing mind full of clean, detailed learning, that learning full of threads and clues, which he could trace and follow out as no one else I ever met could do? Shall I end with words about the lucid, limpid, supremely normal operating mind, almost uncanny in fertility of resource and sureness of stride? On earth I have not seen, and shall not see, his like.

No, let us end by dwelling on, and with, the faithful loving heart, on a love that could not die, and is not dead, on the good Christian, who is happily waiting and watching above.

AVE ATQUE VALE!

Cook, 'The Higher Study of English'[1]

PROFESSOR COOK'S volume is timely. Never, perhaps, since English became a recognized academic study have its teachers manifested greater divergence regarding their function. On its literary side, we are asked, can English be taught at all? Or, a larger question, can any literature be taught? If so, how? Apart from language?—apart from the body in which it is incarnate? Such questions rest, of course, upon a problem still more fundamental, though one that has not in general been sharply defined or patiently meditated: *why* should we study literature, and, notably, why our own? Without making any pretense at being a systematic treatise on the pedagogics of English, the present book does, directly or indirectly, contain well matured answers to these and similar questions; and coming from one who is not merely a scholar of international authority, and not merely a gifted writer and delicate critic, but a powerful and philosophic teacher as well, the answers may be profitably taken to heart and pondered. For he does not speak as the scribes.

The volume is made up of four 'occasional' papers: (1) The Province of English Philology, a presidential address delivered before the Modern Language Association in 1897, and pleading for a larger interpretation (the German) of a much abused term; (2) The Teaching of English, an historical sketch, reprinted from the *Atlantic* for May, 1901; (3) The Relation of Words to Litera-

[1] Boston, Houghton, Mifflin & Company, 1906. Reviewed in *American Journal of Philology* 28 (1907). 217–20. Reprinted by permission.

ture, from an address given at Vassar in February, 1906; and (4) Aims in the Graduate Study of English, a paper read at Princeton the month before. The several essays now come before a wider public without essential change; no attempt has been made to give them artificial correlation. They 'overlap' somewhat, as their author says. They do not in the ordinary sense repeat. However, underlying all their variety of argument and illustration, or rather animating it, there is a philosophy of teaching that is at one with itself, as well as consistent with experience. It is not, like an abstract pedagogy, separable from a knowledge of the subject to be taught, or from the personality of the teacher, or from that of the pupil, or from the concrete practice of great historic teachers; it is at once eclectic and individual.

And what sort of answers will this philosophy afford to the simple questions we have outlined above?

Literature can be taught because it must be; the impulse to orderly and thorough knowledge is inherent in our better natures. It can be taught because it has been; because those who have produced the best literature, above all, the ancients, believed that it ought to be studied. What can be studied can be taught. What the ancients, and the wisest of their followers, taught and learned, Americans can yet learn and teach, if they are trained approximately after the fashion of Milton, Dante, and the Greeks. The answer here is optimistic, though it does not point to the path of least resistance.

Again, *how* is literature to be taught? Apart from the language wherein it is enfleshed? Apart from the national soul that has made and is making the language? The answer is obvious. Yet the obvious answer implies that in order to understand Milton or Shakespeare as either deserves to be understood, we must have among other things a substantial acquaintance with history and historical grammar. But once more: in order to teach literature, must we really teach *litteras?* Does not the letter kill? No, the letter is also alive, has its share of the spirit that informs the whole organism; *spiritus intus alit.* 'Soule is forme, and doth the bodie make'—even to the minutest cell. The teacher and the student of the humanities must count nothing that is human as beneath notice. Every jot and tittle of the law is instinct with life. Those members of the body which seem to be more feeble are necessary; and those parts of the body which we think to be less honorable, upon these we bestow more abundant honor.

On the other hand, shall we study language apart from literature, that is, apart from passion, thought, and sentiment? In the final analysis we cannot. Woe to us if we blindly persist in an effort so unnatural! Nevertheless, for most persons at some time, and by a few specialists much of the time, stress must be laid upon the linguistic side of philology (the only proper term to embrace both linguistics and *belles-lettres*). Such stress is necessary either for the individual or for the general progress in discovering, communicating, and perpetuating what is best in the life of the past and the present.

In the last sentence lies the solution of that more deeply seated yet simple question mooted at the beginning. We study literature through language, we study the past in all its manifestations, in order to discover, to communicate, and to perpetuate what is best in humanity. We study English in order to do this for people of our own blood; the love of letters is patriotic and begins at home. We study English in order that we may have racial life and have it more abundantly.

But what is life? No one can define it. Yet all of us know it. We can at least classify it. First, then, and most important, there is what Wordsworth calls moral life. As the ancients demanded of a poet that he be first of all a good man, so as not to miss the beauty which is inherent in the moral order, similarly the teacher of English must be, however indirectly, a moral teacher. However indirectly, it is the nature of teaching to be didactic. To say that we must teach either truth or beauty by indirection is merely to say that no end can be attained without means. The point is, to keep the end in view.

To summarize as we have done, in our own words, is doubtless to confine Professor Cook's thought within unduly narrow limits, and to rob it of its concreteness—certainly to suppress the specific adaptations it undergoes in the several essays with reference to different aspects and needs of American education. However, instead of marring any of his illustrations by taking them out of their context (where every teacher of English ought to read them), we prefer to cite one or two illustrations which Professor Cook himself might have used, drawing them from sources similar to those on which the best part of his theory and practice is based, that is, from the best poets and critics.

When, for example, it is urged, as in some quarters it has been lately, that literature cannot be taught, or at least that the teacher of English cannot in general propose to himself as his chief and final aim to impart a sense of literary values, we may urge in return the conviction of Wordsworth that literature ought to be studied, and the belief of Coleridge that it can be taught, and taught according to a conscious method suitable to schools.

Thus Wordsworth, dividing all readers into five main classes, credits only the fifth, composed of students, with any sureness of appreciation: 'And, lastly, there are many, who, having been enamoured of this art in their youth, have found leisure, after youth was spent, to cultivate general literature; in which poetry has continued to be comprehended *as a study*.' That his conception of study included inquiry into things small as well as great, and into technical matters which some of our wiseacres nowadays would exclude from the class-room incontinently, is evident; for, having in mind the equipment of the poet and the properly trained reader of poetry, he says of the rest: 'There can be no presumption in saying of most readers that it is not probable they will be so well acquainted with the various stages through which words have passed.' This seems exactly in the tenor of the essay on The Relation of Words to Literature.

And the following, from Coleridge's *Biographia Literaria*, is even more striking in its harmony with the method advocated by Professor Cook throughout; it contains implicitly more than one weighty principle which space has forbidden us to mention.

At school (Christ's Hospital) [says Coleridge] I enjoyed the inestimable advantage of a very sensible, though at the same time, a very severe master, the Reverend James Bowyer. He early moulded my taste to the preference of Demosthenes to Cicero, of Homer and

Theocritus to Virgil, and again of Virgil to Ovid. He habituated me to compare Lucretius (in such extracts as I then read), Terence, and above all the chaster poems of Catullus, not only with the Roman poets of the, so-called, silver and brazen ages; but with even those of the Augustan era; and on grounds of plain sense and universal logic to see and assert the superiority of the former in the truth and nativeness both of their thoughts and diction. At the same time that we were studying the Greek tragic poets, he made us read Shakespeare and Milton as lessons; and they were the lessons too, which required most time and trouble to *bring up*, so as to escape his censure. I learned from him, that poetry, even that of the loftiest and, seemingly, that of the wildest odes, had a logic of its own, as severe as that of science; and more difficult, because more subtle, more complex, and dependent on more, and more fugitive causes. In the truly great poets, he would say, there is reason assignable, not only for every word, but for the position of every word. . . . He sent us to the University excellent Latin and Greek scholars, and tolerable Hebraists. Yet our classical knowledge was the least of the good gifts, which we derived from his zealous and conscientious tutorage.

Unfortunately, these have not been the 'usual courses of learning,' or anything like them, perhaps since the days of Saint Augustine. Were they general now, the author of *The Higher Study of English* might, finally, be supported by the authority of Augustine's mother: 'because she accounted that those usual courses of learning would not only be no hindrance, but even some help towards attaining Thee in time to come.'

W. J. Sedgefield, 'An Anglo-Saxon Book of Verse and Prose'[1]

THIS volume, with one table of Contents, unites in one pagination two previous books, of verse and prose respectively, which it seems can still be separately procured. Thus the Glossary of the 'Verse-Book' is distinct from that of the 'Prose-Book'; and similarly there are two sets of Notes, and two indexes of Names. The editor's fidelity and industry are superior to his taste, and the selections from Old English prose are more useful than those from the poetry. Here the interests of the Old English people are far too largely illustrated from one poem, *Beowulf*, which once again is seen out of perspective. We miss *Genesis B* and *The Dream of the Rood,* which, as R. K. Gordon says (*Anglo-Saxon Poetry,* Everyman's Library, p. xii), are as good as anything in Old English poetry; the same excellent judge says (*ibid.,* p. 261): *'The Dream of the Rood* is the most beautiful of Old English religious poems.' Sedgefield in his Preface (p. v) says of his own volume: 'The requirements of the literary student receive, perhaps for the first time in such a book, as much attention as those of the philologist.' He evidently has not seen very far into the nature of Henry Sweet, nor become familiar with the work of the late Albert S. Cook—whom on p. 99 he calls 'A. Cook' (*cf.* p. 183), as on p. 126 he calls Sievers, 'Edward' (=Eduard). In a writer of English it generally betokens a lack of sympathetic insight into our origins to call Old English 'Anglo-Saxon'; one

[1] Manchester, University Press, 1928. Reviewed in *The Journal of English and Germanic Philology* 28 (1929). 541–2. Reprinted by permission.

feels that the writer who does so is treating the first phase of English life as something alien to him. So Scott's Gael disclosed himself:

And, Saxon—I am Roderick Dhu!

At all events we wish that Sedgefield would follow Gordon (not Gordon's publisher) in saying 'Old English,' and would follow Cook in saying 'student of language,' or the like, instead of 'philologist,' especially when linguistic studies are to be distinguished from literary.

On pp. ix, 300–7, the familiar work of Boethius should be called *Consolatio Philosophiæ*, not *'De Consolatione' Philosophiæ*. On p. 1 is it proper to speak of Bede's *Ecclesiastical History* as one of the 'old Germanic records'? Again, p. 99, how can one be sure that the author of the *Christ* was 'not a man of action'? How many men of action in the period may have shared his contemplative experiences! Alfred later was a man both of action and contemplation.

I have mainly referred to small matters of usage in a solid book. But really, if one accepts the German estimate of *Beowulf*, it would be better to assume that students who could use Sedgefield's volume would own a copy of that poem. In that case his 248 pages devoted to Old English verse, 124 of them text, would have room for samples of much that is omitted, much that is representative—*Andreas* and *Judith*, for example, in addition to *Genesis B* and *The Dream of the Rood*. Cook, in his *First Book in Old English*, p. vi, enunciated the true aim of such a work on the literary side: 'The selections have been made with reference to giving a fairly just, though necessarily incomplete, view of the surroundings, occupations, problems, ideals, and sentiments of our English ancestors.' That, in brief, is the right concept of Old English philology for beginners.

Dr. Johnson on Oats

and Other Grains[1]

JOHNSON'S reference to oats in England and Scotland has aroused more, or broader, smiles than are warranted, at least among persons who have not consulted his book, and who may have heard it misquoted. Many know little more of the great Dictionary than what they suppose Johnson said of this grain on the spur of the moment (in a reference that is not a definition) along with his definition of *network,* which they commonly take at second hand. He does not say that oats never furnish human beings with food in England; like Boswell, he had himself eaten dry oatmeal when a boy; and his statement about oats and people and horses is strictly true. '*Very* true,' Lord Elibank declared.

Of course in what Johnson says about *oats* he is partly in line with tradition, and here, among his predecessors, we should especially note Burton. Two recent writers, Miss Boddy [2] and Mr. Read,[3] have, in fact, made clear Johnson's probable debt to the following passage from the *Anatomy of Melancholy* (1.2.2.1):

Bread that is made of baser grain, as pease, beans, oats, rye, or over-hard baked, crusty, and black, is often spoken against, as causing melancholy juice and wind. Joh. Mayor, in the first book of his History of Scotland, contends much for the wholesomeness of oaten

[1] Published in *Publications of the Modern Language Association of America* 52 (1937). 785–802. Reprinted by permission.

[2] Johnson and Burton, *LTLS,* June 21, 1934.

[3] The History of Dr. Johnson's Definition of Oats, *Agricultural History* 8 (1934). 81–94.

bread. It was objected to him, then living at Paris in France, that his countrymen fed on oats, and base grain, as a disgrace; but he doth ingenuously confess, Scotland, Wales, and a third part of England, did most part use that kind of bread, that it was as wholesome as any grain, and yielded as good nourishment. And yet Wecker (out of Galen) calls it horsemeat, and fitter for juments than men to feed on. But read Galen himself, *Lib.* 1, *De cibus boni et mali succi,* more largely discoursing of corn and bread.[4]

Read Galen, then, in my Note 4 below, since he doubtless begins for Johnson the story of oats in relation to horses and men.

Miss Boddy recalls Johnson's well-known fondness for Burton, and also takes issue with the editor of the *Johnson Handbook* for believing that 'the definition' was not 'intended to reflect upon any one'; she herself refers to it as 'an insult' and thereby goes pretty far in her language for anybody, even a Scot.

Mr. Read's solid article begins on the 'definition' by saying that 'Johnson's taunt about oats' was not created on the spur of the moment, but had a background of centuries. Thus Pliny (*Nat. Hist.* 3. 183 = 18.17.44.149) records that 'the people of Germany are in the habit of sowing oats, and make their porridge of nothing else'—a disgrace, according to Pliny, since he took oats to be a diseased form of wheat. 'By the Middle Ages,' says Read, the reputation of a fondness for oats 'had become attached to the Scots'; he cites Froissart (1.17) for the year 1328; observes that in 1426 the Scottish parliament enacted a law to secure the sowing of wheat as well, and also of pease and beans; and quotes a remarkable passage from John Major's *History of Greater Britain* (1521) defending the use of oaten bread against the aspersions

---

[4] Bullen's ed. (1923), 1. 255; *cf. Galeni de Alimentorum Facultatibus,* Book 14 in his *Opera Omnia,* ed. by Kühn, 6 (1823). 522–3: 'Cap. XIV. [De bromo.] Hoc semen in Asia est frequentissimum, et potissimum in Mysia, quae est supra Pergamum, ubi et tiphae et olyrae uberrimus est proventus. Jumentorum autem est alimentum, non hominum, nisi utique aliquando extrema fame ad panes ex eo quoque semine conficiendos compellantur: citra famem autem coctum ex aqua manditur cum vino dulci, aut sapa, aut mulso, non aliter quam tipha. Calidum autem est admodum, non secus ac illa, quanquam non aeque est durum; ex quo minus quoque corpus nutrit; et panis, qui ex eo fit, alioqui est insuavis, non tamen alvum aut sistit, aut proritat, sed, quod ad id saltem pertinet, medium locum obtinet.'

of a Frenchman who had returned with some from Scotland to France, and 'had shown it about as a monstrosity.' (This is the 'Joh. Mayor' of Burton; for another quotation from him see the excerpt from Lord Hailes below.) According to Major (*Pub. Scot. Hist. Soc.* 10 (1892). 7–9):

Wheat will not grow in every part of the island; and for this reason the common people use barley and oaten bread. And, as many Britons are inclined to be ashamed of things nowise to be ashamed of, I will here insist a little. . . . Just such bread were Christ and his apostles wont to eat, as may be seen from the fourteenth chapter of Matthew and the sixth chapter of John. . . . I say, for my part, that I would rather eat that British oaten bread than bread made of barley or of wheat. I nowhere remember to have seen on the other side of the water such good oats as in Britain, and the people make their bread in the most ingenious fashion. . . . Just eat this bread once, and you shall find it far from bad. It is the food of almost all the inhabitants of Wales, of the northern English (as I learned some seven years back), and of the Scottish peasantry; and yet the main strength of the Scottish and English armies is in men who have been tillers of the soil—a proof that oaten bread is not a thing to be laughed at.[5]

Mr. Read, after other highly interesting quotations in chronological order, takes up the dictionaries prior to Johnson's. Thus Bailey (1721), who gave Johnson a hint he could build on: 'It is forage for horses, generally, and sometimes provision for men.' And similarly Skinner's *Etymologicon* (1671): *Ubique enim Equis, alicubi etiam Hominibus, Esca est.*

It might seem as if Mr. Read had left little for me to do on the head of taunts, insults, and oats. I had, indeed, finished my writing on this subject before learning of his and Miss Boddy's from my friend Professor Pottle. I gladly record my subsequent debt to them all, and now think it likely that Johnson, as he forged ahead in his labor, took a fleeting amusement in beginning his article on *oats* as he did, but never intended an insult. He doubtless expected the reader to read the article through. The evidence I had collected on this and related points I believe should be spread before all who may care to answer for themselves where

[5] Quoted by Read, pp. 82–3.

the truth lies as between Miss Boddy and Miss Struble in *A Johnson Handbook,* p. 123: 'Oats is for him [Bailey] "a grain, food for horses." I do not believe that Johnson's famous line was meant as an aspersion.'

One main author whose work was steadily consulted by Johnson for his Dictionary is barely mentioned by Read, though he had been an assistant to Bailey; it seems strange that so important a writer on agriculture should be neglected in a publication called *Agricultural History.* This writer, it will be seen, I have followed up in some detail; Johnson's use of his work throws much light on what the Dictionary has to say about oats and other grains.

According to Boswell, of course, Johnson did at the age of seventy-four say that by the 'definition of oats' he 'meant to vex them' (the Scottish nation); the date of this reported conversation was some thirty, or perhaps as much as thirty-five, years after the materials for the article on *oats* were put together. Boswell was fifteen years old when the Dictionary appeared; it had been out eight years when he and Johnson met in 1763. On March 23, 1776, he misquoted the wording of the so-called 'definition'; he evidently did not verify this reference at the source; thanks to Bailey and Skinner, perhaps, some misquotation about 'men,' 'food,' and 'horses,' had long since been fastened on Johnson. The words *men* and *food* are not in the 'definition,' though many people now think that they are, and it may well be that in the colloquy of 1783 the word *definition* is Boswell's. I hesitate to question the words *vex them;* but Mr. R. W. Chapman has shown how far Boswell could go in dressing up his own memoranda of conversations when he came to print them.[6]

[6] *Boswell's Note Book,* 1776–1777 (London, 1925), pp. xvi–xvii: 'Secondly, the Notebook shows that Boswell was not content merely to transcribe his memoranda. He was not afraid to be an artist, and to let his knowledge and genius "Johnsonize" what was necessarily raw material. It has hardly been realized how great a licence he permitted himself in this, the most important, part of his task.'—There are possible indications that Boswell makes Johnson use the forms *Scotch* and *Scotchmen* for persons, where present usage and that of a great lexicographer would favor *Scottish, Scot, Scotsmen,* confining the application of *Scotch* to things, as wool, whisky, and the like; yet see the last quotation in footnote 22.

Boswell already had noted under the year 1755, the date of publication of the Dictionary, that out of six amanuenses who helped Johnson in assembling materials for the enterprise five were Scotsmen, and that 'Mr. Andrew Millar, bookseller in the Strand, took the principal charge of conducting the publication of Johnson's Dictionary,' adding: 'It is remarkable that those with whom Johnson chiefly contracted for his literary labours were Scotchmen, Mr. Millar and Mr. Strahan.' [7] Other appropriate extracts bearing on our subject will be found below; the general subject of 'Scotland and the Scotch' fills something like eleven columns in Hill's Index to Boswell's *Life of Johnson,* the biography of an Englishman by a Scot.

Meanwhile, observe what many do not realize, that the Dictionary, as might be expected in its age, is to some extent an encyclopædia. Thus the well-known description of oats, and similar references to barley, buckwheat, maize, millet, panic, rice, rye, and wheat, are meant to give succinct information about the use and distribution of these grains. The same is true of entries for the bean and pea. Quite naturally, the longest account is that of wheat.

For this information, not excepting that on oats, Johnson depends upon good books of reference, including the best book of its sort in his day, one which had been issued half a dozen times before Johnson's work came out in 1755, and which went on reappearing as the standard book on its subject for a very long time thereafter:

The Gardeners Dictionary . . . wherein all the Articles contained in the former Editions of this Work, in Two Volumes, are disposed in One Alphabet; the Sixth Edition. By Philip Miller. London, 1752.

With the author, Johnson had some personal acquaintance; how early, those who are better versed than I in such details of Johnson's life may be able to show. In the *Tour to the Hebrides,* Johnson is reported as saying: 'Philip Miller told me that in Phillips' *Cyder,* a poem, all the precepts are just, and indeed better than

---

[7] *Life of Johnson,* Hill's edition revised by Powell, 1. 287.

in books written for the purpose of instructing.' [8] Johnson says the same thing of *Cyder* in his *Life of John Phillips:* 'This I was told by Miller, the great gardener and botanist.' [9] I cannot now be sure which edition of Miller's work was excerpted for that of Johnson (by one or more of the Scottish amanuenses?), but, taking the sixth as a natural basis, we may infer that Johnson, though faithful in effect, nevertheless when he quoted Miller for substance, and not for idiom, condensed and improved the wording as he went along. Note, however, Miller's word *support,* which he uses of maize and rice; when Johnson says that a grain 'supports' a 'people,' he very likely has picked up the word from Miller. Thus Miller says of maize; 'This plant is seldom propagated in England but as a curiosity in some gardens, but in America it is the chief support of the inhabitants.'

Another work which Johnson made use of was Mortimer's, of which I give, in large part, the title-page (second edition, London, 1708):

The Whole Art of Husbandry, or The Way of Managing and Improving of Land; being A full Collection of what hath been Writ, either by ancient or modern Authors; . . . as also An Account of the particular Sorts of Husbandry used in several Counties. . . .

Yet another systematic book that proved useful in Johnson's enterprise was a medical work by Dr. Arbuthnot, the friend of Pope, possibly in the edition here recorded: *An Essay concerning the Nature of Aliments. . . . By John Arbuthnot, M.D.* Second edition, London, 1732. This treatise throughout supplied Johnson's Dictionary with illustrative quotations, but the following passage (pp. 60–61) was copied piecemeal for the grains:

Barley is emollient, moistning and expectorating. Oats have some of the same qualities. Barley was chosen by Hippocrates as proper food in inflammatory distempers. Rice is the food of, perhaps, two thirds of mankind; it is most kindly and benign to human constitutions, proper for the consumptive, and such as are subject to hæmorrhages. Next to rice is wheat, the bran of which is highly acescent and stimulating; therefore the bread that is not too much purged

[8] In the *Life of Johnson,* Hill's edition 5, 78.   [9] Hill, *ibid.,* Note 3.

from it is more wholesome for some constitutions. Rye is more acid, laxative, and less nourishing than wheat. Millet is diarrhœtick, cleansing, and useful in diseases of the kidneys. Panick affords a soft demulcent nourishment, both for granivorous birds and mankind. Mays affords a very strong nourishment, but more viscous than wheat. Pease being deprived of any aromatick parts, are mild, and demulcent in the highest degree; but being full of aerial particles, are flatulent when dissolved by digestion. Beans resemble them in most of their qualities. All the forementioned plants are highly acescent, except pease and beans.[10]

Such books as these would dispose the mind of Johnson to be what we call 'scientific,' if it were not already scholarly and precise enough, 'objective' enough, for the making of the first great English Dictionary. The foregoing introduction to them should prepare us to take up Johnson on the grains with a better understanding. He is condensing Miller when he says of oats that it is 'A grain, which in England is generally given to horses, but in Scotland supports the people,' and that 'The meal makes tolerable good bread.' Miller does not use *support* in his account of oats, but repeatedly contrasts England and the South of it with Scotland and the North. Johnson is condensing himself when he says in his abridged dictionary, 'abstracted from the folio edition,' [11] merely: 'A grain, which in England is generally given to horses.' In the folio edition, for *Oatmalt* he quotes Mortimer: 'In Kent they brew with one half *oatmalt,* and the other half barleymalt. *Mortimer's Husb.*' And for *Oatmeal* ('Flower made by grinding oats') he quotes Arbuthnot (p. 251): '*Oatmeal* and butter, outwardly applied, dry the scab on the head. *Arbuthnot on Aliment.*' Here he also cites John Gay:

> Our neighbors tell me oft, in joking talk,
> Of ashes, leather, *oatmeal,* bran, and chalk.

These lines 42–3 of Gay's *Second Pastoral* refer to the complexion of the speaker.

I shall now give parallel passages, quoting in each case, first, Johnson's article on a grain (omitting only etymologies, such as

---

[10] And for some other words indicating alimentary values in medicine, as *emollient, diarrhœtick, demulcent, flatulent.*

[11] Abridgment in two volumes, third edition (London, 1766).

Hebrew, which would here give needless trouble to the printer), and then the relevant parts from the *Gardeners Dictionary* of Miller, taking the items in the alphabetical order of Johnson.[12]

Johnson	*Miller*
BARLEY. *n.s.* . . . It hath a thick spike; the calyx, husk, awn, and flower, are like those of wheat or rye, but the awns are rough; the seed is swelling in the middle, and, for the most part, ends in a sharp point, to which the husks are closely united. The species are, 1. Common long-eared *barley.* 2. Winter or square *barley,* by some called *big.* 3. Sprat *barley,* or battledoor *barley.* All these sorts of *barley* are sown in the spring of the year, in a dry time. In some very dry light land, the *barley* is sown early in March; but in strong clayey soils it is not sown till April. The square *barley,* or *big,* is chiefly cultivated in the north of England, and in Scotland; and is hardier than the other sorts. Where *barley* is sown upon new broken up land, the usual method is to plow up the land in March, and let it lie fallow until June; at which time it is ploughed again, and sown with turneps, which are eaten by sheep in winter, by whose dung the land is greatly improved; and then, in March following, the ground is ploughed again, and sown with *barley.* Millar [sic]. *Barley* is emollient, moistening, and expectorating; *barley* was chosen	HORDEUM, barley. The characters are: It hath a thick spike: the calyx, husk, awn, and flower are like those of wheat or rye; but the awns are rough: the seed is swelling in the middle, and, for the most part, ends in a sharp point, to which the husks are closely united. The species are: 1. *Hordeum distichum. Ger.* Common long-eared barley. 2. *Hordeum polystichum, vel hybernum. Park.* Winter or square barley, or Bear barley; by some called Big. 3. *Hordeum distichum, spica breviore et latiori, granis confertis. Raii.* Sprat barley or Battledore barley. These are the sorts of barley which are most commonly cultivated near London; but, besides these three, there are two other sorts which are cultivated in England. . . . All these sorts of barley are sown in the spring of the year, in a dry time; in some very dry light land, the barley is sown early in March; but in strong clayey soils it is not sown till April, and sometimes not until the beginning of May. The square barley or Big is chiefly cultivated in the North of England, and in Scotland, and is hardier than the other sorts. . . . [Three paragraphs intervene.]

[12] Johnson, *A Dictionary of the English Language,* first edition (London, 1755); Philip Miller, *The Gardeners Dictionary,* sixth edition (London, 1752).

by Hippocrates as proper food in inflammatory distempers.

Arbuthnot on Aliments.

Where barley is sown upon new broken-up land, the usual method is to plow up the land in March, and let it lie fallow until June; at which time it is plowed again, and sown with turneps, which are eaten by sheep in winter, by whose dung the land is greatly improved; and then in March following the ground is plowed again, and sown with barley as before.

Johnson

BUCKWHEAT, *n.s.* [*buckweitz,* Germ. *fagopyrum,* Lat.]

The flowers grow in a spike, or branched from the wings of the leaves; the cup of the flower is divided into five parts, and resembles the petals of a flower; the seeds are black and three cornered. The species are, 1. Common upright *buckwheat,* 2. Common creeping *buckwheat.* The first is cultivated in England, and is a great improvement to dry barren lands. The second grows wild, and is seldom cultivated.

Miller.

Miller

FAGOPYRUM, . . . buck-wheat. The characters are: The flowers are specious, growing in a spike, or branched from the wings of the leaves; the cup of the flower is divided into five parts, which resemble the petals of a flower; the seeds are black, and three-cornered.

The species are: 1. *Fagopyrum vulgare erectum. Tourn.* Common upright buck-wheat. 2. *Fagopyrum vulgare scandens. Tourn.* Common creeping buck-wheat. The first of these plants is cultivated in many parts of England, and is a great improvement to dry barren lands. [Three paragraphs intervene.] The second sort is found wild in divers parts of England; but is never cultivated in gardens.

Johnson

MAIZE, or *Indian Wheat. n.s.* The whole *maize* plant has the appearance of a reed; the male flowers are produced at remote distances from the fruit on the same plant, growing generally in a spike upon the top of the stalk; the female flowers are produced from the wings of the leaves,

Miller

MAYS, Indian wheat. The title of this genus is altered by Dr. Linnæus to Zea. The characters are: The whole plant hath the appearance of a reed; the male flowers are produced at remote distances from the fruit on the same plant, growing, for the most part, in a panicle upon the

28

and are surrounded by three or four leaves, which closely adhere to the fruit until it is ripe: this plant is propagated in England only as a curiosity, but in America it is the principal support of the inhabitants, and consequently propagated with great care.   *Miller.*

Maize affords a very strong nourishment, but more viscous than wheat.   *Arbuthnot on Aliments.*

top of the stalk; the female flowers are produced from the wings of the leaves, and are surrounded by three or four leaves which closely adhere to the fruit until it is ripe. The species are: [There follow seven species, and a short paragraph on some other varieties.]

This plant is seldom propagated in England but as a curiosity in some fine gardens; but in America it is one of their greatest supports, and is there cultivated with great care, in the following manner: [An account in four paragraphs follows; and then the spread of maize into Germany, Italy, Turkey, 'and many other countries,' is noted.]

Johnson	*Miller*

MILLET. *n.s.* [*milium,* Lat. *mil* and *millet,* Fr.]

1. A plant.

The *millet* hath a loose divided panicle, and each single flower hath a calyx, consisting of two leaves, which are instead of petals, to protect the stamina and pistillum of the flower, which afterwards becomes an oval, shining seed. This plant was originally brought from the eastern countries, where it is still greatly cultivated, from whence we are annually furnished with this grain, which is by many persons much esteemed for puddings.   *Miller.*

In two ranks of cavities is placed a roundish studd, about the bigness of a grain of *millet.*
         Woodward on Fossils.

Millet is diarrhetick, cleansing, and useful, in diseases of the kidneys.
    Arbuthnot on Aliments.

MILIUM [so called of *Mille, Lat.* a thousand, because of the multitude of its grains], millet.

The characters are: It hath a loose divided panicle; and each single flower hath a calyx, consisting of two leaves, which are instead of petals, to protect the stamina and pistillum of the flower, which afterward becomes an oval shining seed. [Four species are described; then come two paragraphs of added description.]

These plants were originally brought from the Eastern countries, where they are still greatly cultivated, from whence we are furnished annually with this grain, which is by many persons greatly esteemed for puddens, &c.

Johnson

OATS. *n.s.* [*aten,* Saxon.] A grain, which in England is generally given to horses, but in Scotland supports the people.

It is of the grass leaved tribe; the flowers have no petals, and are disposed in a loose panicle: the grain is eatable. The meal makes tolerable good bread.   *Miller.*

The *oats* have eaten the horses.
                              Shakespeare.

It is bare mechanism, no otherwise produced than the turning of a wild *oatbeard,* by the insinuation of the particles of moisture.   *Locke.*

For your lean cattle, fodder them with barley straw first, and the *oat* straw last. *Mortimer's Husbandry.*

His horse's allowance of *oats* and beans was greater than the journey required.   *Swift.*

Miller

AVENA, Oats. . . . The species are: 1. *Avena bulgaris seu alba.* *C.B.P.* Common or white oats. 2. *Avena nigra. C.B.P.* Black oats. 3. *Avena nuda C.B.P* Naked oats 4. *Avena rubra.* Red or brown oats.

The first sort here mentioned is the most common about London; the second sort is more cultivated in the Northern parts of England, and is esteemed a very hearty food for horses; but the first makes the whitest meal, and is chiefly cultivated where the inhabitants live much upon oat-cakes.

The third sort is less common than either of the other, especially in the Southern parts of England; but in the North of England, Scotland, and Wales, it is cultivated in plenty. . . . The red oats are much cultivated in Derbyshire, Staffordshire, and Cheshire; but are never seen in any of the counties near London. . . . The straw of these oats is of a brownish-red colour, as is also the grain, which is very full and heavy, and esteemed better food for horses than either of the former sorts.

Oats are a very profitable grain, and absolutely necessary, being the principal grain which horses love. . . . This grain is a great improvement to many estates in the North of England, Scotland, and Wales; for it will thrive on cold barren soils which will produce no other sort of grain. . . . If they are housed wet, they will not heat in the mow, or become mouldy, as other grain usually do; so is of great advantage in the Northern parts of England, and in

Scotland, where their harvest is generally late, and the autumns wet. The meal of this grain makes tolerable good bread, and is the common food of the country-people in the North.

Johnson

PANNICLE. *n.s.* PANNICK. A plant.

The *pannicle* is a plant of the millet kind, differing from that, by the disposition of the flowers and seeds, which, of this, grow in a close thick spike: It is sowed in several parts of Europe, in the fields, as corn for the sustenance of the inhabitants; it is frequently used in particular places of Germany to make bread.

Miller.

September is drawn with a chearful countenance; in his left hand a handful of millet, oats, and *pannicle*.

Peacham.

Panick affords a soft demulent [*sic*] nourishment. *Arbuth.*

Miller

PANICUM, panic. The characters are: It is a plant of the millet-kind, differing from that by the disposition of the flowers and seeds; which, of this, grow in a close thick spike. [Nine species are then listed.] . . .

The three first sorts are only varieties, which differ in the colour of the grain. These are sowed in several parts of Europe, in the fields, as corn, for the sustenance of the inhabitants; but it is reckoned not to afford so good nourishment as Millet; however, it is frequently used in some parts of Germany, to make puddens, cakes, and bread.

Johnson

RICE. *n.s.* [*oryza*, Lat.] One of the esculent grains: it hath its grains disposed into a panicle, which are almost of an oval figure, and are covered with a thick husk, somewhat like barley: this grain is greatly cultivated in most of the Eastern countries. *Miller.*

Rice is the food of two-thirds of mankind; it is kindly to human constitutions, proper for the consumptive, and those subject to haemorrhages. *Arbuthnot.*

If the snuff get out of the snuffers, it may fall into a dish of *rice* milk.

Swift's Directions to the Butler.

Miller

ORYZA . . . rice. The characters are: It hath its grains disposed into a panicle, which are almost of an oval figure, and are covered with a thick husk, somewhat like barley. . . . This grain is greatly cultivated in most of the Eastern countries, where it is the chief support of the inhabitants; and great quantities of it are brought into England and other European countries every year, where it is in great esteem for puddens, &c.

31

Johnson

RYE. *n.s.* . . .

A coarse kind of bread corn.

Between the acres of the *rye,*
These pretty countryfolks would
 lye.   *Shakesp.*

Rye is more acrid [*sic*], laxative,
and less nourishing than wheat.
   Arbuthnot on Aliments.

Miller

SECALE . . . rye. . . .

The general use of rye is for bread,
either alone or mixed with wheat;
but . . . it is only fit for such persons who have always been used to
this food, few other persons caring
to eat of it.

Johnson

WHEAT. *n.s.* [. . . *triticum,* Lat.]
The grain of which bread is chiefly
made.

It hath an apetalous flower, disposed into spikes; each of them consists of many stamina which are included in a squamose flower-cup,
having awns: the pointal rises in the
center, which afterwards becomes an
oblong seed, convex on one side, but
furrowed on the other: it is farinaceous, and inclosed by a coat which
before was the flower-cup: these are
produced singly, and collected in a
close spike, being affixed to an indented axis. The species are; 1.
White or red *wheat,* without awn.
2. Red *wheat,* in some places called
Kentish *wheat.* 3. White *wheat.* 4.
Red-eared bearded *wheat.* 5. Cone
wheat. 6. Grey *wheat,* and in some
places duck-bill *wheat* and grey pol-
lard. 7. Polonian *wheat.* 8. Many
eared *wheat.* 9. Summer *wheat.* 10.
Naked *barley.* 11. Long grained
wheat. 12. Six rowed *wheat.* 13.
White eared *wheat* with long awns:
Of all these sorts cultivated in this
country, the cone *wheat* is chiefly
preserved, [13] as it has a larger ear
and a fuller grain than any other;

Miller

TRITICUM, . . . wheat. The characters are: It hath an apetalous
flower which is disposed into spikes;
each single flower consists of many
stamina (or threads), which are included in a squamous flower-cup,
which hath awns; the pointal also
rises in the centre, which afterward
becomes an oblong seed, which is
convex on one side, but hath a furrow on the other; is farinaceous, and
inclosed by a coat which was before
the flower-cup; these are produced
singly, and are collected in a close
spike, being affixed to an indented
axis.

[Then follow thirteen kinds of
wheat.]

. . . I have here mentioned the
several variations of this grain
which have been distinguished by
botanists; some of which I take to
be only seminal variations, and not
distinct species; but as many of them
are specifically distinct, and are cultivated by the farmers as such, I
thought it would not be amiss to
enumerate all the varieties.

The six sorts first-mentioned are
what I have commonly observed
growing in divers parts of England;

[13] *Sic;* read 'preferred' after Miller.

but the seeds of all should be annually changed; for if they are sown on the farm, they will not succeed so well as when the seed is brought from a distant country.   *Miller.*

He mildews the white *wheat,* and hurts the poor creature of the earth.
                Shakespeare's King Lear.

Reuben went in the days of *wheat*-harvest.   *Gen. xxx.*

August shall bear the form of a young man of a fierce aspect; upon his head a garland of *wheat* and rie.
                    Peacham.

Next to rice is *wheat,* the bran of which is highly acescent.
            Arbuthnot on Aliments.

The damsels laughing fly: the giddy clown

Again upon a *wheat*-sheaf drops adown.   *Gay.*

but the Cone Wheat is generally preferred, as having a larger ear, and fuller grain, than any other sort; but some of the sorts will thrive best on strong land, and others on a light soil; so that the great skill of the farmer is in adapting the sort of wheat which is the best for his land. [Miller's article on wheat is very long; Johnson abstracts the rest of his thought from the substance of Miller, and only in part uses Miller's language.]

. . . If the farmers have regard to their own interest, they should save this expence of seed, . . . especially when it is to be purchased; which most of the skilful farmers do, at least every other year, by way of change; for they find that the seeds continued long upon the same land will not succeed so well as when they procure a change of seeds from a distant country.

Of the other foods mentioned in the passage I have quoted at length from Arbuthnot—namely, beans and pease—Johnson for the bean takes from Miller a detailed account of 'the principal sorts which are cultivated in England'—the small Lisbon bean, the Spanish, the Tokay, the Sandwich, the Windsor, and the Mazagan bean which 'is brought from a settlement of the Portuguese on the coast of Africa, of the same name.' His geographical interest remains strong; and he again quotes Swift: 'His allowance of oats and *beans* was greater than his journey required.' Under *Pease* he notes that 'Pea, when it is mentioned as a single body, makes *peas;* but when spoken of collectively, as a food or a species, it is called *pease,* anciently *peason'*; he gives the 'Saxon,' French, Italian, and Latin equivalents, quotes *'peason'* and *beans* from Tusser, and closes with our now familiar Arbuthnot as *'Arb.':* '*Pease,* deprived of any aromatick parts, are mild and demulcent, but, being full of aerial particles, are flatulent.'

33

At the end of a similarly crowded line under *Turnip* there is room only for '*Mil.*' References in the earlier part of the alphabet spell the name with an *a*, 'Millar'; but soon the correct spelling, 'Miller,' appears. Glancing here and there, I find an indebtedness of Johnson to this writer for excerpts, short, middling, and long, about the blackberry (by mistake under *Blackberried*), bramble, currant, gooseberry; asparagus, beet, cabbage, carrot, radish; among the trees, the acacia ('Millar'), apple ('Millar'), ash ('Millar'), capivi (*copaiba*—'Miller'), chestnut, citron, elder, oak, orange, peach, pear, pine, and plum; among the flowers, the cowslip, rose, and violet. Much further evidence of Johnson's debt to him can easily be found. Thanks to Miller, Johnson has good articles on flax and cotton, whereas for silk he seems to have no similarly good source of information: '*Silk* . . . 1. The thread of the worm that turns afterwards to a butterfly. . . . 2. The stuff made of the worm's thread.'

In Johnson's careful account of the bagpipe, there is no reference to Scotland; none in his definition of highlander ('from *highland*. An inhabitant of mountains.'); and only this under *Loch:* '*n.s.* A lake. Scottish.' *Scottish* itself he does not list, whereas *English* and *Latin* are recorded and defined; but neither does he list *American, French, German, Greek,* or *Irish.* Here is what he says of haggis:

HAGGESS. *n.s.* (from *hag* or *hack*.) A mass of meat, generally pork chopped, and inclosed in a membrane. In Scotland it is commonly made in a sheep's maw of the entrails of the same animal, cut small, with suet and spices.

It is an amusing task to share the experience of the workshop with the great and noble lexicographer in any one small province of his labors; but the whole performance was gigantic. There is nothing petty about it. The evidence now before us will hardly let one think that Johnson found amusement of the common sort in writing the article on *Oats,* or that the aim of his tireless effort is at this point likely to be quite facetious—or that he gratuitously set out to 'vex' such friends of his as Shiels, the two Macbeans, Stewart, Maitland, and the two Scots, Millar and Strahan, who chiefly helped him to bring out his book. If he had his little joke, and made his smart antithesis, still he was true to the essential facts in a statement which is a model of condensation. But when he reached the age of seventy-four, was his own memory of the way in which he had used the excerpts of an amanuensis for the article on oats somewhat influenced by the undue attention this one article had meanwhile attracted, out of all the grains, from other persons? Or perhaps we should say, *had supposedly attracted,* since what was in the air was something like this: Oats, the food of horses in England, and of men in Scotland. Though the materials for *oats (avena)* may have been collected first, he doubtless wrote the article on *maize,* and had it ready for the printer, before he finished any of the copy for the letter O. Did he mean to vex the Americans as well, when, following what he got through an amanuensis out of Miller, he said of maize, 'This plant is propagated in England only as a curiosity, but in America it is the principal support of the inhabitants'? Did he find amusement in the objectivity of Arbuthnot?—'Panick affords a soft demulcent nourishment, both for granivorous birds and mankind.' Again, if the reference of Arbuthnot to oats had not been colorless, would not Johnson have marked it for one of his half-dozen helpers to copy? Then the Dictionary would have had a slightly different article on oats. Finally, if Boswell cannot give the first statement in this article correctly, and never looked to see what followed, that 'the grain is eatable,' and that 'the meal makes tolerable good bread,' can we be certain that he reports verbatim what the elderly Johnson said about the 'definition'? In the colloquy is not Johnson glad at length to escape from his pursuer? Clearly, it is Boswell's *Life,* and not the article in its entirety, that has kept the vexation or the humor alive. The Scot, and not the Dictionary, has done it.

And now I offer, with comment here and there, a number of passages from which, in conjunction with what has gone before, any one who desires to examine the evidence may form his own opinion on the precise degree or sort of humor, or any lack of it, in this celebrated so-called definition. The references are to the edition of Boswell by Hill revised by Powell as far as that is published, Volumes I–IV, to the last two volumes out of six as published by Hill, and to Johnson's Dictionary, as before, of 1755.

Boswell, Life

(Friday, March 21, 1783)

[Johnson.] 'I wonder how I should have any enemies; for I do harm to nobody.' Boswell. 'In the first place, Sir, you will be pleased to recollect that you set out with attacking the Scotch; so you got a whole nation for your enemies.' Johnson. 'Why, I own that by my definition of *oats* I meant to vex them.' Boswell. 'Pray, Sir, can you trace the cause of your antipathy to the Scotch.' Johnson. 'I can not, Sir.' Boswell. 'Old Mr. Sheridan says it was because they sold Charles the First.' Johnson. 'Then, Sir, old Mr. Sheridan has found out a very good reason.' [14]

Boswell, Life

(Saturday, March 23, 1776)

I saw here [at Lichfield], for the first time, *oat ale;* and oat cakes not hard as in Scotland, but soft like a Yorkshire cake, were served at breakfast. It was pleasant to me to find that *'Oats,'* the *'food of horses,'* were so much used as the *food of the people* in Dr. Johnson's own town.[15]

[Boswell misquotes; see Johnson's actual wording in the article on oats as given above.]

Boswell, Tour

(From a letter of Lord Hailes to Boswell, Feb. 6, 1775)

In J. Major *de Gestis Scotorum,* L.i. C.2. last edition, there is a singular passage:

'Davidi Cranstoneo conterraneo, dum de prima theologiæ licentia foret, duo ei consocii et familiares, et mei cum eo in artibus auditores, scilicet Jacobus Almain Senonensis, et Petrus Bruxcellensis, Prædicatorii ordinis, in Sorbonæ curia die Sorbonico coram commilitonibus suis publice objecerunt, *quod pane avenaceo plebei Scoti* sicut a quodam religioso intellexerant, *vescebantur, ut virum, quem cholericum noverant, honestis salibus tentarent, qui hoc inficiari tanquam patriæ dedecus nisus est.'*

Pray introduce our countryman, Mr. Licentiate David Cranston, to the acquaintance of Mr. Johnson.

---

[14] Hill-Powell 4. 168–9.   [15] *Ibid.* 2. 463.

The syllogism seems to have been this:

> They who feed on oatmeal are barbarians;
> But the Scots feed on oatmeal:
> Ergo—

The licentiate denied the *minor*.[16]

Boswell, *Tour*

(Wednesday, Oct. 13, 1773)

Dr. Johnson and I had each a bed in the cabin. . . . I eat some dry oatmeal, of which I found a barrel in the cabin. I had not done this since I was a boy. Dr. Johnson owned that he too was fond of it when a boy; a circumstance which I was highly pleased to hear from him, as it gave me an opportunity of observing that, notwithstanding his joke on the article of Oats, he was himself a proof that this kind of *food* was not peculiar to the people of Scotland.[17]

[Here again it is clear that Boswell thinks the word 'food' is in the diction of the article.]

Boswell, *Life*

(Autumn, 1747)

But the year 1747 is distinguished as the epoch when Johnson's arduous and important work, his *Dictionary of the English Language*, was announced to the world by the publication of its Plan or Prospectus.[18]

Boswell, *Life*

(1748)

For the mechanical part, he employed, as he told me, six amanuenses; and let it be remembered by the natives of North-Britain, to whom he is supposed to have been so hostile, that five of them were of that country. There were two Messieurs Macbean; Mr. Shiels, who we shall hereafter see partly wrote the Lives of the Poets to which the name of Cibber is affixed; Mr. Stewart, son of Mr. George Stewart, bookseller at Edinburgh; and a Mr. Maitland. The sixth of these humble assistants was Mr. Peyton, who, I believe, taught French, and published some elementary tracts.

To all these painful labourers, Johnson showed a never-ceasing kindness, so far as they stood in need of it. The elder Mr. Macbean

---

[16] Hill 5. 406–7; with two corrections, in the Latin of the *Tour,* supplied by Professor Pottle.

[17] *Ibid.* 5. 308.   [18] Hill-Powell 1. 182.

had afterwards the honour of being librarian to Archibald, Duke of Argyle, for many years, but was left without a shilling. Johnson wrote for him a Preface to 'A System of Ancient Geography'; and, by the favour of Lord Thurlow, got him admitted a poor brother of the Charterhouse. For Shiels, who died of a consumption, he had much tenderness. . . . Peyton, when reduced to penury, had frequent aid from the bounty of Johnson, who at last was at the expence of burying both him and his wife. . . .

The authorities were copied from the books themselves, in which he had marked the passages with a black-lead pencil, the traces of which could easily be effaced. I have seen several of them in which that trouble had not been taken; so that they were just as when used by the copyists. . . .

He is now to be considered as 'tugging at his oar,' as engaged in a steady continued course of occupation, sufficient to employ all his time for some years.[19]

Boswell, Life

(1755)

His introducing his own opinions, and even prejudices, under general definitions of words, while at the same time the original meaning of the words is not explained, as his *Tory, Whig, Pension, Oats, Excise,* and a few more, cannot be fully defended, and must be placed to the account of capricious and humorous indulgence. Talking to me upon this subject when we were at Ashbourne in 1777, he mentioned a still stronger instance of the predominance of his private feelings in the composition of this work than any now to be found in it. 'You know, Sir, Lord Gower forsook the old Jacobite interest. When I came to the work *Renegado,* after telling that it meant "one who deserts to the enemy, a revolter," I added, *Sometimes we say a Gower.* Thus it went to the press; but the printer had more wit than I, and struck it out.'[20]

Johnson never saw reason to change the full article on *Oats,* which in the first American edition (1805), from the eleventh London edition, stands just as it stood in 1755. 'Did you ever hear,' wrote Sir Walter Scott, 'of Lord Elibank's reply when Johnson's famous definition of *oats* was pointed out first to him? . . . "Very true, and where will you find such *men* and such

[19] Hill-Powell 1. 187–90.   [20] *Ibid.* 1. 294–6.

horses?" ' [21] Since this one of the five or six words singled out by Boswell has now been discussed at length, we may as well close by presenting the other four; for Johnson's treatment of them is not fairly seen when, as hitherto has been the custom, the opening of an article is separated from what follows. Each article should be studied as a whole, and, preferably, the articles for any group of words, as the grains, should be compared. Of Boswell's four, *Pension* and *Excise* seem to show more heat than do the other two, but Johnson's authorities seem to like these words, or the ideas, little better than does he. If there is any personal bitterness evinced in any article, is it not in that on *pension?* As for *Tory* and *Whig*, it seems to me that, taken as a whole, the articles on them are excellent, and that, in particular, the extract Johnson quotes for *Whig* from Burnet, a Scot, is admirably chosen for the purpose, and in perfect keeping with the genius and method of his half-encyclopædic dictionary as exemplified by the extracts on grains, trees, and garden vegetables from Arbuthnot and Miller. And with the four let us include Johnson's *renegado* as bettered by the printer.

EXCISE. *n.s.* [*accijs,* Dutch; *excisum,* Latin.] A hateful tax levied upon commodities, and adjuged not by the common judges of property, but wretches hired by those to whom excise is paid.

The people should pay a ratable tax for their sheep, and an *excise* for every thing which they should eat.   *Hayward.*

Ambitious now to take *excise*
Of a more fragrant paradise.   *Cleaveland.*

Excise,
With hundred rows of teeth, the shark exceeds,
And on all trades like Cassawar she feeds.   *Marvel.*

Can hire large houses, and oppress the poor,
By farm'd *excise.*   *Dryden's Juvenal, Sat.* 3.

PENSION. *n.s.* [*pension,* Fr.] An allowance made to any one without an equivalent. In England it is generally understood to mean pay given to a state hireling for treason to his country.

A charity bestowed on the education of her young subjects has

[21] Croker's *Correspondence* as quoted by Hill, Hill-Powell 1. 295 (p. 294, n. 8).

more merit than a thousand *pensions* to those of a higher fortune.
Addison's Guardian, No. 105.

He has liv'd with the great without flattery, and been a friend to men in power without *pensions*.   *Pope.*

RENEGADE.

n.s. [*renegado,* Spanish; *renegat,* Fr.]

RENEGADO.

1. One that apostatises from the faith; an apostate.

There lived a French *renegado* in the same place, where the Castilian and his wife were kept prisoners.   *Addison.*

2. One who deserts to the enemy; a revolter.

Some straggling soldiers might prove *renegadoes,* but they would not revolt in troops.   *Decay of Piety.*

If the Roman government subsisted now, they would have had *renegade* seamen and shipwrights enough.   *Arbuthnot.*

TORY. *n.s.* [A cant term, derived, I suppose, from an Irish word, signifying a savage.] One who adheres to the antient constitution of the state, and the apostolical hierarchy of the church of England, opposed to a whig.

The knight is more a *tory* in the country than the town, because it more advances his interest.   *Addison.*

To confound his hated coin, all parties and religions join whigs, *tories.*   *Swift.*

WHIG. *n.s.* . . . 2. The name of a faction.

The southwest counties of Scotland have seldom corn enough to serve them round the year; and the northern parts producing more than they need, those in the west come in the Summer to buy at Leith the stores that come from the north; and from a word, whiggam, used in driving their horses, all that drove were called the whiggamors, and shorter the *whiggs.* Now in that year before the news came down of Duke Hamilton's defeat, the ministers animated their people to rise and march to Edinburgh; and they came up marching on the head of their parishes with an unheard-of fury, praying and preaching all the way as they came. The marquis of Argyle and his party came and headed them, they being about six thousand. This was called the whiggamor's inroad; and ever after that, all that opposed the court came in contempt to be called *whigs:* and from Scotland the word was brought into England, where it is now one of our unhappy terms of disunion.   *Burnet.*

Whoever has a true value for church and state, should avoid the
extremes of *whig* for the sake of the former, and the extremes of tory
on account of the latter.   *Swift.*

One's respect for Johnson as a lexicographer is likely to grow
upon comparing the articles on Whig and Tory with the corresponding articles in the *Oxford English Dictionary* of to-day,
however much these latter show the fuller information of the
present era. His articles show him to be the right precursor of our
modern scholarship.[22]

[22] Here may be added for completeness two items on oats for which there
seemed to be no good place in the body of my article. According to Hill
(Hill-Powell 4. 168, Note 3), Percival Stockdale records (*Memoirs* 2. 191)
that he heard a Scottish lady, after quoting the 'definition,' say to Johnson:
'I can assure you that in Scotland we give oats to our horses, as well as you
do, to yours, in England.' He replied: 'I am very glad, madam, to find that
you treat your horses as well as you treat yourselves.' The second is from
Boswell (*Tour*, Thursday, Sept. 9, 1773; Hill 5. 167): 'At breakfast this
morning, among a profusion of other things, there were oat-cakes, made of
what is called *graddaned* meal, that is, meal made of grain separated from
the husks, and toasted by fire, instead of being threshed and kiln-dried.'
[Comma after *toasted?*]
    And add this joke on barley from Boswell, *Life*, April 3, 1778 (Hill-
Powell 3. 231): Boswell. 'Yet a misapplication of time and assiduity is not
to be encouraged. Addison, in one of his *Spectators*, commends the judgment of a King, who, as a suitable reward to a man that by long perseverance
had attained to the art of throwing a barleycorn through the eye of a
needle, gave him a bushel of barley.' Johnson. 'He must have been a King
of Scotland, where barley is scarce.'
    Lastly, add these gleanings of Read (p. 86): 'As a schoolboy the young Sam
was given oatmeal porridge for breakfast, and if he was like many children,
this may have given him a mind-set for life. Edmund Hector, an old school-
fellow of Johnson's, told the biographer Boswell about the oatmeal porridge,
and Boswell duly recorded the fact in his notebook [ed. by Chapman, 1925];
but when he came to write up the *Life* he did not see fit to use it. . . . A
colloquial phrase, "to give one his oatmeal," was current in the eighteenth
century. . . . Once after Johnson had administered a public reproof to
Boswell, Boswell came up and said, smiling, "Well, you gave me my oatmeal." Johnson, imagining that he might be vexed, answered: "Digest it,
digest it! I would not have given it you if I thought it would have stuck in
your throat?" ' [*Private Papers of James Boswell from Malahide Castle* 6.
47 (New York, 1929).] Read also quotes (p. 87, n.) Johnson's pleasant letter
to Boswell of May 27, 1775, about his friends in Scotland (Hill-Powell 2.
380): 'I will not send compliments to my friends by name, because I would be
loath to leave any out in the enumeration. Tell them, as you see them, how
well I speak of Scotch politeness, and Scotch hospitality, and Scotch beauty,
and of every thing Scotch, but Scotch oat-cakes, and Scotch prejudices.'

VI

Wordsworth Sources:

Bowles and Keate[1]

THE literary influence of William Lisle Bowles on Coleridge has often been exploited, although not always with enough discrimination and attention to detail. Has the possibility of an influence by Bowles on Wordsworth ever been seriously examined? Wordsworth, who must early have become acquainted with some of Bowles' 'soft strains,' was likely for several reasons to give them a more sympathetic hearing than is nowadays accorded Coleridge's prime favorite.

In Coleridge's lines *To a Young Lady* (1792) the couplet

> My soul amid the pensive twilight gloom
> Mourned with the breeze, O Lee Boo! o'er thy Tomb,

might easily savor of the 'pensive' Bowles, especially if the latter's poem *Abba Thule's Lament for his Son Prince Le Boo* were prior in composition. Lacking the needful editions of Bowles, I cannot answer on the question of priority. However, *Abba Thule* was in existence before a threnody by Wordsworth, to which it bears a resemblance worthy of notice. I refer to *The Affliction of Margaret ——*.

The Fenwick note records, with truthworthy assurance, that *The Affliction of Margaret ——* 'was taken from the case of a

---

[1] Published in *The Athenæum*, London, April 22, 1905, pp. 498–9; the latter part of the article, on Wordsworth's debt to William Bartram, is found in my *Methods and Aims in the Study of Literature*, Ithaca, New York, 1940, pp. 117–32.

poor widow' in Penrith, whose 'sorrow was well known'; 'she kept a shop, and when she saw a stranger passing by, she was in the habit of going out into the street to enquire of him after her son.' Upon such basis in real life Wordsworth builds his eleborate conception of the shadings and fluctuations of hope and fear and uncertainty in the unhappy Margaret, ignorant of the fate of her 'bold,' 'well-born,' 'well-bred,' and 'beauteous' child. Whether or not in the attainment of his idealized picture the poet was at all supported by the inferior yet sometimes admirable imagination of Bowles may be left to the judgment of the reader. The conception of Bowles' *Lament* is roughly the same as that of Wordsworth's poem, centring in Abba Thule's distraction over the inexplicable non-return of his 'brave,' 'bland,' and 'beauteous' prince, and his self-questionings in the effort to explain this grievous enigma:

> Has the fell storm o'erwhelmed him? Has its sweep
> Buried the bounding vessel in the deep?
> Is he cast bleeding on some desert plain?
> Upon his father did he call in vain?
> Have pitiless and bloody tribes defiled
> The cold limbs of my brave, my beauteous child!

a passage badly echoed by the personification of Mania in stanza 24 of Bowles' *Hope: an Allegorical Sketch*:

> Now ravingly she cried: The whelming main—
>   The wintry wave rolls over his cold head;
> I never shall behold his form again;
>   Hence flattering fancies—he is dead, is dead!
> Perhaps on some wild shore he may be cast,
>   Where on their prey barbarians howling rush,
> Oh, fiercer they, than is the whelming blast!
>   Hush, my poor heart! my wakeful sorrows, hush!
> He lives! I yet shall press him to my heart
> And cry, Oh no, no, no,—we never more will part!

Although this feeble stanza may prove not uninteresting on comparison with Wordsworth's poem, it is rather the preceding passage, lines 55–60 of the more praiseworthy *Lament*, that

43

seems to offer a fairly demonstrable parallel to *The Affliction of Margaret* ——, stanza 8:

> Perhaps some dungeon hears thee groan,
> Maimed, mangled by inhuman men;
> Or thou upon a desert thrown
> Inheritest the lion's den;
> Or hast been summoned to the deep,
> Thou, and all thy mates, to keep
> An incommunicable sleep.

Coleridge annotates the name Lee Boo in the couplet quoted above with a reference to a book of travels that turns out to be the source of Bowles' *Lament*. This is, namely, *An Account of the Pelew Islands . . . composed from the Journals and Communications of Captain Henry Wilson* [etc.], by George Keate, London, 1788 (Fourth Edition, 1789). Keate's was a popular narrative in a large contemporary literature of travel, eagerly read by Coleridge and Wordsworth. Coleridge's avidity for such works ought to be more narrowly examined; and Wordsworth's reading of itineraries, for example in 1798, deserves most careful scrutiny. There is no doubt that it formed an essential feature of his preparation for the great poem then incipient. He read, I believe, virtually all voyages by land or sea that friends could place at his disposal, gaining a fund of information that reappears also in his lesser narratives and descriptions. Accordingly, following so obvious a clue as Bowles' and Coleridge's familiarity with Keate, we need not be surprised to find in the *Account* something of possible utility in the study of *The Affliction of Margaret* ——.

Keate's narrative includes a detailed recital of how King Abba Thulle sent his beloved son out from the Pelew Islands to visit England with Capt. Wilson; of Lee Boo's extraordinary 'ease,' 'affability,' and 'good-breeding'; of his success in making friends; finally, of his sudden death (1784), and his burial 'in Rotherhithe church-yard.' It may be that the popular memory of this ingenuous youth was preserved until Wordsworth's acquaintance with London (the grave, it seems, is still marked), for 'the concourse of people at the [funeral] was so great, that it appeared as if the whole parish had assembled to join in seeing the last ceremonies paid to one who was so much beloved by all who had known him in it' (Keate, p. 389). 'The India Company' erected a tablet over his grave, where as a schoolboy Coleridge may indeed have 'mourned,' although he afterwards inexactly recalls the tomb as at Greenwich.

Meanwhile, the trustful father is in total ignorance of his son's mischance. Keate's reflections on the possible feelings of 'the good Abba Thulle' in his far-off home are of peculiar interest, because of their similarity to the alternations of hope and fear in the afflicted Margaret. The island king, having ascertained that Lee Boo was to be gone thirty-six 'moons' at the longest, had contrived a calendar in the shape of a knotted line by which to reckon the elapsing time of separation. Then comes the compiler's gratuitous embellishment:

As the slow but sure steps of Time have been moving onward, the Reader's imagination will figure the anxious parent, resorting to this cherished remembrancer. . . . When verging towards the termination of his *latest* reckoning, he will then picture his mind glowing with parental affection, occasionally alarmed by doubt—yet still buoyed up by hope. . . . Lastly, he will view the good Abba Thulle, wearied out by that expectation, which so many returning moons since his reckoning *ceased* have by this time taught him he had nourished in vain.—But the Reader will bring him back to his remembrance, as armed with that unshaken fortitude that was equal to the Trials of varying life.—He will not in *him,* as in less manly spirits, see the passions rushing into opposite extremes—*Hope* turned to *Despair*—*Affection* converted to *Hatred.*—No—After some allowance for their *natural* fermentation, he will suppose them all placidly subsiding into the *Calm* of Resignation!—Should this not be absolutely the case of our friendly King—as the human mind is far more pained by *uncertainty* than a knowledge of the *worst*— every reader will lament, he should to this moment remain ignorant, that his long-looked-for Son can return no more. [Keate, pp. 392, 393; cf. *The Affliction of Margaret* ——, stanzas 1, 2, 5; *The Forsaken* 1–6.]

What response Keate's appeal to his reader may have found in Wordsworth's imagination will be evident, I think, to all who

45

consult that marvelous study, *The Affliction of Margaret ——*, with its 'overflow,' *The Forsaken*. I shall not discuss the delicate relations between Wordsworth's 'case' in real life and the materials that he amplified from what seems his literary source. Still it may be in place to note that the poet's eye was probably struck by the illustration on p. 364 of Keate's *Account*, representing Prince Lee Boo, second Son of Abba Thulle, 'drawn by Miss Keate,' 'engraved by T. Kirke.' Assuredly it is

An object beauteous to behold.

Wordsworthians will readily bring to mind the connection between the 'Youth from Georgia's shore' in *Ruth* and the frontispiece, 'Mico Chlucco, the Long Warrior, King of the Siminoles,' in Bartram's *Travels*. It is not uncharacteristic of Wordsworth to fuse the lineaments or trappings of an aborigine in his projection of one who 'spake the English tongue.'

VII

A Dissertation upon

Northern Lights[1]

WORDSWORTH'S outspoken contention that Byron had traded freely in Wordsworthian sentiment and diction when he wrote Canto the Third of *Childe Harold* may or may not be dismissed by all as an exhibition of 'wounded vanity' in a 'narrow mind which felt itself eclipsed' (Brandes, *Main Currents* 4. 43, 44). Possibly the view of a man so much in the habit of weighing his statements as Wordsworth deserves a more painstaking examination than the brilliant Danish critic found time to accord it. Such an examination as might now be based partly upon the material in Dr. Oeftering's dissertation, *Wordsworth's und Byron's Natur-Dichtung*, would tend to show that not merely in *Childe Harold*, where Brandes after all sees 'striking and vivid' reminiscences of the Wordsworthian manner, but elsewhere, and frequently, in the later work of Byron unconscious gleanings from the 'narrow' field of his 'eclipsed' predecessor are more or less apparent. The following coincidence in imagery between one of Wordsworth's earlier tales and one of Byron's later, unnoticed, so far as I can discover, by Dr. Oeftering, looks like a case in point. It has not escaped the eye of Byron's editor, Mr. Ernest H. Coleridge.

In stanza 11 of *Mazeppa,* near the beginning, Byron in an

[1] Published in *Modern Language Notes* 21 (1906). 44–6. Reprinted by permission. [For recent scientific information concerning the Aurora, and beautiful illustrations of it, in color as well as in black and white, see Carl W. Gartlein, Unlocking Secrets of the Northern Lights, in the *National Geographic Magazine* for November, 1947, pp. 673–704.]

abrupt, confused figure alludes to the northern lights as giving out a sound of 'crackling':

> We sped like meteors through the sky,
> When with its crackling sound the night
> Is chequer'd with the northern light.

Now Wordsworth had already employed this same remarkable conceit of an audible aurora, in his *Complaint of a Forsaken Indian Woman*. Indeed, but for some commentary like this prior use and Wordsworth's note upon it, we might thoughtlessly misconstrue Byron's loosely written lines, on the supposition that the night, rather than the light, made the 'crackling.' Wordsworth is explicit. He does not, it is true, personally vouch for the reality of a phenomenon which he could not test with his own eyes and ears, and whose actual occurrence is still among meteorologists subject to dispute. Rather, pursuing a method similar to that of Coleridge in *The Ancient Mariner,* he puts the report of this supposed freak of nature in the mouth of a deranged dreamer. In his note, however, he refers his allusion to an authority that he seems to respect. The first eight lines of *The Complaint,* which we are to imagine as chanted by a deserted squaw, now run thus:

> Before I see another day,
> Oh let my body die away!
> In sleep I heard the northern gleams;
> The stars, they were among my dreams;
> In rustling conflict through the skies,
> I heard, I saw the flashes drive,
> And yet they are upon my eyes,
> And yet I am alive.

In earlier versions, lines 5 and 6 were printed:

> In sleep did I behold the skies,
> I saw the crackling flashes drive.

For the local coloring in these lines Wordsworth was dependent upon Samuel Hearne's *Journey from Prince of Wales's Fort in Hudson's Bay, to the Northern Ocean,* a book which both

Coleridge and he must have read about the same time (1797), and which he may have borrowed from Coleridge. A copy (Dublin, 1796) used by the latter is said to be in the possession of Dr. James B. Clemens, of New York City; the 'marginalia on the fly-leaf' mentioned by Dr. Haney (*Bibliography of Coleridge*, p. 115) might furnish a clue to its private history.[2] In connection with his 'Ballad-tale,' *The Three Graves* (*Poetical Works*, ed. by Campbell, p. 590), Coleridge speaks of 'Hearne's deeply interesting anecdotes of the Copper Indians,' with a recommendation that the reader consult the original. In his note to *The Complaint* Wordsworth cites 'that very interesting work, Hearne's Journey,' as follows:

In the high northern latitudes, as the same writer informs us, when the northern lights vary their position in the air, they make a rustling and a crackling noise.

He evidently has in mind a passage in Hearne which I quote from the edition of 1795 (London) (p. 224):

I do not remember to have met with any travellers into high northern latitudes, who remarked their having heard the Northern Lights make any noise in the air as they vary their colours or position; which may probably be owing to the want of perfect silence at the time they made their observations on those meteors. I can positively affirm, that in still nights I have frequently heard them make a rustling and crackling noise, like the waving of a large flag [3] in a fresh gale of wind.

Not to burden the pages of *Modern Language Notes* with too much physical science, I may yet for the sake of comparison transcribe a few sentences from a standard work, Angot's *Aurora Borealis* (New York, 1897, pp. 46–7), showing more recent opin-

[2] I observe later that Wordsworth's library in 1850 contained a copy of Hearne in the edition of 1795; and for other reasons I am now inclined to think that Coleridge may have learned of the book through Wordsworth.

[3] Compare Coleridge, *Ancient Mariner* 313–17:

> The upper air burst into life!
> And a hundred fire-flags sheen,
> To and fro, they were hurried about!
> And to and fro, and in and out,
> The wan stars danced between.

49

ion about this alleged occurrence, and offering further commentary on Wordsworth and Byron:

Sound of the aurora.—Another physical phenomenon about which there is considerable disagreement is the sound which, according to some observers, sometimes accompanies the aurora borealis.

It is a very general belief in certain countries—for instance, in the Orkneys, in Finmark, and among the Indians of the territories round Hudson Bay—that the aurora is accompanied by a particular sound, somewhat resembling the rustling of silk. The Lapps, who also believe in the existence of this sound, compare it to the 'cracking' which may be heard in the joints of the reindeer when in movement. A great number of trustworthy observers maintain that they have distinctly heard this sound during very vivid auroras. Others, on the contrary, have never remarked any sound which in their opinion could reasonably be attributed to the aurora; we must note, however, that purely negative results cannot be set against a single positive and certain fact.

The observations which Angot seems to heed in this connection are subsequent to the account in Hearne. It is not impossible, of course, that Byron drew his information from some other, earlier source, as it is not impossible that he had read Hearne,[4] for he was both a traveler and a reader of travels. Is it not more likely that he involuntarily hit off the cadence of Wordsworth's *Complaint?* There is a certain similarity to this in his jingle.

A flitting note like the present may at least conclude where it began, with a suggestion about Wordsworth's mental calibre. This may be gaged more accurately by the measure of a serious record like *The Prelude,* which the author of *Main Currents* has hardly consulted enough for a proper understanding of his man, than by undue attention to the small talk of Moore and Emerson. However limited Wordsworth's horizon may have appeared to Emerson in 1833, or to an admirer of Nietzsche and Byron many years later, his conception thirty years earlier of what a poet ought to see and do was not restricted. Witness *The Prelude* to-

---

[4] He might have known about Hearne through Edward Ellice, who was connected with the Hudson's Bay Company.

ward the end of Book Fifth (lines 523 ff.); in spite of a grammatical hitch the mental sweep of the passage is untrammeled:

> Ye dreamers, then,
> Forgers of daring tales! we bless you . . .
> we feel
> With what, and how great might ye are in league,
> Who make our wish, our power, our thought a deed,
> An empire, a possession,—ye whom time
> And seasons serve; all Faculties to whom
> Earth crouches, the elements are potter's clay,
> Space like a heaven filled up with northern lights
> Here, nowhere, there, and everywhere at once.

VIII

Pleonastic Compounds

in Coleridge[1]

IN COLERIDGE and other 'romantic' poets one sign of their release from tradition is the free use and coinage of hyphened adjectives and nouns. Coleridge, for example, is very rich in compound nouns; richer at all events than Bowles and Wordsworth, with whom he is naturally to be compared; and like Carlyle showing his tendency toward original word-building before any hypothetical influence from the study of German. His translation of *Wallenstein* is not rich in compound words. I wish to call attention to a peculiar section of his poetical vocabulary. Coleridge possesses a set of tautological compounds the nature of which can be traced, so far as I am aware, to no external source. The usage in question may for the present be considered an idiosyncrasy.

More than one reader must have been surprised at the strange ligature in *The Rime of the Ancient Mariner* 41:

> And now the STORM-BLAST came, and he
> Was tyrannous and strong.

Coleridge repeated the noun in the latest version (1829) of his *Monody on the Death of Chatterton* 17:

> Too long before the vexing Storm-blast driven.[2]

---

[1] Published in *Modern Language Notes* 19 (1904). 223–4. Reprinted by permission.

[2] Compare Bayard Taylor's translation of Goethe's *Faust* 2885–6:
> And when roars
> The howling storm-blast through the groaning wood.

Blast, of course, is the stock 'romantic' word for powerful wind. With Coleridge, Wordsworth, and Bowles, the element seldom blows in other terms. So Wordsworth (Oxford Edition, p. 154):

> A whirl-blast from behind the hill
> Rushed o'er the wood with startling sound.

The peculiar smack of Coleridge comes from the underlying repetition in his compound; *storm* (German *sturm*) anticipating the conception of *blast.* In fact, his phraseology as it now stands is a partial compression of an earlier (Oxford Edition, p. 1031):

> Listen, Stranger! Storm and Wind
> A Wind and Tempest strong!

where the epic reiteration is even more obvious. The Biblical savor of the context (cf. Job 21.18; Is. 25.4; Ps. 107.25, 148.8: 'Stormy wind fulfilling his word') is preserved also in *squally blast, Dejection* 14. Compare also *snowy blast, To Charity* 4, and Milton's *stormy blast, Paradise Regained* 4. 418.

This cumulative effect is paralleled in many similar combinations where there is an approximate equivalence in the hyphened terms. Thus in *The Ancient Mariner* 78 (as also *snow-fog* in the marginal gloss to line 64):

> Whiles all the night, through fog-smoke white,
> Glimmered the white moon-shine;

a collocation that may have impressed Sir Walter Scott, since the Oxford Dictionary gives but one instance of the word: 'fog-smoke white as snow,' *Marmion* 2, Introd. ix. (Cf. Oxford Dictionary *fog-cloud.*)

Again, note the unusual conveyance in which Coleridge's 'Hermit good' approaches the Mariner's ship (line 523):

> The *skiff-boat* neared: I heard them talk.

Here we have a case of virtual identity, as in *harbour-bay* (line 472) we find partial equivalence:

> The *harbour-bay* was clear as glass.

With these examples one should compare an indefinite number of like formations; some with, and some without the hyphen

53

—for Coleridge is free also from the restraint of consistent punctuation; the majority composed of two nouns, a few others of an adjective and a noun, where the second half of the expression more or less clearly echoes the idea of the first. Take, for instance, *The Ancient Mariner* 395:

> But ere my *living life* returned.

Similarly in the following. *Christabel* 46, *ringlet curl;* 191, *cordial wine;* 649, *minstrel bard. Destiny of Nations* 184, *Pilgrim-man* (cf. *Ancient Mariner* 490, *seraph-man*). *The Picture* 45, *thorn-bush;* 89, *willow-herb;* 115, *cavern-well;* 176, *coppice-wood. The Nightingale* 101, *orchard-plot. Addressed to a Young Man of Fortune* 6, *fog-damps. Catullian Hendecasyllables* 15, *canoe-boat.* With *skiff-boat, canoe-boat,* and *living life* we may class *mountain-hills,* from *Fears in Solitude* 184, as a noteworthy illustration of this strange touch in Coleridge. I have marked, and may here record, the following compound words in *The Rime of the Ancient Mariner:*

Wedding-guest, bright-eyed, storm-blast, mast-high, thunder-fit, fog-smoke, moon-shine, cross-bow, death-fires, water-sprite, dungeon-grate, night-mare, Life-in-Death, far-heard, spectre-bark, life-blood, star-dogged, hoar-frost, water-snakes, fire-flags, a-dropping, sky-lark, honey-dew, charnel-dungeon, meadow-gale, light-house, harbour-bar, harbour-bay, seraph-man, seraph-band, oak-stump, skiff-boat, forest-brook, ivy-tod, she-wolf, a-feared, garden-bower, bride-maids, marriage-feast, morrow-morn.

Naturally, some of the expressions cited are not confined to this one author. *Coppice-wood* is in good usage elsewhere. *Cordial* wine, if it belongs in our list at all, has a close parallel in Milton's *Comus* 672:

> And first behold this cordial julep here.

For others, as *skiff-boat,* no authority is recorded. Altogether, they make a distinctive part of Coleridge's strange diction, well worth special scrutiny. In *The Ancient Mariner* and kindred narratives they add their grateful flavor to the numerous devices of echo and repetition with which the poet intensifies his general epic effect.

54

An Aquatic in 'The Rime of the Ancient Mariner'[1]

IN LINES 131–4 of *The Ancient Mariner,* Coleridge vaguely reveals, through a fitting atmosphere of unreality, the malign agent that has begun to wreak vengeance on the slayer of the Albatross:

> And some in dreams assured were
>> Of the Spirit that plagued us so;
> Nine fathom deep he had follow'd us
>> From the Land of Mist and Snow.

So the lines ran in the first edition of *Lyrical Ballads:* they suffered no material change in later versions.

However, when he subsequently added the curious marginal gloss that accompanies *The Ancient Mariner* in *Sibylline Leaves,* the poet gave this stanza a peculiar emphasis, reinforcing it by next to the longest and perhaps the most grandiloquent passage in the entire commentary. He explains:

A Spirit had followed them; one of the invisible inhabitants of this planet, neither departed souls nor angels; concerning whom the learned Jew, Josephus, and the Platonic Constantinopolitan, Michael Psellus, may be consulted. They are very numerous, and there is no climate or element without one or more.

Does not this gloss itself call for commentary?

Strangely enough, in the sporadic efforts that have been made

[1] Published in *Modern Language Notes* 20 (1905). 107–8. Reprinted by permission.

during the past sixty years to trace Coleridge's 'indebtedness' in
The Ancient Mariner to various 'sources,' one or two of which,
for all his discursive reading, he may never have seen, his specific
recommendation to consult Josephus and Psellus has passed un-
heeded. Possibly a latent touch of humor has made his advice
seem irrelevant. His reference to 'the learned Jew,' it is only fair
to say, does not seem to be a clue of remarkable value. If he really
means Flavius Josephus, he is apparently either napping or pur-
posely misleading. So far as I can discover, there is nothing in the
well-known historian that serves in any way to explain the demonology of *The Rime;* although Josephus' account of Eleazer ex-
orcising evil spirits before Vespasian and his army would in other
connections have attracted Coleridge, had he read it.[2] Very likely
the author of a recent fascinating article on *Demonology* in *The
Jewish Encyclopedia*[3] could decide whether the poet did not
rather have in mind some forgotten erudite of the Middle Ages.[4]

His allusion to 'the Platonic Constantinopolitan,' on the other
hand, is easily identified. Coleridge refers to Michael Psellus, sur-
named 'The Younger' (1018–79), a late Neoplatonist, who,
though in all probability not a native of Constantinople, became
a teacher there, and ranks in Byzantine literature as 'the great
literary light and philosopher of the eleventh century.'[5] Among
his numerous writings is a polemical dialogue directed against
the obscure sect of the Euchites, and entitled Περὶ ἐνεργείας
δαιμόνων—evidently one of the treatises of which Coleridge was
thinking when he put together his marginal gloss. Illustrative
of some unusual tendencies in Coleridge's reading, this dialogue
might well be quoted extensively for the light it throws upon his
studies in mediæval theology and revived Platonism. Here, however, we must restrict ourselves to a few briefer excerpts bearing
more obviously upon the gloss in question. There is no need of

[2] *Antiq. Jud.* 8. 2. 5; cf. *B. J.* 7. 6. 3.

[3] Vol. 4, pp. 514 ff.

[4] Later:—Could he by any possibility have meant 'the learned Jew,' Philo?
Cf. Coleridge's *Works*, ed. by Shedd, 5. 449 ff., and the article on *Angelology*
in *The Jewish Encyclopedia*.

[5] Krumbacher *Gesch. d. Byzantinischen Lit.*, in Iwan Müller's *Handbuch
d. Klass. Altertumswissenschaft* (1897), 9.1, ss. 79, 80, 433 ff.

wasting words in introducing the characters of Psellus' dialogue; a certain *Thrax* is supposed to be retailing to *Timotheus* the occult lore of a Mesopotamian named *Marcus:* [6]

'Marcus,' continued I, 'are there many kinds of demons?'

'Many?' said he; 'there are demons of every possible variety in form and body; for the upper air is full of them, as well as the air immediately around us; likewise the land and the sea and the nethermost abysses.'

'Well,' said I, 'if it be not too laborious, enumerate them severally.'

'It would be laborious,' answered he, 'merely to recall those that I myself have cast out. However, if you insist, I shall do my best to satisfy you.'

Whereupon he enumerated many kinds of demons, including their names and their forms and the regions they inhabit. . . . In general, so he said, there are six main varieties of demons. . . . First, what he called in his local barbarian gibberish 'Leliourion,' a name signifying *igneous;* this sort roams the atmosphere above us; though from the sacred regions around the moon every demon is banished as a thing profane. Second, the sort that wanders in the air directly about us, a kind often simply called *aerial.* In addition to these, third, the *terrestrial.* Fourth, the *aqueous* and *marine.* Fifth, the *subterranean.* Last, the *lightloathing* and *insensate.* These varieties of demons all hate God and are hostile to men. They are, so to speak, incomparably evil. But the aqueous and the subterranean, and still more the lightloathing are malignant and baleful to the last degree.

So far as concerns lines 131–4 of *The Ancient Mariner,* the baleful genius that 'had followed them' would belong in Marcus' fourth division, the aqueous or marine; just as the 'dæmons of the earth or middle air' mentioned in the gloss to lines 345–9 belong respectively in his third and first. In the gloss to lines 393–7, however, there might seem to be a confusion of species: here 'The Polar Spirit's fellow-dæmons, the invisible inhabitants of the element,' are heard talking in the air above. Still whether or not their proper abode is the water, an escape from their usual habitat should give us no concern. Coleridge's poetic master also —his demonology is far more definitely articulated than Cole-

[6] I translate from the edition by J. F. Boissonade, Nuremberg, 1838, pp. 15–18.

ridge's—permits the evil powers of all the 'elements' to gather
and parley in the upper atmosphere:

> For Satan with slye preface to return
> Had left him vacant, and with speed was gon
> Up to the middle Region of thick Air,
> Where all his Potentates in Council sate;
> There without sign of boast, or sign of joy,
> Sollicitous and blank he thus began.
>   Princes, Heavens antient Sons, Ætherial Thrones,
> Demonian Spirits now, from the Element
> Each of his reign allotted, rightlier call'd,
> Powers of Fire, Air, Water, and Earth beneath,
> So may we hold our place and these mild seats
> Without new trouble.[7]

Psellus, I am told, was a main avenue through which oriental
demonology passed into Europe. Is it improbable that Milton in
his 'industrious and select reading' became acquainted with the
dialogue Περὶ ἐνεργείας δαιμόνων? It is by no means impossible
that both Milton and Coleridge knew also of a shorter treatise
by the same 'Constantinopolitan': τινὰ περὶ δαιμόνων δοξάζουσιν
Ἕλληνες.

These references to Psellus and Milton are casual hints for the
next editor of *The Ancient Mariner*. Let us hope that he will
dive through the flotsam and jetsam of so many previous note-
mongers, and morosely follow Coleridge 'nine fathom deep' to
his real sources.

[7] *P.R.* 2.115–26; cf. *Il Pens.* 93–6; *P.R.* 1. 39–47; 4.201.

X

The Abyssinian Paradise in

Coleridge and Milton[1]

IN HIS *Poems of Coleridge,* p. 292, Dr. Garnett annotates the allusion to Abyssinia in *Kubla Khan* as follows:

L. 40. *Singing of Mount Abora.* There seems to be no mountain of this name in Abyssinia at the present day, though one may be mentioned by some ancient traveler. Whether this be the case, or whether the mountain be Coleridge's invention, the name must be connected with the river Atbara, the Astaboras of the ancients, which rises in Abyssinia and falls into the Nile near Berber. The principal affluent of this river is the Tacazze = *terrible,* so called from the impetuosity of its stream. If Coleridge knew this, an unconscious association with the impetuosity of the river he had been describing may have led to the apparently far-fetched introduction of the Abyssinian maid into a poem of Tartary.

Abora might be a variant spelling, not only of *Atbara,* but of *Amara* in some old itinerary or, say, in one of the seventeenth- and eighteenth-century books that touch on the location of the paradise terrestrial. I have not, however, been able to find the variant in anything that Coleridge read. Presumably he read many both of the earlier and of the later travelers. One of the later, the best authority that he could have for his knowledge of Abyssinia, was James Bruce, whose *Travels to Discover the Sources of the Nile* fell into Coleridge's hand perhaps as early

[1] Published in *Modern Philology* 3 (1906). 327–32. Reprinted by permission.

59

as 1794.[2] It is barely possible that Coleridge borrowed the book from Southey, for the latter's library in 1844 contained a copy of the Dublin (1790) edition. Bruce, of course, mentions the river *Astaboras* or *Atbara,* as well as Atbara, a peninsula, and *Amhara* (compare *Amara*), a 'division of country.' He speaks of the *Tacazzè* also, remarking on the contrast between its placidity at one season [3] and its turbulence when swollen with rain:

> But three fathoms it certainly had rolled in its bed; and this prodigious body of water, passing furiously from a high ground in a very deep descent, tearing up rocks and large trees in its course, and forcing down their broken fragments scattered on its stream, with a noise like thunder echoed from a hundred hills, these very naturally suggest an idea, that, from these circumstances, it is very rightly called the *terrible.*[4]

Some of the diction and imagery here reminds one of Coleridge's tumultuous river *Alph.* However, there is in general not enough of the fabulous about Bruce to warrant the supposition that Coleridge is indebted to him for much of *Kubla Khan,* full though that poem be of the spirit of the 'old travellers.' In any case, I cannot believe that Dr. Garnett has hit upon the 'unconscious association' that brought Abyssinia into 'a poem of Tartary.'

For that matter, I cannot regard 'poem of Tartary' as an entirely fitting name for Coleridge's sensuous vision. This might preferably be termed a dream of the terrestrial, or even of the 'false,' paradise; since, apart from its unworthy, acquiescent admission of demoniac love within so-called 'holy' precincts,[5] it reads like an arras of reminiscences from several accounts of natural [6] or enchanted parks, and from various descriptions of that elusive and danger-fraught garden which mystic geographers

---

[2] *Coleridge's Poems: Facsimile Reproduction,* p. 173.
[3] Edinburgh edition (1790), Vol. 3, p. 157.
[4] Edinburgh edition (1790), Vol. 3, p. 158.
[5] A savage place! as holy and enchanted
    As e'er beneath a waning moon was haunted
    By woman wailing for her demon-lover!
                   —*Kubla Khan* 14–16.
[6] For example, Bartram's descriptions of Georgia and Florida in his *Travels,* etc. (Philadelphia, 1791).

have studied to locate from Florida to Cathay.[7] Like the Tartar paradise at the beginning of *Kubla Khan* and the bewitched inclosure of the Old Man of the Mountain which seems to appear toward the end,[8] this Abyssinian hill in the middle is simply one of those 'sumptuous' retreats whose allurements occupied the imagination of a marvel-hunter like Samuel Purchas. It is certainly not 'Coleridge's invention.' The Portuguese Alvarez passed by the mountain *Amara* in Abyssinia and was acquainted with the myth concerning it.[9] Incidentally he speaks of a city in that region, called *Abra,* the name of which may in some way be connected with Coleridge's *Abora.*

However, if we do not demand unusual exactitude in the poet's handling of proper names, we need not go far afield to discover his mountain; no farther, in fact, than the volume which he says he was reading before he fell asleep and dreamed his *Kubla Khan.* Purchas has an entire chapter of his *Pilgrimage,* entitled Of the Hill Amara, in which he has collected the substance of the stories about that fabulous spot. An excerpt or two from him may serve in identification:

The hill Amara hath alreadie been often mentioned, and nothing indeed in all Ethiopia more deserueth mention. . . . This hill is situate as the nauil of that Ethiopian body, and center of their Empire, vnder the Equinoctiall line, where the Sun may take his best view thereof, as not encountering in all his long iourny with the like Theatre, wherein the Graces & Muses are actors, no place more graced with Natures store, . . . the Sunne himself so in loue with the sight, that the first & last thing he vieweth in all those parts is this hill. . . . Once, Heauen and Earth, Nature and Industrie, have all been corriuals to it, all presenting their best presents, to make it of this so louely presence, some taking this for the place of our Fore-fathers Paradise. And yet though thus admired of others, as a Paradise, it is made a Prison to some [i. e., the princes of Abyssinia], on whom Nature had bestowed the greatest freedome.[10]

This, then, is the *Mount Abora* of which Coleridge (or his slave-girl) sings, a paradise which he is led to compare with that

---

[7] See the authorities cited in Pierre Daniel Huet's *La situation du paradis terrestre* (Paris, 1711).

[8] Compare *Purchas his Pilgrimage* (1617), p. 428.

[9] See his account (chap. 54) in Ramusio.   [10] Purchas (1617), p. 843.

of Tartary by the most intimate of mental associations. It is also the *Mount Amara* of Milton's *Paradise Lost,* occurring in a section of that poem with which I can fancy the author of *Kubla Khan* as especially familiar; in the Fourth Book, where Milton offers his marvelous description of the authentic paradise terrestrial, distinguishing it carefully from sundry false claimants:

> Nor, where Abassin kings their issue guard,
> Mount Amara (though this by some supposed
> True Paradise) under the Ethiop line
> By Nilus' head, enclosed with shining rock
> A whole day's journey high, but wide remote
> From this Assyrian garden.[11]

When the industrious Todd [12] pointed out a connection between these lines and Purchas' chapter on Mount Amara, quoting the passage given below from the *Pilgrimage,* he failed to note that later on in the Fourth Book Milton had, in spite of his distinction, to all appearances levied on Purchas' description of the false Abyssinian garden for embellishment of the true 'Assyrian.' Purchas goes on with the account of his 'hill.'

It is situate in a great Plaine largely extending it selfe every way, without other hill in the same for the space of 30. leagues, the forme thereof round and circular, the height such, that it is a daies worke to ascend from the foot to the top; round about, the rock is cut so smooth and euen, without any vnequall swellings, that it seemeth to him that stands beneath, like a high wall, whereon the Heauen is as it were propped: and at the top it is over-hanged with rocks, iutting forth of the sides the space of a mile, bearing out like mushromes, so that it is impossible to ascend it. . . . It is above twenty leagues in circuit compassed with a wall on the top, well wrought, that neither man nor beast in chase may fall downe. The top is a plaine field, onely toward the South is a rising hill, beautifying this plaine, as it were with a watch-tower, not seruing alone to the eye, but yeelding also a pleasant spring which passeth through all that Plaine . . . and making a Lake, whence issueth a River, which hauing from these tops espied Nilus, never leaves seeking to find him, whom he cannot

---

[11] *Paradise Lost* 4. 280–6.
[12] *Milton's Poetical Works,* ed. by Todd (1809), 3. 101–2.

leave both to seeke and finde. . . . The way vp to it is cut out within the Rocke, not with staires, but ascending by little and little, that one may ride vp with ease; it hath also holes cut to let in light, and at the foote of this ascending place, a faire gate, with a *Corpus du Guarde*. Halfe way vp is a faire and spacious Hall cut out of the same rocke, with three windowes very large vpwards: the ascent is about the length of a lance and a halfe: and at the top is a gate with another gard. . . . There are no Cities on the top, but palaces, standing by themselves, in number four and thirtie, spacious, sumptuous, and beautifull, where the Princes of the Royall bloud have their abode with their Families. The Souldiers that gard the place dwell in Tents.[13]

This sunlit and symmetrical hill, with its miracle of inner carven passages, may partially explain Coleridge's 'sunny dome' and 'caves of ice,' which must have puzzled more than one reader in *Kubla Khan*. The preceding lines from Milton should also be compared, and, as I have hinted, the following as well:

> The setting Sun
> Slowly descended, and with right aspect
> Against the eastern gate of Paradise
> Levelled his evening rays. It was a rock
> Of alabaster, piled up to the clouds,
> Conspicuous far, winding with one ascent
> Accessible from Earth, one entrance high;
> The rest was craggy cliff, that overhung
> Still as it rose, impossible to climb.
> Betwixt these rocky pillars Gabriel sat,
> Chief of the angelic guards.[14]

There are, it is true, too many points of similarity in the various paradises of the Fathers and geographers to permit the critic to say with great assurance that Milton or Coleridge borrowed this or that embellishment of his mystical inclosure from any one prior writer. We are dealing here, I presume, with a world-old effort of imagination showing certain reappearing essentials of an inherited conception, such as a fountain with outflowing 'sinuous rills,' a symmetrical mountain, a disappearing 'sacred

[13] Purchas (1617), p. 844.   [14] *Paradise Lost* 4. 540–9.

river,' all within a wall of measured circuit, and the like, the chief of which may be found in a poem of small compass like *Kubla Khan* [15]—probably all of them in the fourth book of *Paradise Lost*. In how far Milton may be indebted to Purchas' compendium for all sorts of quasi-geographical lore, in addition to the slight obligations already indicated, is a question lying rather in the province of the professed student of Milton. For the present writer, whose interest here is more particularly in Coleridge, it seems enough to point out the relationship between Coleridge's beautiful fragment and Milton's completed masterpiece; to indicate, in passing, Milton's greater distinctness and mastery in handling his material; finally, to suggest, on the basis of this brief paper, that, instead of continuing to treat *Kubla Khan* as a sort of incomparable *hapax legomenon,* wholly unexplainable, because incomparable, we shall understand it and its author better if we seek to trace the subtle, yet no less real, connection between them and the literature to which they belong. Specifically, let the reader of Coleridge be also a reader of Coleridge's master, Milton, and the lover of *Kubla Khan* a lover also of that 'pleasant soil' in which 'his far more pleasant garden God ordained.' [16]

[15] Compare, for example, Coleridge's 'mighty fountain,' 'sinuous rills,' and 'meandering' river with the following, quoted by Todd: 'In ipso hortorum apice *fons* est eximius, qui primum argenteis aquarum vorticibus ebulliens, mox diffusus in fluvium sinuosis flexibus, atque mæandris concisus *oberrat,* et felicia arva perennibus fœcundat rivulis.'—P. Causinus, *de Eloq.,* lib. XI, edit. 1634 (Todd, *Milton's Poetical Works* [1809] 3. 95–6). Cf. Milton, *Paradise Lost* 4. 223 ff., and the first part of *Kubla Khan.*

[16] *Paradise Lost* 4. 215. [The most helpful collection of references I ever met on paradises is found in the work of Edoardo Coli, *Il Paradiso terrestre Dantesco,* Florence, 1897.]

XI

The Power of the Eye

in Coleridge[1]

EVERY one will recall what a distinctive mark of the chief personage in *The Rime of the Ancient Mariner* is his 'glittering eye'; and it will not be forgotten that in a stanza contributed by Wordsworth to the opening of the ballad by his friend, the Mariner is represented as exercising through the gleam of his eye a notable power of hypnotic fascination:

> He holds him with his *glittering eye*—
> The Wedding-Guest *stood still,*
> And listens like a three years' child:
> The Mariner hath his will.[2]

That is, the Mariner has his own way with the Wedding-Guest, as the Sun, later in the poem, has his way with the ship:

> The sails at noon left off their tune,
> And the ship *stood still* also.

[1] Reprinted from *Studies in Language and Literature in Celebration of the Seventieth Birthday of James Morgan Hart,* New York, Henry Holt and Company, 1910, pp. 78–121. Reprinted by permission.

[2] *A.M.* 13–16. Throughout this paper italics are used in order to draw attention to certain catchwords or stock phrases in the poet's vocabulary, *e.g., bright, bright-eyed, glitter, glittering, fixed, stood still,* etc. And the following abbreviations are employed: *A.M.* (= *The Rime of the Ancient Mariner,* in the final text of 1829 as reprinted by Campbell); *A.M.,* 1 ed. (= the original text of the same poem in *Lyrical Ballads,* 1798, as reprinted by Campbell); *P.W.* (= the *Poetical Works* of Coleridge, edited by Campbell); and *P.B.* (= Wordsworth's *Peter Bell*).

> The Sun, right up above the mast,
> Had *fixed* her to the ocean.[3]

At first reading, one might suppose the meaning to be that the Mariner had control of the Wedding-Guest's will—which of course is true. But it is not precisely what is said, as may be gathered from a stanza, subsequently omitted, in the original version of the ballad:

> Listen, O listen, thou Wedding-guest!
>   'Marinere! thou hast thy will:
> For that which comes out of thine *eye* doth make
>   My body and soul to be *still*.'[4]

The Wordsworthian lines beginning, 'He holds him with his glittering eye,' and the general Coleridgean notion in them, are sufficiently familiar, as is also the gloss which accompanies them: 'The Wedding-Guest is *spell-bound* by the *eye* of the old seafaring man, and constrained to hear his tale.'[5]

However, it is not probable that among students of Coleridge the frequency with which the idea of an ocular hypnosis or the like arises in the mind of the poet has been duly observed, so that his full meaning in several otherwise well-known passages may easily escape the general reader. Accordingly, I propose to collect a number of extracts from Coleridge in which this notion is altogether patent; to add to these certain other extracts in which it may be only suggested, or is concealed, proceeding in such a way that the less may receive light from the more obvious; and to supply still further material, some of it drawn from remoter sources, that can be made to bear upon the particular subject of this study. Our study, therefore, will involve an examination of passages from *Lewti, The Three Graves, Kubla Khan, The Rime of the Ancient Mariner* in the first as well as the final and accepted version, *Christabel, The Nightingale, Osorio,* etc.; it will include some description of Coleridge's appearance—for example, the look of his eye—and some account of his interest in animal magnetism and ocular fascination; it

---

[3] *A.M.* 381–4.   [4] *A.M.,* 1 ed., 362–5.
[5] Marginal gloss to *A.M.* 13–16.

will touch upon the widespread interest during the earlier part of Coleridge's life in Friedrich Anton Mesmer and his cult of magnetizers; and, among other things, it will allude to certain differences, casual as well as intended, between Coleridge and Wordsworth in their treatment of what is called the 'supernatural.' It hardly needs to be said that the present writer, being neither an adept in the secrets of animal magnetism, nor versed in the immense body of writings on this and related topics, does not concern himself with any question as to the reality of the hypnotic influences issuing, or thought to issue, from the human eye, but only with Coleridge's opinion as to their reality or likelihood. For the history of the subject the reader may consult the standard work by Binet and Féré,[6] Charles Mackay's *Memoirs of Extraordinary Popular Delusions*,[7] or, if they are accessible, some of the older treatises of which Coleridge himself makes mention—among them, and especially, that by Kluge.[8] I have not been able to obtain this.

As for Coleridge himself, it may be assumed that he was conscious of a power that seemed to dwell in his own eye. Thus in the *Hexameters* addressed to William and Dorothy Wordsworth, and written, as their author says, 'during a temporary blindness in the year 1799,' he exclaims:

O! what a life is the eye! what a fine and inscrutable essence! [9]

And even in ordinary conversation he must have experienced, to an unusual degree, the sense of control over his audience which in the born orator we often attribute to his direct, or, as we call it, 'piercing' glance. In fact, Carlyle bears testimony to something of the sort in Coleridge, when the latter was an elderly and broken man, long after the halcyon days when *The Rime of the Ancient Mariner* and *Christabel* were taking shape. Says Carlyle: 'I have heard Coleridge talk, with eager musical energy,

[6] *Animal Magnetism*, New York, Appleton, 1890. See also the historical sketch at the beginning of Albert Moll's *Hypnotism*, New York, 1890.

[7] London, Routledge, 1869 (volume 1, pp. 262–95, *The Magnetizers*).

[8] Carl Alexander Kluge, *Versuch einer Darstellung des animalischen Magnetismus*, Berlin, 1815 (first edition, 1811). The work was widely translated.

[9] *P.W.*, p. 138.

two stricken hours, his face radiant and moist, and communicate no meaning whatsoever to any individual of his hearers—certain of whom, I for one, still kept eagerly listening in hope.' [10] The Sage of Highgate evidently needed to lay no hand upon that chosen guest whom he would detain from the pleasures of the world at his feast of reason and flow of soul. In his prime he was not less magnetic. 'From Carlyon we learn that Coleridge dressed badly, "but I have heard him say, fixing his prominent eyes upon himself (as he was wont to do whenever there was a mirror in the room), with a singularly coxcombical expression of countenance, that his dress was sure to be lost sight of the moment he began to talk, an assertion which, whatever may be thought of its modesty, was not without truth." ' [11]

That there was something unusual, if not captivating, in his look may be inferred, if only from the strange and conflicting reports (brought together by Dr. Haney) as to the actual color of his eyes. They were, of course, large and gray, as his most intimate friends specifically affirm. Wordsworth calls him

A noticeable man, with large gray eyes.[12]

And Dorothy Wordsworth, writing to a friend a year or so before the composition of *The Rime of the Ancient Mariner,* says of Coleridge: 'His eye is large and full, not dark but gray; such an eye as would receive from a heavy soul the dullest expression, but it speaks every emotion of his animated mind. It has more of "the poet's eye in a fine frenzy rolling" than I ever witnessed. He has fine dark eyebrows, and an overhanging forehead.' [13] Several other references to Coleridge's eyes may be given summarily. Carlyle: 'The deep eyes, of a light hazel, were as full of sorrow as of inspiration.' Carlyle (on another occasion): 'A pair of strange, brown, timid, yet earnest-looking eyes.' Emerson:

[10] Carlyle, *Life of John Sterling: Works* (1904) 11.56.

[11] Campbell, *Samuel Taylor Coleridge,* p. 99.

[12] *Stanzas Written in my Pocket-copy of Thomson's 'Castle of Indolence'* 39.

[13] *Letters of the Wordsworth Family,* ed. by Knight, 1.109. For other references to Coleridge's appearance I am indebted to the interesting article by Dr. John Louis Haney, 'The Color of Coleridge's Eyes,' *Anglia* 23.424 ff.

'Bright blue eyes, and fine clear complexion.' Armstrong: 'The quick, yet steady and penetrating greenish-gray eye.' Winter (an imaginary portrait): 'The great, luminous, changeful blue eyes.' Leapidge Smith: 'Eyes not merely dark, but black, and keenly penetrating.' De Quincey (who, like the following, was a more trustworthy observer than some of the foregoing): 'His eyes were large, and in color were gray.' Hazlitt: 'Large, projecting eyebrows, and his eyes rolling beneath them like a sea with darkened lustre.' Henry Nelson Coleridge: 'His large gray eyes, at once the clearest and the deepest that I ever saw.' Harriet Martineau: 'His eyes were as wonderful as they were represented to be—light gray, extremely prominent, and actually "glittering." '

Much of the discrepancy in these reports may be set down to haste and carelessness in observation—Emerson, for example, is not always trustworthy on minor details; but, as we may gather from Dorothy Wordsworth, Coleridge's eyes, even before he began to take opium, might, under varying stress of emotion, go through a considerable range of appearance. As often happens with emotional subjects, his pupils were likely to suffer a striking dilatation, followed by intense contraction, the latter state having the effect which we know as a 'glitter.' At all events it doubtless is right to believe that in a measure the 'glittering eye' of the Ancient Mariner is the counterpart of an effect sometimes visible in the poet; and, if there be such a thing as the hypnotic glance, there is nothing unreasonable in imagining that Coleridge possessed it.

In any case, if the existence of such a thing were affirmed, Coleridge was bound to be interested, as in any of those mysterious phenomena which he termed 'facts of mind.' Thus in a compendious description of himself which he sent to Thelwall in 1796, he remarks: 'Metaphysics and poetry and "facts of mind," that is, accounts of all the strange phantasms that ever possessed "your philosophy" . . . are my darling studies.' [14] Though any systematic account of the studies in animal magnetism entered into by so discursive and unmethodical a reader as Coleridge is scarcely

[14] Letter of Nov. 19, 1796. *Letters of Samuel Taylor Coleridge*, ed. by E. H. Coleridge, 1.181.

possible, there is some ground for supposing that in his earlier years he was more prone to believe in a 'fact of mind,' such as ocular hypnosis, than he was in later life. His allusions to cures by suggestion among the American Indians, as recorded in Hearne's *Hudson's Bay,* and to similar occurrences among the Negroes of whom he read in Bryan Edwards' *West Indies,*[15] and indeed the use to which he puts his information on these matters in *Osorio* and the poems designed for *Lyrical Ballads,* all point to a less critical attitude in the young Coleridge than we find in the Coleridge of *Table Talk* and Highgate. At Highgate he has become the cautious philosopher. It is therefore characteristic of him to say, under *Table Talk* for April 30, 1830: 'My mind is in a state of philosophical doubt as to animal magnetism. Von Spix, the eminent naturalist, makes no doubt of the matter, and talks coolly of giving doses of it.' Yet he goes on: 'The torpedo affects a third or external object, by an exertion of its own will; such a power is not properly electrical; for electricity acts invariably under the same circumstances.' And he adds: 'A steady gaze will make many persons of fair complexions blush deeply. Account for that.' [16]

However, he had already given as it were his final utterance on this head some years before 1830. Between 1820, when Southey's *Life of Wesley* appeared, and August, 1825, when Coleridge wrote the words in which he bequeathed his personally annotated copy of this work to its author, he had composed a long marginal memorandum on the similarity of the religious trances among the Wesleyan Methodists to the trances induced by the magnetizers. On the credibility of the phenomena said to occur during the magnetic trances, he observes:

Among the magnetizers and attesters are to be found names of men . . . of integrity and incapability of intentional falsehood . . . Cuvier, Hufeland, Blumenbach, Eschenmeyer, Reil, etc. . . . Nine years has the subject of zoömagnetism been before me. I have traced it historically, collected a mass of documents in French, German, Italian, and the Latinists of the sixteenth century, have never neg-

[15] *P.W.,* p. 590. Cf. Hearne, pp. 193 ff., 218 ff.; Edwards, Book 4, Chap. 3.
[16] Coleridge, *Works,* ed. by Shedd, 6.302.

lected an opportunity of questioning eye-witnesses, *e.g.*, Tieck, Treviranus, De Prati, Meyer, and others of literary or medical celebrity, and I remain where I was, and where the first perusal of Klug's work had left me, without having moved an inch backward or forward. The reply of Treviranus, the famous botanist, to me, when he was in London, is worth recording: . . . 'I have seen what I am certain I would not have believed on *your* telling and, in all reason, I can neither expect nor wish that you should believe on mine.' [17]

If the perusal of C. A. Kluge's (= 'Klug's') work left him in an enduring state of 'philosophical doubt,' to track Coleridge through the labyrinth of his subsequent futile investigations would not seem to be urgently demanded; and we may merely observe that he owned a copy of this treatise in the edition of 1815.[18] If he read this edition in the year of its issue, the 'nine years' of persistent study would bring the date of his marginal note in Southey's volume down to 1824. But even if he had seen Kluge in the edition of 1811, how are we to explain the long gap in his interest between 1797–98, when he had read Hearne and Edwards, and was writing *The Three Graves* and *The Rime of the Ancient Mariner,* and 1811, or later, when he began his alleged comprehensive researches? [19] It may, indeed, be the case that the date of his marginal note is the same as that of the bequest to Southey, 1825, and that his preoccupation with animal magnetism began just nine years earlier than this, namely, 1816, when he put himself under medical care, and was received under

[17] Coleridge, *Works,* ed. by Shedd, 6.303.
[18] See Haney's *Bibliography of Coleridge,* under 'Marginalia' (p. 119, No. 180).
[19] See, however, Mackay, *Extraordinary Popular Delusions* 1.291: 'During the first twelve years of the [nineteenth] century little was heard of animal magnetism in any country of Europe. Even the Germans forgot their airy fancies, recalled to the knowledge of this every-day world by the roar of Napoleon's cannon and the fall or the establishment of kingdoms. During this period a cloud of obscurity hung over the science, which was not dispersed until M. Deleuze published, in 1813, his *Histoire Critique du Magnétisme Animal.* This work gave a new impulse to the half-forgotten fancy. Newspapers, pamphlets, and books again waged war upon each other on the question of its truth or falsehood; and many eminent men in the profession of medicine recommenced inquiry with an earnest design to discover the truth.'

71

the roof of James Gillman at Highgate. In the library of a well-to-do physician, who was also a man of no slight intellectual curiosity, the poet would at that time be almost certain to find a number of books dealing with the subject.[20] However this may be, it is clear, as Dykes Campbell points out, that by June, 1817, Coleridge had become deeply enough engrossed to think of writing a popular work of his own on animal magnetism, 'a proposal which he renewed (to Curtis) eighteen months later, when his old teacher, Blumenbach, had recanted his [dis]belief' in it. And since he thereupon 'offered to contribute a historical treatise to the *Encyclopedia Metropolitana*,' the idea may possibly not have been so easily relinquished as were some of his numerous other literary projects. Campbell also refers to a contemporary letter (August, 1817) in which Southey, writing to his wife, anticipates the nature of a visit which he is about to pay Coleridge: 'He will begin as he did when last I saw him, about Animal Magnetism, or some equally congruous subject, and go on from Dan to Beersheba in his endless loquacity.' [21] Coleridge's letter of December 1, 1818, to Curtis, though rather long, may be quoted in full:

Dear Sir: Some time ago, I ventured to recommend an article on Animal Magnetism, *purely historical,* for the *Encyclopedia Metropolitana*. Since then the celebrated Professor Blumenbach, for so many years the zealous antagonist of Animal Magnetism, has openly recanted his opinion in three separate paragraphs of his great work on Physiology, which is a text-book in all the hospitals and Medical Universities in Europe; and this too happens to be in the edition from which Dr. Elliotson has recently translated the work into English. Cuvier had previously published his testimony, viz. that the facts were as undeniable as they were difficult to be explained on the present theory. The great names of Hufeland, Meckel, Reil, Autenrieth, Soemerring, Scarpa, etc., etc., appear as attesters of the facts, and their independence of the imagination of the patients. To these must be added the reports delivered in the courts of Berlin and Vienna by the several committees appointed severally by the Prus-

[20] Compare Coleridge, *Miscellanies*, etc., ed. by Ashe, 1885, pp. 351, 365 (footnote), 408, 410, etc.

[21] *P.W.*, Introduction, p. cii.

sian and Austrian governments, and composed of the most eminent physicians, anatomists, and naturalists of the Prussian and Austrian States. In this country, the rising opinion of our first-rate medical men is that the subject must sooner or later be submitted to a similar trial in this country, in order that so dangerous an implement (if it should prove to be a new physical agent akin to the galvanic electricity) may be taken out of the hands of the ignorant and designing, as hath already been done on the Continent by very severe Laws. Putting the truth or falsehood of the theory wholly out of the question, still it is altogether unique, and such as no history of the present age dare omit. Nay, it may be truly said that it becomes more interesting, more important, on the supposition of its falsehood than of its truth, from the great number and wide dispersion of celebrated individuals, of the highest rank in science, who have joined in attesting its truth; especially as the largest part of these great men were for a long time its open opponents, and all, with the single exception of Cuvier, its avowed disbelievers. Add to this that as an article of entertainment, and as throwing a new light on the oracles and mysteries of Greek, Roman, and Egyptian Paganism, it would not be easy to point out its rival. These are the grounds on which I rest my continued recommendation of such an article as well worthy the attention of the conductors of your great work. One other motive will not be without its weight in *your* mind. I have some grounds for believing that a work of this kind is in *contemplation* by persons from whose hands it ought, if possible, to be rescued by anticipation, as it will, I know, be a main object with them to use the facts in order to undermine the *divine* character of the Gospel history, and the superhuman powers of its great founder; a scheme which can be rendered plausible only by misstatements, exaggeration, and the confounding of testimonies—those of fanatics and enthusiasts with the sober results of guarded experiment, given in by men of science and authority.[22]

When they are put together, the marginal note and this letter suggest a fairly extensive list of volumes with which Coleridge might be presumed to have had some acquaintance. Doubtless he had access to other important works which he does not happen to cite. He must, of course, have dipped into Mesmer; a copy of

[22] 'Some Unpublished Letters of Samuel Taylor Coleridge,' *Lippincott's Magazine* 13.710 (June, 1874).

Mesmerismus, Berlin, 1814, annotated by the poet, was among the books that came into the possession of Lord Coleridge.[23] He could scarcely have missed the passage on the evil eye in Bacon's essay *Of Envy,* or the passage on fascination in *The Advancement of Learning.*[24] He may in all likelihood have read more than one of the Latin treatises on fascination of the sixteenth and seventeenth centuries, such as that by Christian Frommann.[25] There is, however, at least in the marginal note, an element of grandiloquence which will lead the knowing to suspect that in regard to this, as to other domains of research, Coleridge gives the impression that he has mastered more of the pertinent writings than has actually been the case. Under any circumstances, it would not at present be advisable to attempt a more detailed account of his investigations, especially if they left him in the position where he began.

For an understanding of his poetry, it seems advantageous to turn from his own later studies, however extended, to the general interest in mesmerism evinced by the contemporaries of Coleridge during the formative period of his boyhood and youth. This interest was lively on the Continent, because of the vogue of Mesmer and his immediate disciples (his paper on the discovery of magnetism having been published in 1779), and because of the stir aroused by the commissions appointed in France to inquire into the validity of his pretensions; [26] and it was lively in England shortly after, for example at London and Bristol, through the vogue of mesmerists like the celebrated Dr. John Bell and Dr. J. B. de Mainauduc.[27] This latter personage left an extraordinary reputation at Bristol, so that Coleridge should ulti-

[23] Haney, *Bibliography of Coleridge,* p. 121, No. 206. See also p. 112, No. 108; p. 124, No. 229.

[24] Book 2. *Works of Bacon,* ed. by Spedding, Ellis, and Heath, 6.256–7.

[25] *Tractatus de Fascinatione Novus et Singularis, in quo Fascinatio vulgaris profligatur, naturalis confirmatur, & magica examinatur,* etc., *Norimbergæ,* 1675. Among 'the Latinists of the sixteenth century' Coleridge would doubtless first of all include Paracelsus.

[26] In 1784.

[27] See the *History of Animal Magnetism; its Origin, Progress, and Present State; as Delivered by the late Dr. De Mainauduc,* etc. By G. Winter. Bristol, 1801.

mately have heard about him there; though it seems probable that he must have known something of the great magnetizer while a schoolboy at Christ's Hospital in London.

The methods by which the different magnetizers attracted a following, did not, in all likelihood, vary to any great extent in their essentials, and must often have resembled the procedure of Mesmer himself in detail. He 'carried a long iron wand, with which he touched the bodies of the patients; . . . often, laying aside the wand, he magnetized them with his eyes, fixing his gaze on theirs.' [28] In fact, he seems to have made use of the principle described by Binet and Féré as 'hypnotization by sensorial excitement,' that is, (1) 'by excitement of the sense of sight'—not (a) 'strong and sudden excitement, by luminous rays, by solar or electric light'—but (b) 'slight and prolonged excitement, by fixing the eyes on an object, brilliant or otherwise, which is placed near the eyes, and somewhat above their level.' [29] The eye of the magnetizer, would, if unusually brilliant, constitute a suitable object for the patient's gaze; hence, as Mackay notes, with the mesmerists and animal magnetizers in general, fixing with the eye was an established element in the practice: 'First, request [the patient] to resign himself; to think of nothing; not to perplex himself by examining the effects which may be produced. . . . After having collected yourself, take his thumbs between your fingers in such a way that the internal part of your thumbs may be in contact with the internal part of his, *and then fix your eyes upon him!*' [30]

Some conception of the stir created by the magnetizers in London while Coleridge was at school there, and at Bristol, which he subsequently visited, may be gathered from the following extracts, the first being supplied by Mackay:

So much curiosity was excited by the subject, that, about [1788] a man named Holloway gave a course of lectures on animal magnet-

[28] Binet and Féré, *Animal Magnetism,* p. 10.
[29] *Animal Magnetism,* p. 93. Compare Albert Moll, *Hypnotism* (1890), pp. 28 ff.; p. 72.
[30] *Extraordinary Popular Delusions* 1.293; Mackay quotes from the instructions of the magnetizer Deleuze (1813).

ism in London, at the rate of five guineas for each pupil, and realized a considerable fortune. Loutherbourg the painter and his wife followed the same profitable trade; and such was the infatuation of the people to be witnesses of their strange manipulations, that at times upwards of three thousand persons crowded around their house at Hammersmith, unable to gain admission. The tickets sold at prices varying from one to three guineas.[31]

In 1786, as recorded by Sir Gilbert Elliot, many well-known people were experiencing the magnetic treatment, among them the wife of Richard Brinsley Sheridan:

I am going with [Mrs. Crewe] to-day to Dr. Bell, one of the magnetizing quacks, and the first whom I shall have seen. Lady Palmerston, Mrs. Crewe, Mrs. Sheridan, and Miss Crewe have been twice at Mainaduc's. They were all infidels the first day, except Mrs. Crewe, who seemed staggered a little by the number and variety of the people she saw affected by the *crisis*. The next time, Mrs. Sheridan and Mrs. Crewe were both magnetized, and both had what is called a crisis—that is, they both fell into a sort of trance, or waking sleep, in which they could hear what passed, but had no power of speaking or moving, and they described it as very like the effects of laudanum. . . .

All the fine people have been magnetized, and are learning to magnetize others. The Prince of Wales had a crisis—that is to say, became sick and faint.[32]

The next quotation, from Mackay, bears witness to the further renown of De Mainauduc at Bristol:

In the year 1788 Dr. Mainauduc, who had been a pupil, first of Mesmer and afterwards of [Deslon], arrived in Bristol, and gave public lectures upon magnetism. His success was quite extraordinary. People of rank and fortune hastened from London to Bristol to be magnetized, or to place themselves under his tuition. Dr. George Winter, in his *History of Animal Magnetism*, gives the following list of them: 'They amounted to one hundred and twenty-seven, among whom there were one duke, one duchess, one marchioness, two countesses, one earl, one baron, three baronesses, one bishop, five

---

[31] *Extraordinary Popular Delusions* 1.287–8.
[32] *Life and Letters of Sir Gilbert Elliot, First Earl of Minto*, 1.111–13.

right honorable gentlemen and ladies, two baronets, seven members of parliament, one clergyman, two physicians, seven surgeons, besides ninety-two gentlemen and ladies of respectability.' He afterwards established himself in London, where he performed with equal success.[33]

Coleridge was at school in London from 1782 until 1791; it seems impossible that he should have escaped all knowledge of what was in the air, especially as it was about 1788 when 'his brother Luke came to walk the London Hospital, and Coleridge then thought of nothing but how he too might become a doctor. He read all the medical and surgical books he could procure.' [34]

The extracts that have just been given will suffice to indicate the amount of attention which was popularly bestowed upon 'facts of mind' during the youth of Coleridge and Wordsworth, and will help to explain the number of allusions to hypnotic fascination, hypnotic trances and suggestion, and the emergence from psychological 'crises,' to be found in the poems designed by Wordsworth, and, more especially, by Coleridge, for the *Lyrical Ballads* of 1798. The *Lyrical Ballads* were not merely an experiment in adapting a selection from the language of humble and rustic life to the expression of the chief human emotions; to a large extent they represented studies in the psychology of the abnormal, in which Wordsworth treated such diverse types as *The Idiot Boy*, the *Forsaken Indian Woman*, and *Peter Bell*— cases in actual life, or such as might have occurred in actual life, though he was to invest them with the light of the poetical imagination. Coleridge, on the other hand, who was to deal with 'supernatural' events as if they were real, works within a much narrower range of subject-matter. To tell the truth, so far as his salient ideas are concerned he hardly goes beyond the province of animal magnetism; and the notion of 'fixing,' and then of a sudden release, keeps getting the mastery over him after the fashion of a hobby bestriding its rider. Add to this conception of 'fixing' the readily associated idea of a good or an evil will in the magnetizer, which may naturally extend to blessing or cursing

[33] *Extraordinary Popular Delusions* 1.287.
[34] Campbell, *Samuel Taylor Coleridge*, p. 12.

the person who is 'fixed,' and we have the dominant notions in *The Three Graves, The Rime of the Ancient Mariner, Christabel,* and much of the contemporary *Osorio*. There is, of course, a certain amount of Miltonic, Spenserian, and mediæval demonology interwoven or adumbrated, and therefore a further variation according as one decides the question mooted by 'the Latinists' of the sixteenth and seventeenth centuries, that is, whether 'fascination' is ever accomplished without demoniac assistance. Let the reader who can at every point in the story say whether the lady Geraldine is a witch, or 'an angel beautiful and bright' and yet 'a fiend,' or a mere unsubstantial phantasm in the mind of Christabel, decide how Coleridge might have wished to settle this question. Presumably, in his effort to render the 'supernatural' more 'real,' he failed to distinguish accurately for himself just when he believed, and when he did not believe, in dubious or impossible phenomena; that is, he tried to steer a middle course between 'subjectivity' and 'objectivity.' Indeed, Coleridge's wavering on this point—his 'philosophical doubt,' even thus early, whether to present the strange occurrences of *The Rime of the Ancient Mariner* as frankly supernatural, or as in some measure capable of a rational explanation, on the ground that they existed only as mental hallucinations on the part of the main character, who saw them in a hypnotic trance, or as the vagaries of 'A Poet's Reverie,' that is, the impalpable substance of trances seen within a trance, a dream of a dream— involves his poem in an unfortunate want of self-consistency.

When we examine particular instances, however, the characteristics of the ever-recurring magnetic trance for Coleridge betray a remarkable resemblance. One person, or personified object, 'fixes' another; the 'fixed' person or object thereupon remains so for a sharply defined period:

> Seven days, seven nights, I saw that curse,
> And yet I could not die.[35]

Then, without warning, the spell is 'snapt,' and the hitherto

[35] *A.M.* 261–2. Compare Dante, *Inferno* 34.25–7. This may suggest other references in Dante, *e.g., Purgatorio* 32.7–9, 67–72.

motionless subject of the spell may be thrown into violent activity. Or, if the fascinated person or object has been set in motion by the fascinator, the motion is suddenly retarded or wholly arrested when the trance of itself comes to an end, or when some other kind of magnet gains the ascendency:

> Till noon we quietly sailed on,
> Yet never a breeze did breathe:
> Slowly and smoothly went the ship,
> Moved onward from beneath.

> Under the keel nine fathom deep,
> From the land of mist and snow,
> The spirit slid: and it was he
> That made the ship to go.
> The sails at noon left off their tune,
> And the ship stood still also.

> The Sun, right up above the mast,
> Had fixed her to the ocean:
> But in a minute she 'gan stir,
> With a short uneasy motion—
> Backwards and forwards half her length
> With a short uneasy motion.

> Then like a pawing horse let go,
> She made a sudden bound.[36]

With Coleridge, for example in *The Rime of the Ancient Mariner,* one may almost say that any being or thing can 'fix' any other, so long as he or it may be supposed to have or be a face or an eye. Thus the Mariner fixes the Wedding-Guest, and holds him so to the end of the story; the Sun, which is at one time a face and perhaps at another an eye, in a certain position, namely the equatorial zenith, fixes the ship, which is also personified; the Moon is a face—or is she a benevolent eye?—so influential that the 'great bright eye' of the Ocean is caught and swayed by her; in the Hermit's description the wolf seems to be 'pointing' the owl; and the Pilot's boy is fixed by the Mariner. Furthermore, in this same ballad there is an immense amount of apparently casual

[36] *A.M.* 372–90.

looking and watching and eyeing, or of refusing and being unable to look, of good and evil looks, of glances direct and askance, of brilliant and alluring light and color, of glistening and glimmering, attractive and repulsive objects, all of which becomes suggestive when connected with the more evident cases of fascination. All or nearly all the looking is enforced, or is done in order to avoid the peril of fixation:

> My head was turned perforce away,
> And I saw a boat appear.[37]

Probably no other noun is so frequently employed in the ballad as the word *eye* (or *eyes*); and the repetition of words like *bright, bright-eyed, glitter, glittering, fixed, still, trance,* having been mentioned in a footnote, requires no further discussion.

In order to make the preceding remarks on Coleridge more intelligible, we need only scrutinize the following extracts from his poetry. Here and there a line or two of explanation, or a footnote, will be added, when either may seem to be desirable; for order and transition in this material I may trust to a somewhat mechanical grouping—even though the groups patently overlap, and sometimes include mere verbal resemblances between passages where the hypnotic influence is not alluded to and those in which it is.

1. The bright flashing or glittering eye:

(a) It is an ancient Mariner,
    And he *stoppeth* one of three.
    'By thy long grey beard and *glittering eye,*
    Now wherefore *stopp'st* thou me?' *A.M.* 1–4.

(b) *Bright-eyed* Mariner. *A.M.* 20, 40.

(c) 'I fear thee and thy *glittering eye,*[38]
    And thy skinny hand so brown.' *A.M.* 228–9.

(d) The Mariner, whose *eye* is *bright,*
    Whose beard with age is hoar,
    Is gone. *A.M.* 618–20.

[37] *A.M.* 502–3.
[38] 'And constrained by that *glittering eye,* Hypatia knelt before her [Miriam].' Kingsley, *Hypatia.*

(e) Again the wild-flower wine she drank:
   Her *fair large eyes* 'gan *glitter bright*.   *Christabel* 220–1.

(f) And both blue *eyes* more *bright* than clear,
   Each about to have a tear.

   With *open eyes* (ah woe is me!)
   Asleep, and dreaming fearfully.   *Christabel* 290–3.

(g)   I see thy heart!
   There is a frightful *glitter* in thine *eye*,
   Which doth betray thee.   *Osorio* 5.149–51.

(h) *Maria.* O mark his *eye!* he hears not what you say.
   Osorio (pointing at vacancy). Yes, mark his *eye!* There's
      fascination in it.   *Osorio* 5.255–6.

(i) And all should cry, Beware! Beware!
   His *flashing eyes*, his floating hair!
   Weave a circle round him thrice,
   And *close your eyes* with holy dread.   *Kubla Khan* 49–52.

2. The dull eye:

   (a) There passed a weary time. Each throat
      Was parched, and *glazed* each *eye*.
      A weary time! a weary time!
      How *glazed* each *weary eye*.   *A.M.* 143–6.

   (b) A snake's small *eye blinks dull* and *shy*.   *Christabel* 583.

3. The wild look:

   (a) 'God save thee, Ancient Mariner!
      From the fiends, that plague thee thus—
      Why *look'st* thou so?'—With my cross-bow
      I shot the Albatross.   *A.M.* 79–82.

   (b) A gust of wind sterte up behind
         And whistled thro' his bones;
      Thro' the holes of his *eyes* and the hole of his mouth
         Half-whistles and half-groans.   *A.M.*, 1 ed., 195–8.

   (c) I moved my lips—the Pilot shrieked
      And fell down in a fit;
      The holy Hermit *raised his eyes*,
      And prayed where he did sit.

I took the oars: the Pilot's boy,
Who now doth crazy go,
Laughed loud and long, and all the while
His eyes went to and fro.
'Ha! Ha!' quoth he, 'full plain I see,
The Devil knows how to row.'   *A.M.* 560–9.

(d) Behold! her bosom and half her side—
A sight to dream of, not to tell!
O shield her! shield sweet Christabel!

Yet Geraldine nor speaks *nor stirs;*
Ah! what a *stricken look* was hers!   *Christabel* 252–6.

(e) Alas! what ails poor Geraldine?
Why stares she with *unsettled eye?*
Can she the bodiless dead espy?   *Christabel* 207–9.

(f) His heart was cleft with pain and rage,
His cheeks they quivered, his *eyes* were *wild.*
                                    Christabel 640–1.

(g) Then when he *fix'd* his obstinate *eye* on you,
And you pretended to *look strange* and tremble.
Why—why—what ails you now?
      Osorio (with a stupid stare). Me? why? what ails me?
A pricking of the blood—it might have happen'd
At any other time.   *Osorio* 3.175–9.

(h) She started up—the servant maid
      Did see her when she rose;
And she has oft declared to me
      The blood within her froze.   *Three Graves* 172–5.

4. The evil look:

(a) Ah! well-a-day! what *evil looks*
Had I from old and young!   *A.M.* 139–40.

(b) Beneath the lamp the lady bowed,
And slowly *rolled her eyes around.*   *Christabel* 245–6.

(c) And in her arms the maid she took,
      Ah wel-a-day!

And with low voice and *doleful look*
These words did say:
'In the touch of this bosom there worketh a spell,
Which is lord of thy utterance, Christabel.'

Christabel 263–8.

(d) Geraldine in maiden wise
Casting down her *large bright eyes,*

.   .   .   .   .

And folded her arms across her chest,
And couched her head upon her breast,
And *looked askance* at Christabel—
Jesu, Maria, shield her well!   *Christabel* 573–4, 579–82.

(e) And sometimes starting up at once
In green and sunny glade—

There came and *looked him in the face*
An angel beautiful and *bright;*
And that he knew it was a Fiend,
This miserable Knight!   *Love* 47–52.

5. The eye and the curse; *e. g.,* the mother's, brother's, widow's, or orphan's curse, and the dead man's curse:

(a) Beneath the foulest mother's curse
No child could ever thrive:
A mother is a mother still,
The holiest thing alive.   *Three Graves* 255–9.

(b) To him no word the mother said,
But on her knee she fell,
And fetched her breath while thrice your hand
Might toll the passing-bell.

'Thou daughter now above my head,
Whom in my womb I bore,
May every drop of thy heart's blood
Be curst for ever more.'   *Three Graves* 134–41.

(c)   What if his spirit
Re-enter'd its cold corse, and came upon thee,

.   .   .   .   .

83

What if, his *steadfast eye* still beaming pity
And brother's love, he turn'd his head aside,
Lest he should *look* at thee, and with one *look*
Hurl thee beyond all power of penitence? [39]

Osorio 3. 80–1, 83–6.

(d) *Alhadra*. . . . I shall curse thee then!
Wert thou in heaven, my curse would pluck thee thence.

Osorio 5. 287–8.

(e) Not all the blessings of an host of angels
Can blow away a desolate widow's curse;
And tho' thou spill thy heart's blood for atonement,
It will not weigh against an orphan's tear.

Osorio 5. 203–6.

(f) 'The curse liveth for him in the *eye* of the dead men.'

The cold sweat melted from their limbs,
Nor rot nor reek did they:
The *look* with which they *looked* on me
Had never passed away.

An orphan's curse would drag to hell
A spirit from on high;
But oh! more horrible than that
Is a curse in a dead man's eye!
Seven days, seven nights, I saw that curse,
And yet I could not die.   *A.M.* 257–62.

(g) All stood together on the deck,
For a charnel-dungeon fitter:
All *fixed* on me their *stony eyes,*
That in the moon did *glitter.*

The pang, the curse, with which they died,
Had never passed away:
I could not draw my *eyes* from theirs,
Nor turn them up to pray.

And now this spell was snapt: once more
I viewed the ocean green,

[39] See also *Osorio* 1.10–13, 20–21, 40–41, 80–81 (cf. *P.W.*, p. 458, No. 52), 144, 185; 2.22–3, 84, 99–100, 106–7, etc.

And *looked* far forth, yet little *saw*
Of what had else been seen.   *A.M.* 434–45.

—This is because what is behind him has the same effect as the eye of a fiend upon the sinner whom he is pursuing.

6. Enforced looking, refusal to look, and the effort to look away:

(a) He holds him with his skinny hand,
'There was a ship,' quoth he.
'Hold off! unhand me, grey-beard loon!'
Eftsoons his hand dropt he.[40]   *A.M.* 9–12.

(b) Listen, O listen, thou Wedding-guest!
'Marinere! thou hast thy will:
'For that, which comes out of thine *eye,* doth make
'My body and soul to be still.' [41]   *A.M.,* 1 ed., 362–5.

(c) Lines 45–50 of *A.M.* represent a pursuit where we are to imagine the pursuer with his eyes fastened upon the back of the head of him who is being pursued. The pursued does not look round.

(d) And in *A.M.,* lines 149–52, the Mariner's eye is fixed upon a distant object, which, as it approaches, assumes the form of a ship.

[40] *Eftsoons his hand dropt he:* Though this may mean that the Wedding-Guest at first takes hold of the Mariner's hand in order to free himself, and then desists as the spell begins to work, it may otherwise mean that the Mariner drops his hand, since he now can hold the Wedding-Guest by the power of the glittering eye.

[41] The Wedding-Guest clearly refers to a magnetic emanation from the body of the Mariner. Mackay says: 'The assertions made in the celebrated treatise of Deleuze are thus summed up: "There is a fluid continually escaping from the human body," and "forming an atmosphere around us," which, as "it has no determined current," produces no sensible effects on surrounding individuals. It is, however, "capable of being directed by the will"; and, when so directed, "is sent forth in currents," with a force corresponding to the energy we possess. Its motion is "similar to that of the rays from burning bodies." . . . The will of the magnetizer . . . can fill a tree with this fluid. . . . Some persons, when sufficiently charged with this fluid, fall into a state of somnambulism, or magnetic ecstasy; and when in this state, "they see the fluid encircling the magnetizer like a halo of light." ' *Extraordinary Popular Delusions* 1.291.

(e) All stood together on the deck,
  For a charnel-dungeon fitter:
  All *fix'd* on me their *stony eyes*
   That in the moon did *glitter*.

  The pang, the curse, with which they died,
   Had never pass'd away:
  I *could not draw my een* from theirs
   Ne turn them up to pray.

  And in its time the spell was snapt,
   And I *could move my een*.   *A.M.*, 1 ed., 439–48.

(f) I *looked* upon the rotting sea,
  And drew my *eyes* away;
  I *looked* upon the rotting deck,
  And there the dead men lay.

  I *looked* to heaven, and tried to pray.

  I closed my lids, and kept them close,
  And the *balls* like pulses beat;
  For the sky and the sea, and the sea and the sky
  Lay like a load on my weary *eye*,
  And the dead were at my feet.   *A.M.* 240–4, 248–52.

(g) Beneath the *lightning* and the *Moon*
  The dead men gave a groan.

  They groaned, they stirred, they all uprose,
  Nor spake, *nor moved their eyes*.   *A.M.* 329–32.

  The body of my brother's son
  Stood by me, knee to knee;
  The body and I pulled at one rope
  But he said nought to me.   *A.M.* 341–4.

(h) The Marineres all 'gan pull the ropes,
  But look at me they n'old:
  Thought I, 'I am as thin as air—
   They cannot me behold.'   *A.M.*, 1 ed., 374–7.

(i) I turn'd my head in fear and dread,
  And by the holy rood,
  The bodies had advanc'd, and now
   Before the mast they stood.

They lifted up their stiff right arms,
    They held them straight and tight;
And each right-arm burnt like a torch,
    A torch that's borne upright.

Their *stony eye-balls glitter'd on*
    In the red and smoky light.

I pray'd and turn'd my head away
    Forth looking as before.   *A.M.,* 1 ed., 489–500.

(j) But soon I heard the dash of oars,
    I heard the Pilot's cheer;
    My head was turned perforce away,
    And I saw a boat appear.   *A.M.* 500–03.

(k) The boat came closer to the ship,
    But I nor spake nor stirred.   *A.M.* 542–3.

(l) I pass, like night, from land to land;
    I have strange power of speech;
    That moment that his *face* I *see,*
    I know the man that must hear me:
    To him my tale I teach.   *A.M.* 586–90.

7. The bright and flashing object:

(a) I cannot chuse but *fix* my *sight*
    On that small vapor, thin and white!
        Variant lines in *Lewti, P.W.,* p. 568.

(b) The brands were flat, the brands were dying,
    Amid their own white ashes lying;
    But when the lady passed, there came
    A *tongue of light,* a *fit of flame,*

And Christabel saw the lady's *eye,*
And nothing else saw she thereby,
Save the *boss of the shield* of Sir Leoline tall.[42]
        Christabel 156–62.

[42] That is, besides the eye-like boss of the shield, Christabel sees what we often observe in the lower animals, cats, for example, but more rarely in human beings, when a beam of light is properly reflected from the retina of the animal or person into the eye of the observer. Compare the use made by Poe of this phenomenon in *The Tell-tale Heart.*

(c)   The smooth thin lids
        Close o'er her eyes; and tears she sheds—
        Large tears that leave the lashes bright!
        And oft the while she seems to smile
        As infants at a sudden light!
        Yea, she doth smile, and she doth weep. *Christabel* 314–19.

(d) A little distance from the prow
        Those crimson shadows were:
        I turned my *eyes* upon the deck—
        Oh, Christ! what saw I there!

    Each corse lay flat, lifeless and flat,
    And, by the holy rood!
    A man all light, a seraph-man,
    On every corse there stood.

    This seraph-band, each waved his hand:
    It was a heavenly sight!
    They stood as signals to the land,
    Each one a lovely light.[43]   *A.M.* 488–95.

(e) With the images in Coleridge's description of the flaming seraph-band compare the fascination produced by the 'fire-flags' (*aurora borealis*) in *A.M.* 313–7; the parti-colored water in *A.M.* 269–71; and the glistening 'water-snakes' in *A.M.* 272–81.

8. The Sun personified, and represented as having a face or an eye with the power of fascination:

(a) The sun came up upon the left,
        Out of the sea came he!
        And he shone *bright,* and on the right
        Went down into the sea.   *A.M.* 25–8.

(b) The Sun now rose upon the right:
        Out of the sea came he,
        Still hid in mist, and on the left
        Went down into the sea.   *A.M.* 83–6.

[43] Compare Milton, *Paradise Lost* 6.579–881:
                        At each behind
            A Seraph stood, and in his hand a Reed
            Stood waving tipt with fire.

(c) Nor dim nor red, like God's own head,
    The glorious sun uprist.   *A.M.* 97–8.

(d) The women sat down by his side,
    And talked as 'twere by stealth.

'The Sun peeps through the close thick leaves,
    See, dearest Ellen! see!
'Tis in the leaves, a little sun,
    No bigger than your ee;

'A tiny sun, and it has got
    A perfect glory too;
Ten thousand threads and hairs of light,
Make up a glory gay and bright
    Round that small orb, so blue.'   *Three Graves* 503–13.

(e) The western wave was all a-flame.
    The day was well nigh done!
    Almost upon the western wave
    Rested the broad *bright* Sun;
    When that strange shape drove suddenly
    Betwixt us and the Sun.

And straight the Sun was flecked with bars,
    (Heaven's Mother send us grace!)
As if through a dungeon-grate he peered
    With broad and burning face.   *A.M.* 171–80.

(f) The thought is repeated in lines 185–6, the gloss to which
reads: 'And its [the spectre-ship's] ribs are seen as bars on the face
of the setting sun.'

(g) 'The ship hath suddenly been becalmed.'

And we did speak only to break
    The silence of the sea!
All in a hot and copper sky,
    The bloody Sun, at noon,
Right up above the mast did stand,
    No bigger than the Moon.[44]

[44] And at mid-day from the mast
    No shadow on the deck is cast.
                              Bowles, *Camöens* 40–1.

89

Day after day, day after day,
We stuck, nor breath nor motion;
As idle as a painted ship
Upon a painted ocean.   *A.M.* 109–19.

(h) The sails at noon left off their tune,
And the ship stood still also.

The *Sun,* right up above the mast,
Had *fixed* her to the ocean: [45]
But in a minute she 'gan stir,
With a short uneasy motion—
Backwards and forwards half her length
With a short uneasy motion.

Then like a pawing horse let go,
She made a sudden bound.   *A.M.* 381–90.

9. The fascination of the Moon, which is personified, and represented as a face or eye:

(a) Mother of wildly-working visions! hail!
I watch thy gliding, while with watery light
Thy weak eye glimmers through a fleecy veil.
                    Sonnet to the Autumnal Moon 2–5.

(b) 'At the rising of the Moon,'

We listened and looked sideways up!   *A.M.* 202.

—namely, at the star-dogged Moon. Whereupon,

One after one, by the star-dogged Moon,
Too quick for groan or sigh,
Each turned his face with a ghastly pang,
And cursed me with his eye.   *A.M.* 211–14.

(c) 'In his loneliness and *fixedness,* he yearneth towards the journeying Moon.'

The moving Moon went up the sky,
And no where did abide.   *A.M.* 263–4.

[45] For the sun as an eye, compare:
No longer . . . may I behold yon day-star's sacred eye.
                    Sophocles, *Antigone* 880–1.

I. e., after a seven day's gazing at the eyes of the dead men, he fixes his eye on the Moon, which is, like the Sun, a face or an eye. Then he turns his face to the ocean, and watches the water-snakes as they glisten. He blesses them, the spell is 'snapt,' and he is able to pray.

(d) 'Still as a slave before his lord,
　　The ocean hath no blast;
　　His *great bright eye* most *silently*
　　Up to the Moon is cast—

　　If he may know which way to go;
　　For she guides him smooth or grim.
　　See, brother, see! how graciously
　　She *looketh down* on him.' [46]　　　　　　*A.M.* 414–21.

(e)　　*Osorio (with great majesty).* O woman!
　　I have stood silent like a slave before thee.
　　　　　　　　　　　　　　　　　　Osorio 5. 302–3.

(f) The moonlight steeped in silentness
　　The steady weathercock.　　　　　*A.M.* 478–9.

(g)　　　　　　　　　　Silent icicles,
　　Quietly shining to the quiet Moon.
　　　　　　　　　　　　Frost at Midnight 73–4.

(h)　　　　　　　　On moonlight bushes,
　　Whose dewy leaflets are but half-disclosed,
　　You may perchance behold them on the twigs,

---

[46] For lo the Sea that fleets about the Land,
　And like a girdle clips her solide waist,
　Musike and measure both doth understand;
　For his great chrystall eye is alwayes cast
　Up to the Moone, and on her fixèd fast;
　　And as she daunceth in her pallid spheere,
　　So daunceth he about his Center heere.
　　　　　　　　　Sir John Davies, *Orchestra*, stanza 49.
The parallel to Coleridge was noted by Mrs. Humphry Ward, in *Ward's English Poets*, 1880, 1.550.
See also:
　　　　In the broad open eye of the solitary sky.
　　　　　　　　　　Wordsworth, *Stray Pleasures* 16.

Their bright, bright eyes, their eyes both bright and full,
Glistening, while many a glow-worm in the shade
Lights up her love-torch.   *The Nightingale* 64–9.

(i) And he beheld the moon, and, hushed at once,
Suspends his sobs, and laughs most silently,
While his fair eyes, that swam with undropped tears,
Did glitter in the yellow moon-beam! Well!—
It is a father's tale.[47]   *The Nightingale* 102–6.

10. Fascination of animals:

(a) 'When the ivy-tod is heavy with snow,
And the owlet whoops to the wolf below,
That eats the she-wolf's young.'   *A.M.* 535–7.

(b) And what can ail the mastiff bitch?
Never till now she uttered yell
Beneath the *eye* of Christabel.[48]   *Christabel* 149–51.

(c) When lo! I saw a bright green snake . . .
Close by the dove's its head it crouched; . . .
This dream it would not pass away—
It seems to live upon my eye!
          Christabel 549, 552, 558–9.

(d) A snake's small *eye* blinks *dull* and shy,
And the lady's *eyes* they shrunk in her head,
Each shrunk up to a serpent's *eye,*
And with somewhat of malice, and more of dread,
At Christabel she *look'd askance!*—
One moment—and the sight was fled!

But Christabel in *dizzy trance*
Stumbling on the unsteady ground
Shuddered aloud, with a hissing sound;
And Geraldine again turned round,
And like a thing, that sought relief,
Full of wonder and full of grief,

---

[47] Cf. *P.W.*, p. 456, No. 37.

[48] A searching study of Coleridge's use of the supernatural in *Christabel* is to be found in Mr. Ernest Hartley Coleridge's edition of the poem (London, 1907). See also the comprehensive treatise, in two volumes, on the evil eye, by Dr. S. Seligman: *Der Böse Blick*, Berlin, 1910.

She rolled her *large bright eyes* divine
Wildly on Sir Leoline.

The maid, alas! her thoughts are gone,
She nothing *sees,—no sight but one!*
The maid, devoid of guile and sin,
I know not how, in fearful wise,
So deeply had she drunken in
That *look,* those shrunken serpent *eyes,*
That all her features were resigned
To this sole image in her mind:
And passively did imitate
That *look* of dull and treacherous hate!

. . . . .

And when the *trance* was o'er, the maid
Paused awhile, and inly prayed.
Christabel 583–606, 613–14.

It may throw a further light on Coleridge's conception of the power of the eye, if we briefly examine Wordsworth's use of a similar conception in *Peter Bell,* especially if we remember that this poem was written as a sort of counter to *The Rime of the Ancient Mariner.* Wordsworth employs the idea of ocular fascination, but in such a way that we can see its explanation on wholly rational grounds. Peter fancies that he is under the control of supernatural influences, but the reader knows that Peter is fascinated, not from without, not by spirits or emanations from persons or things external, but from within by his own fears, that is, by the 'spirits of the mind,' reacting upon the outer environment. Wordsworth makes use of a sort of 'facts of mind,' the existence of which has never been disputed. Furthermore, with Wordsworth, ocular fascination is only one device out of many whereby the hero's conversion is effected. There are a dozen other means to his salvation, with which, however, we have no present concern. To be compared, then, with the passages from Coleridge are the following passages from *Peter Bell.*

First, the one in which the 'shining hazel eye' of the Ass is turned toward Peter, and again turned away from him to the object in the water. Next, the one in which Peter's eye becomes

93

fixed upon the object in the water, the fixation being accompanied by a host of images of the most diverse kinds, that flash and throng through Peter's brain. Next, the one in which

> The mosques and spires change countenance,
> And look at Peter Bell! [49]

Nor may we forget the good soul whose eye is fascinated by the ghostly apparition of a word (unnamed) formed by the wick of the taper falling on the page of his book. This account, of course, has a more or less humorous intention, as has also the description of the Ass turning his head to grin at Peter, while Peter eyes the Ass and grins back. Two representative passages from the ballad may be quoted:

> He looks, he cannot choose but look;
> Like some one reading in a book—
> A book that is enchanted.
>
> Ah, well-a-day for Peter Bell!
> He will be turned to iron soon,
> Meet Statue for the court of Fear. [50]
>
> And now the Spirits of the Mind
> Are busy with poor Peter Bell;
> Upon the rights of *visual sense*
> Usurping, with a prevalence
> More terrible than *magic spell*.
>
> .   .   .   .   .
>
> The sweat pours down from Peter's face,
> So grievous is his heart's contrition;
> With agony his *eye-balls* ache
> While he beholds by the furze-brake
> This miserable vision! [51]

That the normal emotions of the human spirit may endure sufferings more terrible than those produced by 'magic spell' is Wordsworth's tacit criticism upon some of the devices employed by Coleridge. A more prolonged comparison than can here be made between *The Rime of the Ancient Mariner* and *Peter Bell*

---

[49] *P.B.* 689–90.   [50] *P.B.* 518–23.   [51] *P.B.* 916–20, 931–5.

would bring out further interesting differences in the treatment of detail by the two poets. It is enough to say that in the happy fitting of details into a general plan, and the transition from one incident to the next, the superiority lies altogether on the side of Wordsworth. For one thing, since he is more fertile he is not compelled to make the same notion do duty, under various disguises, for the machinery throughout an entire ballad. If he does repeat himself, the repetition is not of a questionable and, after all, unimportant phenomenon, such as that of ocular hypnosis. As for Coleridge, one can scarcely maintain that the passages here collected tend to ennoble one another in such a fashion as to increase our respect for this author. It is disappointing to find his 'poet's eye' continually 'fixed' by so trivial a 'fact of mind.'

Wordsworth's Conception of

the 'Ancient Mariner'[1]

THE contributions made by Wordsworth to Coleridge's *The Rime of the Ancient Mariner* would furnish an alluring subject for investigation, both with respect to the general course of the story, and in regard to various details and the embellishment of individual stanzas. But upon such an investigation, however fascinating, I shall not enter, partly because it would involve a long and delicate comparison between Coleridge's ballad and the ballad which is its counterpart in Wordsworth, namely *Peter Bell;* partly because it is not clear that either poet in later years could give a precise account of all the elements in *The Rime* that at first were distinctly attributable to Wordsworth. The Advertisement in the first edition of *Lyrical Ballads* shows a disposition on the part of 'the author' (with a little *a*) of *The Thorn* not to allow his manner of writing to be confused with that of 'the Author' of *The Rime of the Ancyent Marinere*—the first sign, it may be, of his dissatisfaction with the poem by Coleridge. As time went on, and Wordsworth's taste improved through study, reflection, and practice, he came to rate this poem at something like its true worth, and felt less and less inclined to take upon himself any large share of responsibility for its production, especially after his temporary estrangement from its author; the result of his disclaimers, and of Coleridge's partial silence, being that most readers, and even students, of the poem have little no-

---

[1] Published in *Archiv für das Studium der Neueren Sprachen und Literaturen* 125 (1910). 89–92.

tion how important Wordsworth's share in it really was. Actually he gave Coleridge the very kernel of the plot, furnished him with a working basis, without which the author of the fragmentary *Kubla Khan*, the unfinished *Three Graves*, those scattered members entitled *The Wanderings of Cain,* and *Christabel,* it is conceivable, might never have brought *The Rime of the Ancient Mariner* to a conclusion. However, it is not with the plot that we are concerned, but with the main character—and with the main character not strictly as he is represented in the poem, but approximately as Wordsworth might have desired to represent him, had the two authors been able to continue their joint effort as they began.

In a criticism which, in spite of Lamb's strictures upon it, still remains the most decisive ever uttered with reference to Coleridge's ballad, Wordsworth chiefly complained of the lack of characterization in the Ancient Mariner himself—the 'Old Navigator,' as Coleridge loved to call him. In a 'note' in the second edition of *Lyrical Ballads* Wordsworth observes: 'The poem of my friend has indeed great defects; first, that the principal person has no distinct character, either in his profession of mariner, or as a human being who having been long under the controul of supernatural impressions might be supposed himself to partake of something supernatural: secondly, that he does not act, but is continually acted upon.' One is forced to think that, in his intense sympathy with Coleridge, Dykes Campbell too lightly dismisses these and other discriminating remarks of Wordsworth as 'patronising.' [2] Doubtless Wordsworth had attempted to give distinctness to the character at the very beginning of his collaboration with Coleridge. In fact, of the lines in the poem which are known to have been composed by Wordsworth, four (9–12) contain the clearest suggestion of the power of ocular hypnosis which is the most definite psychological trait of the Ancient Mariner; and two (226–7) give the clearest picture of his outward physique:

> And thou art long, and lank, and brown, .
> As is the ribbed sea-sand.

[2] *Poetical Works* of Coleridge, ed. by James Dykes Campbell, p. 596.

Accordingly, as I am disposed to maintain that Wordsworth furnished Coleridge with a manageable plot which Coleridge, deficient in architectonic power, could elaborate only in such a way as to merit Wordsworth's censure—'the events have no necessary connection, do not produce each other'; so I am led to believe that Wordsworth's power of characterization may have had much to do with whatever clearness of conception does accompany us in reading the passages which describe the main personage of the ballad. Not a little support for this belief may be derived from two or three descriptions in Wordsworth's own narratives—passages seemingly unconnected with *The Rime of the Ancient Mariner*. And yet I cannot divest myself of the notion that the germ in Wordsworth's lines, 'And thou art long, and lank, and brown,' is to be found full-grown in his account of the ghostly apparition in Book 4 of *The Prelude* (lines 379 ff.):

> My homeward course led up a long ascent,
> Where the road's watery surface, to the top
> Of that sharp rising, glittered to the moon
> And bore the semblance of another stream
> Stealing with silent lapse to join the brook
> That murmured in the vale. All else was still;
> No living thing appeared in earth or air,
> And, save the flowing water's peaceful voice,
> Sound there was none—but, lo! an uncouth shape,
> Shown by a sudden turning of the road,
> So near that, slipping back into the shade
> Of a thick hawthorn, I could mark him well,
> Myself unseen. He was of stature tall,
> A span above man's common measure, tall,
> Stiff, lank, and upright; a more meagre man
> Was never seen before by night or day.
> Long were his arms, pallid his hands; his mouth
> Looked ghastly in the moonlight: from behind,
> A mile-stone propped him; I could also ken
> That he was clothed in military garb,
> Though faded, yet entire. Companionless,
> No dog attending, by no staff sustained,
> He stood, and in his very dress appeared

A desolation, a simplicity,
To which the trappings of a gaudy world
Make a strange back-ground. From his lips, ere long,
Issued low muttered sounds, as if of pain
Or some uneasy thought; yet still his form
Kept the same awful steadiness—at his feet
His shadow lay, and moved not. From self-blame
Not wholly free, I watched him thus; at length
Subduing my heart's specious cowardice,
I left the shady nook where I had stood
And hailed him. Slowly from his resting-place
He rose, and with a lean and wasted arm
In measured gesture lifted to his head
Returned my salutation; then resumed
His station as before; and when I asked
His history, the veteran, in reply,
Was neither slow nor eager; but, unmoved,
And with a quiet uncomplaining voice,
A stately air of mild indifference,
He told in few plain words a soldier's tale—
That in the Tropic Islands he had served,
Whence he had landed scarcely three weeks past;
That on his landing he had been dismissed,
And now was travelling towards his native home.
This heard, I said, in pity, 'Come with me.'
He stooped, and straightway from the ground took up
An oaken staff by me yet unobserved—
A staff which must have dropped from his slack hand
And lay till now neglected in the grass.
Though weak his step and cautious, he appeared
To travel without pain, and I beheld,
With an astonishment but ill suppressed,
His ghostly figure moving at my side;
Nor could I, while we journeyed thus, forbear
To turn from present hardships to the past,
And speak of war, battle, and pestilence,
Sprinkling this talk with questions, better spared,
On what he might himself have seen or felt.
He all the while was in demeanour calm,
Concise in answer; solemn and sublime

He might have seemed, but that in all he said
There was a strange half-absence, as of one
Knowing too well the importance of his theme,
But feeling it no longer. Our discourse
Soon ended, and together on we passed
In silence through a wood gloomy and still.

By its contrast to the portrait in the ballad of Coleridge, this description seems to illustrate precisely what Wordsworth meant when he wished that the Ancient Mariner had a more distinct character either in his profession, or as a human being acting in such a way as to produce the effect of the supernatural. To the genius of Wordsworth, which is often allied to that of Rembrandt, the task of portraying the shadowy and evanescent by tangible and easily recognized means—which nevertheless escape the unobservant—is always grateful; one thinks of the poet's masterly selection of details in his representation of old age in the Leech-gatherer. Another instance, out of many, is the sketch called *Animal Tranquillity and Decay*, written about the time, possibly just before, Coleridge and Wordsworth began the composition of *The Rime of the Ancient Mariner:*

The little hedgerow birds,
That peck along the road, regard him not.
He travels on, and in his face, his step,
His gait, is one expression: every limb,
His look and bending figure, all bespeak
A man who does not move with pain, but moves
With thought.— He is insensibly subdued
To settled quiet: he is one by whom
All effort seems forgotten; one to whom
Long patience hath such mild composure given,
That patience now doth seem a thing of which
He hath no need. He is by nature led
To peace so perfect that the young behold
With envy, what the Old Man hardly feels.

The 'Forest Hermit' in

Coleridge and Wordsworth[1]

THE romantic imagination, we are to understand, lays emphasis upon the part as against the whole; upon the poetic detail as against the large and unified poetical conception; upon the individual element in poetry—so Aristotle might put it—as against the universal; upon the individual man also as against the State in and for itself. Hence, in a measure, arises the phenomenon of the beautiful fragment, like *Christabel* or *Kubla Khan,* which its author is powerless to finish; for want of a dominant architectonic idea, for want of an original and compelling unity, he is unable to subordinate each separate phrase, each accretion of images, to the inexorable evolution of a complete and harmonious masterpiece. Hence also, if we may make such a leap, comes in part the romantic idealization of the solitary, the anchoret, the recluse; of the individual who withdraws from the social organism and tries to exist alone and for himself.

His retreat, of course, must be voluntary. If it is forced, or forcibly prolonged, he will shortly be heard lamenting with Cowper's Selkirk:

> O Solitude! where are the charms
> That sages have seen in thy face?

And even if it be altogether of his own volition, he can by no means deny himself the social joy of telling others about his pref-

---

[1] Published in *Modern Language Notes* 24 (1909). 33–6. Reprinted by permission.

erence. Thus in a dozen places De Quincey reveals the secret of his carefully nourished 'passion' for solitude. His passion, of course, represents a mood that every one feels now and then. But undoubtedly the air was surcharged with the mood after the time of that natural man Rousseau. Even Charles Lamb, most affable and accessible of mortals, confesses to a like 'passion,' though his confession has the faintest aroma of literary inheritance. The mood was a part of the literary bequest from a generation preceding.

Undoubtedly, too, there is an element here of revived mediævalism. The romantic solitary carries about him some reminder of the cloister or the staff and scrip. In any case, retire or wander as far as he will, he can never quite succeed in being a creature sundered from the generality, for after all there are many like him; and in spite of his cry, 'I am myself, myself alone!' if we drag him and his nearest neighbor from their respective mossy cells, the sunlight may disclose similarities between them amounting to the fixed characteristics of a type.

In reading *The Rime of the Ancient Mariner*, the present writer long imagined that the Hermit who appears in Part VI to shrive the hero had an original in some real personage. And this may still be true. The moment the Mariner reaches shore, he enters a landscape, along the Somerset coast of the Severn Sea, with which Coleridge and his erstwhile collaborator, Wordsworth, were thoroughly familiar; it may be that somewhere in their ramblings among the Quantock Hills one or both of the poets had seen a recluse corresponding, after a fashion, to the Hermit of the Wood. At the same time, this Hermit has such first-class literary antecedents, and such clear and occasionally artificial parallels in Wordsworth and Coleridge themselves, as to shake one's belief that either poet necessarily had 'his eye on the object' when the holy man of the *Rime* was taking shape. The hermits in English literature are numerous. It might be interesting to compare this one with a Spenserian character whom he greatly resembles (albeit the latter is a pious fraud); for it will be recalled that both Coleridge and Wordsworth were eagerly reading Spenser in Quantockian days. First, however, it may be well to compare him and his habitat with other hermits as conceived by the two modern poets; since, whatever his origin, he is without doubt a stereotyped figure in both, and for Wordsworth a stock poetical resource, not unlike several of the pseudo-classic devices which Wordsworth eschewed.

Save for a traditional slip in the printing,[2] the description of the 'forest Hermit' in the final text of the *Ancient Mariner* (lines 508–41, 560–63, 570–77) is substantially the same as that first given in the *Lyrical Ballads* of 1798. Coleridge had indeed introduced a touch of something similar in a poem which Dykes Campbell assigns to the year 1793, entitled *Lines to a Beautiful Spring in a Village:*

> Nor thine unseen in cavern depths to dwell,
> The Hermit-fountain of some dripping cell! [3]

—where the context savors of an influence from Virgil or even Theocritus. And it is believed that he had in mind the same scene as that just cited from the *Ancient Mariner,* when he put together certain lines in a 'ballad-tale' for which Wordsworth gave him the subject in 1797, *The Three Graves:*

> 'Tis sweet to hear a brook, 'tis sweet
> To hear the Sabbath-bell,
> Deep in a woody dell.
>
> His limbs along the moss, his head
> Upon a mossy heap,
> With shut-up senses, Edward lay;

[2] This slip is worth noting. In most of the recent versions, including the standard text of Dykes Campbell, lines 529–30 of the *Ancient Mariner* are made to run:

> The planks looked warped! and see those sails,
> How thin they are and sere!

[So also in the definitive edition by Ernest Hartley Coleridge (1912), 1. 206.]

Apart from the impossible past tense, *looked warped* is an odd bit of cacophony to foist upon the author of *Christabel*; it is about as melodious as the celebrated elegiac line composed—says De Quincey—by Coleridge's old pedagogue, Jemmy Boyer:

> 'Twas thou that smooth'd'st the rough-rugg'd bed of pain.

[3] Coleridge, *Poetical Works*, 1893, p. 24.

> That brook e'en on a working day
> Might chatter one to sleep.[4]

Again, we may not be far from the holy Hermit's cushion plump, when we are taken in the midnight wood to watch Christabel praying under the traditional mossy oak:

> The sighs she heaved were soft and low,
> And nought was green upon the oak
> But moss and rarest mistletoe:
> She kneels beneath the huge oak tree,
> And in silence prayeth she.[5]

Finally, there is a direct reference to the traditional hermit, with a general reminiscence of his sylvan dwelling, in Coleridge's *Mad Monk*, a poem written about three years after the *Ancient Mariner*, and, like the *Lines to a Beautiful Spring in a Village*, indebted to a bucolic source in the Classics. The familiar oak has changed to a tree of equally good literary parentage, the Sicilian chestnut:

> I heard a voice from Etna's side;
> Where o'er a cavern's mouth
> That fronted to the south
> A chestnut spread its umbrage wide:
> A hermit or a monk the man might be;
> But him I could not see:
> And thus the music flow'd along,
> In melody most like to old Sicilian song:
>
> 'There was a time when earth, and sea, and skies,
> The bright green vale, and forest's dark recess,
> With all things, lay before mine eyes
> In steady loveliness:
> But now I feel, on earth's uneasy scene,
> Such sorrows as will never cease;—
> I only ask for peace;
> If I must live to know that such a time has been!'

---

[4] *The Three Graves* 492–500, *Poetical Works*, p. 92; see Hutchinson's edition of *Lyrical Ballads*, pp. 217, 258.
[5] *Christabel* 32–6, *Poetical Works*, p. 116.

The rest is not now to the point. The tale closes abruptly, with a hint of the hermit's customary environment:

> Here ceased the voice. In deep dismay,
> Down through the forest I pursu'd my way.[6]

So much for sylvan hermits in Coleridge; now for a few in Wordsworth. The first that we come upon in the latter poet is scarcely typical—he is a man with a family; but he is fairly artificial. He dwells on the border of Lake Como, where Wordsworth with careful circumstantiality pictures him in the *Descriptive Sketches* of 1793:

> Once did I pierce to where a cabin stood,
> The red-breast peace had bury'd it in wood,
> There, by the door a hoary-headed sire
> Touch'd with his wither'd hand an aged lyre;
> Beneath an old-grey oak as violets lie,
> Stretch'd at his feet with stedfast, upward eye,
> His children's children join'd the holy sound,
> A hermit—with his family around.[7]

Whatever reality lay beneath this description, the artificial side of it becomes apparent the instant we examine Wordsworth's subsequent revision. For example, the Popian lyre gives place to a 'rude viol,' which may or may not have been a real element in the original 'delicious scene':

> But once I pierced the mazes of a wood
> In which a cabin undeserted stood;
> There an old man an olden measure scanned

[6] *The Mad Monk* 1–16, 46–47. This poem, by the way, ought sometime to be compared with Wordsworth's *Intimations of Immortality* and Coleridge's *Dejection;* for the discovery will yet be made that they are all three

> In melody most like to old Sicilian song.

The conventional turn, 'There was a time . . . But now' . . . (cf. *Dejection,* Stanza 6, *Intimations of Immortality,* Stanza 1) is the same modulation that we find in *Lycidas:*

> But O the heavy change, now thou art gon.

[7] *Descriptive Sketches,* 1793, lines 168–175, *Poetical Works,* ed. by Dowden, 7. 285; cf. *An Evening Walk* 219, *Poetical Works* 7. 272.

On a rude viol touched with withered hand.
As lambs or fawns in April clustering lie
Under a hoary oak's thin canopy,
Stretched at his feet, with stedfast upward eye,
His children's children listened to the sound;
—A Hermit with his family around.[8]

However, so far as I have observed, the typical Hermit of the
Wood does not appear in Wordsworth until after his emancipa-
tion from the general artificiality of *Descriptive Sketches,* or until
his alliance with Coleridge in *Lyrical Ballads.* We have noted the
type in the first of the *Ballads,* that is, in the *Ancient Mariner;* we
may note it also in the poem with which the collection closes—in
Tintern Abbey. Revisiting the sylvan Wye, the devotee of nature
glances over a pastoral landscape, descrying here and there

> Wreaths of smoke
> Sent up, in silence, from among the trees!
> With some uncertain notice, as might seem,
> Of vagrant dwellers in the houseless woods,
> Or of some Hermit's cave, where by his fire
> The Hermit sits alone.[9]

Here, one might fancy, is the identical holy man of the *Ancient
Mariner,* dwelling, not along the sylvan Wye, but somewhere
among the Quantock Hills, and transferred for the nonce to the
neighborhood of Tintern Abbey. And in the following description one might be tempted to find the same holy man's woodland
chapel; for the 'sheltering cove' or recess in the mountains is almost certainly in the vicinity of Alfoxden or Nether Stowey:

> A spot where, in a sheltering cove
> A little chapel stands alone,
> With greenest ivy overgrown,
> And tufted with an ivy grove.[10]

—only this happens to be the chapel of Wordsworth's fervent

[8] *Descriptive Sketches* (final version) 145–153, *Poetical Works,* 1. 27.
[9] *Lines Composed a few Miles above Tintern Abbey* 17–22, *Poetical Works* 2. 146.
[10] *Peter Bell* 852–5, Poetical Works 2. 248.

Methodist in *Peter Bell*. Very likely it may be identified with the woodland chapel in *The Three Graves*.

Is there, then, no hermit in *Peter Bell?* Wordsworth himself seems to expect one. Having conducted his hero to a suitable glade in the very heart of the woods, he inquires:

> And is there no one dwelling here,
> No hermit with his beads and glass? [11]

No, there is no hermit; none, at least, in the ordinary sense. The sole inhabitant of this deep and quiet spot is—

> A solitary Ass.

Peter himself is surprised. It was just the place for a real, *human* eremite. Wordsworth's query supplies one of the many points of contact between his poem and the *Ancient Mariner;* for *Peter Bell* is the ballad of the supernatural which Wordsworth was constrained to write when he found himself unable to proceed conjointly with Coleridge in making the *Rime*.

Still other poems of Wordsworth describe this character in terms that remind us of Coleridge. In both poets, of course, the really curious thing about these holy men is the fact that they always dwell in the woods. They do not perch on pillars; they are not enamored of the heath or the sandy waste. They are lovers of shade, of ivy, moss, and oak. They are amateurs in the contemplation of foliage. Thus the confessor of the *Ancient Mariner* likens those sails, so thin and sere, to

> Brown skeletons of leaves that lag
> My forest-brook along;

and thus Wordsworth, rebelling against the complicated life of London, observes that

> living men
> Are ofttimes to their fellow-men no more
> Than to the forest Hermit are the leaves
> That hang aloft in myriads.[12]

[11] *Peter Bell*, 376–7, *Poetical Works* 2. 232.
[12] *Ancient Mariner* 533–4; *Recluse* 605–08, Wordsworth, *Poetical Works*, ed. by Morley, p. 342. Cf. *Iliad* 6. 146–9; Dante, *Paradiso* 26. 137–8.

These lines were written in the year 1800. No especial connection is to be traced between the thought in them and that in the familiar sonnet commencing:

> Nuns fret not at their convent's narrow room;
> And hermits are contented with their cells; [13]

—the date of which has not been ascertained. Nor does it seem possible to establish any precise relation between the *Inscriptions supposed to be found in and near a Hermit's Cell* (five of them composed in 1818) and the earlier material that we have been studying. The lines, again, *For the Spot where the Hermitage stood on St. Herbert's Island, Derwent-Water*, which belong to the earlier, Grasmere period, are contemporary with the *Recluse;* yet their atmosphere does not seem closely allied to that of the *Recluse* or *Tintern Abbey.* St. Herbert is interesting because he gives a local habitation and a name to one of Wordsworth's hermits, and because Wordsworth knew something of his history. But as yet I see no ground for imagining that either he or any other particular recluse of the middle ages underlies the general conception in Wordsworth and Coleridge. St. Herbert, for example, was not a forest type; he lived on an island.

The holy men of the type here examined appear in Coleridge and Wordsworth chiefly in poems written between 1797 and 1804. A final example, representing the latter date, might be taken from the *Prelude,* where Wordsworth is relating his experiences in France during the year 1792, when he walked along the Loire in company with Beaupuy:

> From earnest dialogues I slipped in thought,
> And let remembrance steal to other times,
> When, o'er those interwoven roots, moss-clad,
> And smooth as marble or a waveless sea,
> Some Hermit, from his cell forth-strayed, might pace
> In sylvan meditation undisturbed. [14]

All these passages would gain in significance, if we set beside them several stanzas from Spenser, a few well-known lines from

[13] Wordsworth, *Poetical Works,* ed. by Dowden, 3. 3.
[14] *Prelude* 9. 438–43, *Poetical Works,* 7. 182.

Milton, and a quotation from some eighteenth-century poet—
say Parnell. The hermit of the nineteenth-century romantic poets
is necessarily in large part the creature of tradition. How much
of him is an inheritance, and how much is due to the originality
of Wordsworth and Coleridge, may be learned as well, perhaps,
by a brief as by an extended comparison. I would call particular
attention to the similarity between the first two stanzas in Part
VII of the *Ancient Mariner* and the following stanza from the
Faerie Queene:

> A litle lowly Hermitage it was,
> Down in a dale, hard by a forests side,
> Far from resort of people that did pas
> In traveill to and froe: a litle wide
> There was an holy chappell edifyde,
> Wherein the Hermite dewly wont to say
> His holy thinges each morne and eventyde:
> Thereby a christall streame did gently play,
> Which from a sacred fountaine welled forth alway.[15]

We may close our list with the first six lines of Parnell's *Hermit*, in many ways a fair example of what Wordsworth is supposed
to have disliked in the age of Pope:

Were there space, two passages from Milton might be added:
Il Penseroso, 167–172, *Comus*, 385–992. There are reminiscences
from both in Wordsworth's *Ecclesiastical Sonnets* XXI, XXII.

We may close our list with the first six lines of Parnell's *Hermit*, in many ways a fair example of what Wordsworth is supposed
to have disliked in the age of Pope:

> Far in a wild, unknown to public view,
> From youth to age a reverend hermit grew;
> The moss his bed, his drink the crystal well;
> Remote from man, with God he pass'd the days,
> Prayer all his business, all his pleasure praise.[16]

Here is artificiality with a vengeance. Yet, after all, is not the
type in Wordsworth almost as conventional?

---

[15] *F.Q.* 1. 1. 34. Compare Tasso, *Ger. Lib.* 8. 27, 28, 41, 42; Ariosto, *Orl. Fur.* 8. 29 ff.

[16] Parnell, *Poetical Works,* Aldine Edition, p. 100.

XIV

On Wordsworth's 'To Joanna'[1]

IN CHAPTER 20 of the *Biographia Literaria*,[2] Coleridge selects a number of examples from Wordsworth with which to illustrate 'a poet whose diction, next to that of Shakespeare and Milton, appears to me of all others the most individualised and characteristic.' Among these examples, adds Coleridge, 'the second shall be that noble imitation of Drayton (if it was not rather a coincidence) in the Joanna.'

Let me be pardoned for bringing together the lines in Drayton and Wordsworth to which Coleridge alludes, so as to refer with more convenience to certain passages from various sources, which, for one reason or another, may be associated with them. First, then, the lines from Canto 30 of Drayton's *Polyolbion*, 'The Thirtieth Song' being an account of 'Westmerland':

> Wherefore as some suppose of Copper Mynes in me,
> I *Copper-land* was cald, but some will have 't to be
> From the old *Britans* brought, for *Cop* they use to call
> The tops of many Hils, which I am stor'd withall.
> Then *Eskdale* mine Ally, and *Niterdale* so nam'd,
> Of Floods from you that flow, as *Borowdale* most fam'd,
> With *Wasdale* walled in, with Hills on every side,
> Hows'ever ye extend within your wasts so wide,
> For th' surface of a soyle, a *Copland, Copland* cry,
> Till your shouts the Hills with Ecchoes all reply.
>
> Which *Copland* scarce had spoke, but quickly every hill,
> Upon her Verge that stands, the neighbouring Vallies fill;
> *Helvillon* from his height, it through the Mountaines threw,

---

[1] Published in *The Academy* (London), Jan. 9, 1910, pp. 108–10.
[2] *Biographia Literaria*, ed. by Shawcross, 2. 82.

From whom as soone againe, the sound *Dunbalrase* drew,
From whose stone-trophied head, it on to *Wendrosse* went,
Which tow'rds the Sea againe, resounded it to *Dent*,
That *Broadwater* therewith within her Banks astound,
In sayling to the Sea, told it to *Egremound*,
Whose Buildings, walks, and streets, with Ecchoes loud and long,
Did mightily commend old *Copland* for her Song.[3]

Since the time of Coleridge's suggestion, it has been generally allowed that the similarity between these lines and the subsequent passage which corresponds to them in *To Joanna* is not a mere coincidence. Thus Lienemann (*Die Belesenheit von William Wordsworth*, p. 17) without qualification assumes an influence from *Polyolbion* upon Wordsworth; though the specific instance may appear to be substantiated by the other evidences which Lienemann has collected in order to show that the later poet was acquainted with the works of the earlier. Nothing, however, is more likely than that the author of *A Guide Through the District of the Lakes*, who is known to have been familiar with many topographical works on the region, should have read Drayton's verses on 'Westmerland' with attention, or that, with his unusual powers of memory, he might have retained much more than the substance of 'Old Copland's' song. As in the case of Burns, it is more often safe than unsafe to believe that a passage of singular felicity in Wordsworth owes its excellence in part to the justice and freedom with which an earlier model has been chosen and adapted by him, however subconsciously, for a new purpose. Wordsworth's *Ode to Duty*, for example, surpasses Gray's *Hymn to Adversity* and Horace's *Ode to Fortune*, and possibly a choral ode in the *Agamemnon* of Æschylus, because in some sense or measure it is founded on all of them.[4]

Whether they were consciously imitated by Wordsworth or not, the lines of Drayton can hardly be thought to suffer from the charge of being humorously intended. In dealing with the

---

[3] *Polyolbion* 30. 145–64. Publications of the Spenser Society, New Series, No. 1 (1889), 3. 164. Coleridge quotes lines 155–64.

[4] Cf. *The Poems of William Wordsworth*, ed. by Nowell C. Smith, 2. 528. Horace 1. 35. Æschylus, *Agamemnon*, 170 ff. Milton, *Paradise Lost* 9. 652–4.

lines *To Joanna,* on the other hand, we must bear in mind that they represent a humorous intention, and that Wordsworth on occasion was not unmoved by a Chaucerian impulse to 'blere' the eye of an acquaintance (and even of the gentle reader?)—an impulse to which he yields in gravely describing to the astonished vicar the circumstances of Miss Hutchinson's morning walk, and the marvelous effect of her laugh among the mountain echoes:

> Our pathway led us on to Rotha's banks;
> And, when we came in front of that tall rock
> That eastward looks, I there stopped short—and stood
> Tracing the lofty barrier with my eye
> From base to summit. . . .
>
> —When I had gazed perhaps two minutes' space,
> Joanna, looking in my eyes, beheld
> That ravishment of mine, and laughed aloud.
> The Rock, like something starting from a sleep,
> Took up the Lady's voice, and laughed again;
> That ancient Woman seated on Helm-crag
> Was ready with her cavern; Hammar-scar,
> And the tall Steep of Silver-how, sent forth
> A noise of laughter; southern Loughrigg heard,
> And Fairfield answered with a mountain tone;
> Helvellyn far into the clear blue sky
> Carried the Lady's voice—old Skiddaw blew
> His speaking-trumpet; back out of the clouds
> Of Glaramara southward came the voice;
> And Kirkstone tossed it from his misty head.[5]

'The effect of her laugh,' said Wordsworth to Miss Fenwick,[6] many years after the poem was written, 'is an extravagance, though the effect of the reverberation of voices in some parts of the mountains is very striking.' Indeed, within the poem itself he is careful not to vouch for the surprising echo as an objective fact:

> —Now whether (said I to our cordial Friend,
> Who in the hey-day of astonishment

---

[5] *To Joanna* 41–65, Oxford Wordsworth, p. 147.
[6] *Poems of William Wordsworth,* ed. by Knight (1896), 2. 157.

Smiled in my face) this were in simple truth
A work accomplished by the brotherhood
Of ancient mountains, or my ear was touched
With dreams and visionary impulses
To me alone imparted, sure I am
That there was a loud uproar in the hills.

And in the Fenwick note he goes on to say that 'there is in *The Excursion* an allusion to the bleat of a lamb thus reëchoed, and described without any exaggeration, as I heard it, on the side of Stickle Tarn, from the precipice that stretches on to Langdale Pikes' (*Excursion* 4. 402 ff.)

'List!— I heard,
From yon huge breast of rock, a voice sent forth
As if the visible mountain made the cry.
Again!'—The effect upon the soul was such
As he expressed: from out the mountain's heart
The solemn voice appeared to issue, startling
The blank air—for the region all around
Stood empty of all shape of life, and silent
Save for that single cry.

Then comes the spiritual interpretation of the objective fact, in the truest Wordsworthian style.

Unfortunately the manifest artistic device used by Wordsworth in *To Joanna,* and his characteristic apology for the pleasure which he was capable of taking in the sheer exercise of a refined technique, have not preserved him from being partially misunderstood. Coleridge, I believe, though he seems to have been acquainted with the poem from a time when it was little more than a week old,[7] seems also to have set a wrong value upon it, or on the lines concerning the echo, when in the *Biographia Literaria* he offers the quotation as a sample of Wordsworth's purest style, without allowing for the 'extravagance.' Even the subtle Charles Lamb may have gone partly astray. In defending his love of the great nature whose spirit moves in the heart of mighty cities, Lamb girds at that Wordsworthian ravishment which stirred the lungs of Miss Hutchinson, and observes: 'I

[7] *Journals of Dorothy Wordsworth,* ed. by Knight, 1. 45–6.

should certainly have laughed with dear Joanna.' But the point
is that Wordsworth laughs with her, too. Indeed, one can imagine him smiling with or at every one connected with the poem,
from the Vicar in the heyday of astonishment to the guileless
reader who fails to appreciate the 'merry banter' that runs
throughout, as well as the delicate irony and artistically introduced exaggeration in the passage about the echo. Rightly considered, of course, this is an admirable bit of art, so that we may
well agree with Lamb in setting a high, though not the highest,
value upon 'the description of these continuous echoes in the
story of "Joanna's Laugh," where the mountains, and all the
scenery, absolutely seem alive.' [8] But we must not forget the final
utterance of Wordsworth himself: 'The effect of her laugh is an
extravagance.'

So much for the poet and his friends. The disaffected writers
for the *Anti-Jacobin* were not the sort of persons to let slip many
extravagances, conscious or unconscious, in what they took to
be the nature-worship of the 'Lakists.' Accordingly, some years
after the *Anti-Jacobin* had ceased, we still find Hookham Frere
pursuing the vein which he and his associates had so gleefully
worked in their palmiest days. Yet I fail to discover that any one
has noted the delicious imitations of Wordsworth in Frere's *King
Arthur and His Round Table,* by 'William and Robert Whistlecraft,' or in particular of the lines describing the triumphal progress of Joanna's laugh. In *King Arthur* the presence of the monks
is disclosed to the giants by the new bells in the convent—'bells
of larger size and louder tone':

> Meanwhile the solemn mountains that surrounded
>   The silent valley where the convent lay,
> With tintinnabular uproar were astounded,
>   When the first peal burst forth at break of day;
> Feeling their granite ears severely wounded,
>   They scarce knew what to think, or what to say;
> And (though large mountains commonly conceal
>   Their sentiments, dissembling what they feel,

[8] This and the preceding quotation from Lamb are to be found in his
letters to Wordsworth, dated January 30, 1801, and February, 1801; see
The Works of Charles Lamb, ed. by Macdonald, *Letters* 1. 191.

Yet) Cader-Gibbrish from his cloudy throne
   To huge Loblommon gave an intimation
Of this strange rumour, with an awful tone,
   Thundering his deep surprise and indignation;
The lesser hills, in language of their own,
   Discuss'd the topic by reverberation;
Discoursing with their echoes all day long,
Their only conversation was, 'ding-dong.'

Those giant mountains inwardly were moved,
   But never made an outward change of place:
Not so the mountain-giants—(as behoved
   A more alert and locomotive race),
Hearing a clatter which they disapproved,
   They ran straight forward to besiege the place
With a discordant universal yell,
Like house-dogs howling at a dinner-bell.[9]

Now is it too fanciful to suggest that in so far as these various passages from Drayton, Wordsworth, and Frere have an ultimate literary model in the classics, this may be the striking account, familiar to every student of Greek, which Æschylus puts into the mouth of Clyæmnestra, telling of the way in which the signal of the fall of Troy was heralded from mountain to mountain, through the entire distance from Ida to Mycene? I quote the lines of Æschylus in the translation by Plumptre:

Chorus: What herald could arrive with speed like this?
Clytæmnestra: Hephæstos flashing forth bright flames from Ida:
Beacon to beacon from that courier-fire
Sent on its tidings; Ida to the rock
Hermæan named, in Lemnos: from the isle
The height of Athos, dear to Zeus, received
A third great torch of flame, and lifted up,
So as on high to skim the broad sea's back,
The stalwart fire rejoicing went its way;
The pine-wood, like a sun, sent forth its light
Of golden radiance to Makistos' watch;
And he, with no delay, nor unawares
Conquered by sleep, performed his courier's part:

---

[9] *King Arthur and His Round Table,* stanzas 17, 18, 19, *Works* of J. H. Frere 2. 248–9.

Far off the torch-light, to Eurîpos' straits
Advancing, tells it to Messapion's guards:
They, in their turn, lit up and passed it on,
Kindling a pile of dry and aged heath.
Still strong and fresh the torch, not yet grown dim,
Leaping across Asôpos' plain in guise
Like a bright moon, towards Kithæron's rock,
Roused the next station of the courier flame.
And that far-travelled light the sentries there
Refused not, burning more than all yet named:
And then the light swooped o'er Gorgôpis' lake,
And passing on to Ægiplanctos' mount,
Bade the bright fire's due order tarry not;
And they enkindling boundless store, send on
A mighty beard of flame, and then it passed
The headland e'en that looks on Saron's gulf,
Still blazing. On it swept, until it came
To Arachnæan heights, the watch-tower near;
Then here on the Atreidæ's roof it swoops,
This light, of Ida's fire no doubtful heir.
Such is the order of my torch-race games.[10]

It has been questioned whether or not the phenomenon described by Æschylus was intended by him to be understood as objectively true, and if intended as an extravagance whether it is a deliberate lie on the part of Clytæmnestra. Such questions concern us here but indirectly.[11]

That the tragedies of Æschylus were familiar to Wordsworth is sufficiently attested by the quotations and other references collected by Lienemann. However, the extent of Wordsworth's indebtedness to the classics is an interesting problem that still awaits an investigator—one who can divest himself of the crude traditional notion that the so-called Lake Poet had no teacher nor master save Nature and solitude.

---

[10] Æschylus, *Agamemnon* 271–302, trans. by Plumptre; cf. also Scott, *Lady of the Lake* 3. 1. 18, 24.

[11] Cf. *The Agamemnon of Æschylus*, ed. by Verrall, Introduction, pp. xv. ff.; J. R. S. Sterrett, The Torch-Race, *American Journal of Philology* 23. 393 ff. [Cf. also Lowell, *Commemoration Ode*.]

XV

Wordsworth's Translation of

the Harmodius Hymn[1]

IN HIS collection of modern renderings of the Harmodius and Aristogiton Hymn (*Classical Weekly* 9.82–86), Dr. Mierow has not included the version by the poet Wordsworth, which might have been found at a glance with my Concordance under the name of either hero; but a classical scholar would be more likely to note the Wordsworthian lines in the *Classical Review* 15.82, where they were first published by Professor William Knight in February, 1901. Professor Knight calls this 'the second of more attempts than one on [Wordsworth's] part to deal with the subject of Harmodius and Aristogeiton,' and ascribes it to 'the first decade' of the nineteenth century. Mr. Nowell Smith, in his edition of *The Poems of William Wordsworth* 3.586, says:

> The verses are a fairly close, but somewhat expanded, translation of the well-known Athenian Scolion, or drinking song. . . . The first line should probably begin, 'I will bear'; the 'and' represents nothing in the Greek. In line 16 'myrtle' should probably be 'myrtle's,' as in line 2.

Wordsworth, however, as the Concordance shows, elsewhere writes 'myrtle leaf,' 'myrtle groves,' 'myrtle wreaths,' and 'myrtle shores.' Of an infelicity like 'myrtle's boughs' he would not, I believe, be guilty twice within so few lines. One is therefore tempted to doubt the accuracy of Professor Knight's transcription in line 2, and, both here and in line 16, to read:

[1] Published in the *Classical Weekly* 9 (1916). 109–10. Reprinted by permission.

With the myrtle boughs arrayed.

Yet I give the translation as it appears in the edition of Nowell Smith (3.442):

> And I will bear my vengeful blade
> With the myrtle's boughs arrayed,
> As Harmodius before,
> As Aristogiton bore,
>
> When the tyrant's heart they gor'd
> With the myrtle-braided sword,
> Gave to triumph Freedom's cause,
> Gave to Athens equal laws.
>
> Where, unnumbered with the dead,
> Dear Harmodius, art thou fled?
> Athens sings 'tis thine to rest
> In the islands of the blest,
> Where Achilles swift of feet
> And the brave Tydides meet.
>
> I will bear my vengeful blade
> With the myrtle boughs arrayed,
> As Harmodius before,
> As Aristogiton bore,
> When in Athens' festal time
> The tyrant felt their arm sublime.
>
> Let thy name, Harmodius dear,
> Live through Heaven's eternal year:
> Long as Heaven and Earth survive,
> Dear Aristogiton, live;
> With the myrtle-braided sword
> Ye the tyrant's bosom gor'd,
> Gave to Triumph Freedom's cause,
> Gave to Athens equal laws.

We do not know the grounds upon which Professor Knight based his conjecture as to the date of Wordsworth's rendering. Dr. Mierow's allusions to the translation by Archdeacon Wrangham remind one that in the years 1795–1796 Wrangham and Wordsworth collaborated in an imitation of Juvenal which was

to strike at contemporary tyrants in England; but, so far as I
know, the first reference made by Wordsworth to Harmodius
and Aristogiton occurs in Book Tenth of *The Prelude,* and is
to be dated October–December, 1804. The passage (*Prelude*
10.191–208), if it does only a little to substantiate Knight's conjecture, may yet be quoted by way of commentary on the translation:

> On the other side, I called to mind those truths
> That are the commonplaces of the schools—
> (A theme for boys, too hackneyed for their sires,)
> Yet, with a revelation's liveliness,
> In all their comprehensive bearings known
> And visible to philosophers of old,
> Men who, to business of the world untrained,
> Lived in the shade; and to Harmodius known
> And his compeer Aristogiton, known
> To Brutus that tyrannic power is weak,
> Hath neither gratitude, nor faith, nor love,
> Nor the support of good or evil men
> To trust in; that the godhead which is ours
> Can never utterly be charmed or stilled;
> That nothing hath a natural right to last
> But equity and reason; that all else
> Meets foes irreconcilable, and at best
> Lives only by variety of disease.

119

Eigerman, 'The Poetry of Dorothy Wordsworth'[1]

THIS book, three-quarters or more of it blank paper, does not contain the authentic poetry of Dorothy Wordsworth that is included in the published works of her brother. It consists of a 'Foreword' by Hoxie Neale Fairchild, a Preface by the editor, and 84 selections of (mostly) cadenced prose taken from the *Journals* of Dorothy Wordsworth as published by that incredibly bad editor William Knight. If the present book was worth doing at all, Mr. Eigerman should have tried to secure his text from the manuscript sources. He has extracted as well as he could, omitting some, but not all, of the prosy connective tissue of Dorothy's better passages, and has cut and printed them in lines of such length, uneven length, as may content him and others, which we are now asked to regard as verse. Like all the proponents of 'free verse' known to me, he gives no sign of knowing anything about the history of rhythmical prose from the time of the Greeks, and of Plato and his students above all, down to Ruskin and De Quincey and others of our time. As for Dorothy Wordsworth, her poetic prose, with its pleasing metaphors and similes mainly drawn from the realm of external nature, is not an ornate prose of the highest order, and will not endure comparison with the best of her brother's prose and verse. Is it ungracious to say that as a poet she has been overrated in the vulgar effort to dis-

[1] 'Edited from the *Journals*'; New York, Columbia University Press, 1940. Reviewed in *Modern Language Notes* 56 (1940). 636. Reprinted by permission.

parage her brother? We do well to point out what is excellent in her daily words and thoughts; perhaps there is excellence enough to warrant the display of her cadences by the present disproportionate use of blank pages and spaces. Most of the excerpts do not occupy a third of a page apiece. The warm affection of her brother leads us to share his gratitude to her. If he had not expressed it generously, she would not have had so many warm tributes from other sources.

Spenser, Ovid, Chester,

Cowper, on Trees[1]

IN the *Classical Weekly* 22 (1929). 91–2 Mrs. Ada Hume Coe drew attention to a parallel between Ovid, *Metamorphoses* 10. 86–105, and Spenser, *Faerie Queene* 1.1. 8–9. In the year 1894 W. W. Skeat made clear the relation between these two passages and Chaucer, *Parlement of Foules* 176–82:

> The bilder ook, and eek the hardy ashe;
> The piler elm, the cofre unto careyne;
> The boxtree piper; home to whippes lasshe;
> The sayling firr; the cipres, deth to pleyne;
> The sheter ew, the asp for shaftes pleyne;
> The olyve of pees, and eek the drunken vyne,
> The victor palm, the laurer to devyne.

On the lines in the *Parlement of Foules* Skeat comments as follows (*Complete Works of Geoffrey Chaucer* 1. 511–12, Oxford, 1894):

Imitated by Spenser, *F.Q.* 1.1. 8–9, Chaucer's list of trees was suggested by a passage in the *Teseide* 11. 22–4; but he extended his list by help of one in the *Roman de la Rose* 1338–68; especially lines 1363–8, as follows:

> Et d'*oliviers* et de *cipres,*
> Dont il n'a gaires ici pres;
> *Ormes* y ot branchus et gros,

[1] Published in the *Classical Weekly* 22 (1929). 166. Reprinted by permission.

> Et avec ce charmes et fos,
> Codres droites, *trembles* et *chesnes,*
> Erables haus, *sapins* et *fresnes.*

Here *ormes* are elms; *charmes,* horn-beams; *fos,* beeches; *codres,* hazels; *trembles,* aspens; *chesnes,* oaks; *erables,* maples; *sapins,* firs; *fresnes,* ashes. Hence this list contains seven kinds of trees out of Chaucer's thirteen. See also the list of twenty-one trees in *Knight's Tale,* A 2921. Spenser has:

> The builder oake, sole king of forrests all.

This tree-list is, in fact, a great curiosity. It was started by Ovid, *Metam.* 10. 90; after whom, it appears in Seneca, *Oedipus* 532; in Lucan, *Phars.* 3.440; in Statius, *Thebaid,* 6. 98; and in Claudian, *De Raptu Prosperpinae,* 2. 107. Statius was followed by Boccaccio, *Tes.* 11. 22–4; *Rom. de la Rose* 1361; Chaucer (twice) ; Tasso, *Ger. Lib.* 3.73; and Spenser. Cf. Virgil, *Aen.,* 6.179.

Skeat continues with separate notes on the individual trees, some of which should interest the student of Spenser and Ovid. The accumulation of references to intermediary Latin writers is old; citations may be found in the *Works of Edmund Spenser,* edited by Henry John Todd, 2. 13–15, London, 1805. Todd, again, is indebted to Thomas Warton's *Observations on Spenser's Faerie Queene,* pp. 100–02, London, 1754, where the Chaucerian parallel passages are given in full; Warton makes due acknowledgment to John Jortin's *Remarks on Spenser's Poems,* pp. 4–5, for the references to Ovid, Seneca, Lucan, Statius, and Claudian. Jortin's work was published in London in 1734.

The editions of Ovid I have consulted do not suggest that there was a Greek original of his 'tree-list,' or even that we should compare his descriptions with those given by Theophrastus; yet here (as elsewhere) Ovid probably had a source, in the writings of the Alexandrian age, and ultimately, one might guess, in a comedy of the Middle period, unless the list goes back to prehistoric antiquity. Such lists, like the 'points' of a horse, are very ancient. But we must not get out of our depth. Let me note the list of trees in the *Culex* 123–45, and that by Robert Chester in *Love's Martyr, or Rosalyn's Complaint,* 1601 (edited by Alexander B. Grosart, New Shakespeare Society, Series VIII, Miscellanies, No. 2.95–6, London, 1878). Chester has thirty-five items: oak, vine, rose-tree, pine, hawthorn, Christ's-thorn, rosemary, tamarisk, willow, almond, holly, cork, gooseberry, olive, filbert, barberry, mastic, Judas-tree, ash, maple, sycamore, pomegranate, apricot, juniper, turpentine, quince, pear, medlar, fig, orange, lemon, nutmeg, plum, citron, myrtle.

No doubt there are a great many other instances of this Ovidian device. I will close with a fairly modern example from Cowper, *The Task* 1.307–20:

> No tree in all the grove but has its charms,
> Though each its hue peculiar; paler some,
> And of a wannish gray; the willow such,
> And poplar, that with silver lines his leaf,
> And ash far-stretching his umbrageous arm;
> Of deeper green the elm; and deeper still,
> Lord of the woods, the long-surviving oak.
> Some glossy-leav'd, and shining in the sun,
> The maple, and the beech of oily nuts
> Prolific, and the lime at dewy eve
> Diffusing odours: nor unnoted pass
> The sycamore, capricious in attire,
> Now green, now tawny, and, ere autumn yet
> Have chang'd the woods, in scarlet honours bright.

Notes on Byron and Shelley[1]

Adonais, STANZA 20; *Don Juan,* CANTO 11, STANZA 60

UNDER the impression that Keats owed his death to anonymous censure in the *Quarterly Review,* Shelley in 1821 wrote (*Adonais* 177–80):

> Nought we know, dies. Shall that alone which knows
> Be as a sword consumed before the sheath
> By sightless lightning?—the intense atom glows
> A moment, then is quenched in a most cold repose.

A year or so later, Byron, accepting Shelley's mistaken belief, and gratuitously deeming Milman author of the pernicious attack in the *Quarterly,* gives impetus to this tradition about the quenching of Keats' vital spark, in Canto 11 of *Don Juan.* Has the following parallel to Shelley's 'intense atom'—*i.e.* the mind of Adonais —ever been noted (*Don Juan,* Canto 11, Stanza 60)?—

> John Keats, who was killed off by one critique,
>   Just as he really promised something great,
> If not intelligible, without Greek
>   Contrived to talk about the gods of late,
> Much as they might have been supposed to speak.
>   Poor fellow! His was an untoward fate;
> 'T is strange the mind, that very fiery particle,
> Should let itself be snuffed out by an article.

In his edition of *Don Juan* (1906, p. 446), Ernest Hartley Coleridge annotates 'fiery particle' with a reference to Horace (*Sat.*

[1] Published in *Modern Language Notes* 23 (1908). 118–19. Reprinted by permission.

2. 2. 79): '*divinæ particulam auræ.*' So far as Latin literature is concerned, a reference to Lucretius might be equally in place (*De Rer. Nat.* 3. 177–236); though he conceives of the soul, not as being a single atom, but as composed of many, 'exceedingly small, smooth, and round.' Yet he adds the quality of heat, which is missing in Horace. Lucretius, however, immediately throws us back upon the Greek atomists. An excerpt from Aristotle may be in point (*De An.* 1. 2. 403^b 30), in which he sums up the theories of Leucippus and Democritus; I quote Wallace's translation as given in Bakewell's *Source Book in Ancient Philosophy* (pp. 65–6):

There are some who maintain that fundamentally and primarily the soul is the principle of movement. They reasoned that that which is not itself in motion cannot move anything else, and thus they regarded the soul as one of those objects which were in motion. Democritus, whose view agrees with that of Leucippus, consequently maintained soul to be a sort of fire and heat. For as the forms of the atoms are as the atoms themselves unlimited, he declares that those which are spherical in shape constitute fire and soul, these atoms being like the so-called motes which are seen in the sunbeams that enter through doorways, and it is in such a mixed heap of seeds that he finds the elements of the whole natural world. The reason why they maintain that the spherical atoms constitute the soul, is that atoms of such configuration are best able to penetrate through everything, and to set the other things in motion at the same time as they are moved themselves, the assumption here being that the soul is that which supplies animals with motion. This same assumption led them to regard respiration as the boundary with which life was coterminous. It was, they held, the tendency of the encircling atmosphere to cause contraction in the animal body and to expel those atomic forms, which, from never being at rest themselves, supply animals with movement. This tendency, however, was counteracted by the reënforcement derived from the entrance from outside of new atoms of a similar kind. These last in fact—such was their theory—as they united to repel the compressing and solidifying forces, prevented those atoms already existing in animals from being expelled from them: and life, they thought, continued so long as there was strength to carry on this process.

126

Adonais, Stanza 55

In the fourth stanza of *Adonais,* Shelley seems to liken the spirit of Milton to one of the heavenly bodies:

> But his clear Sprite
> Yet reigns o'er earth; the third among the sons of light.

Somewhat similarly, at the end of the poem, he declares:

> The soul of Adonais, like a star,
> Beacons from the abode where the Eternal are.

This description of Keats reminds one of Wordsworth's apostrophe to Milton (*London, 1802*):

> Thy soul was like a Star, and dwelt apart.

—Compare the Homeric description of the infant Astyanax (*Iliad* 6. 401):

> Ἑκτορίδην ἀγαπητὸν, ἀλίγκιον ἀστέρι καλῷ

—'like to a beautiful star.'

But my attention has been called to the well-known lines by Ben Jonson on Shakespeare:

> But stay, I see thee in the hemisphere
> Advanced, and made a constellation there!
> Shine forth, thou Star of poets, and with rage,
> Or influence, chide, or cheer the drooping stage;
> Which, since thy flight from hence, hath mourn'd like night,
> And despairs day, but for thy volume's light.

Jonson, of course, is here adapting the fable of the Dioscuri, who were metamorphosed into the constellation of Gemini (Hyginus, *Poetikon Astronomikon* 2. 22).

Fuess, 'Lord Byron

as a Satirist'[1]

THE 'noble minor' whose *Hours of Idleness* received the lash in the *Edinburgh Review* of 1807, and who was stung by the censure (of Jeffrey, as he thought) into becoming a poet more worthy of consideration, had enjoyed little training of the proper sort for the career of letters—as indeed he afterwards disclosed:

> And thus, untaught in youth my heart to tame,
> My springs of life were poisoned.

It is common to make a sharp antithesis between 'life' and 'books' —between the discipline in school and the discipline without; but it is also vulgar, and we cannot justify the antithesis by reason. Unfortunate in his early surroundings, unsettled in his schooling, Byron grew up an omnivorous and uncritical, though biased, reader, with a long memory for the substance of history, epic poetry, and the drama; but he had a slipshod verbal memory that interfered with the precision of his acquirements, and he lacked the fine sense for the use of words which represents an inner clarity of thought and definiteness of emotion, and which distinguishes the poet from the occasionally felicitous rhymester —which distinguishes Horace, whom as a boy he 'hated so,' from the author not only of *English Bards and Scotch Reviewers*, but of *Beppo, Don Juan, The Vision of Judgment,* and even *Hints*

---

[1] *Lord Byron as a Satirist in Verse.* By Claude M. Fuess. New York, Columbia University Press. Reviewed in *The Dial*, Chicago, Jan. 16, 1913, pp. 48–51.

from Horace, written at a time when the Roman poet had become an object of Byron's admiration. If one's springs of life are so poisoned as to be permanently vitiated, if mind and heart are so undisciplined that the brain at length becomes

> In its own eddy boiling and o'erwrought,
> A whirling gulf of phantasy and flame

(whatever that may mean), the flow of language from such a well is unlikely to be English pure and undefiled.

The truth is, even when he has become more stoical, Byron is no literary artist; he often loses control of his medium, and often carelessly abuses it. If Tennyson and Milton, for example, in the use of words and figures, and indeed in every element of style, exhibit the sureness of touch that characterizes a great painter like Rembrandt or Da Vinci in the laying on of pigments, or a great composer such as Beethoven in the choice and arrangement of musical notes, Byron by comparison is lacking in sensitiveness as to the details of the English language and its syntax. Now, to return, this sensitiveness is largely a matter of early discipline of heart and head, and in the mature writer is an element of his personality. It is an element in Swift, as in Juvenal or Horace. It is an element in the character of a great satirist, as it is in that of a tragic or an epic poet. Even though the satirist debases his medium, and for his own purposes departs from the accepted usage, he must do so with a full, and not a fumbling, sense of what is right.

And yet, if he was trained for anything, Byron was trained for the writing of satire. His poetry has its immediate roots in the poetry of *The Anti-Jacobin;* its models, so far as the native literature is concerned, are to be found in Pope and Dryden; his best efforts sprang from the influence, direct or indirect, of the Italian school of Berni and Pulci; he was not untouched by the severer part of Dante; and he ultimately harks back to Juvenal and Horace. With the main body of European satire, outside of the Middle Ages, Byron was more or less familiar; some authors, as Horace and Pulci, he studied with attention. Nor is it without significance that the opening of *English Bards and Scotch Re-*

viewers is an imitation of the first two lines in Juvenal. Byron had also seen the world, as the saying goes—not Plato's world, nor more than a third of Dante's, and hardly so much as the world of Lucian. He knew 'life'—not an abundant life, not life seen steadily and as a whole, but life externally diversified and shifting. He knew men, including certain good men like Scott and Moore, and was interested in them—though not in Christian men as such nor in virtuous women. In the region where satire has interests in common with literary criticism (which is also a criticism of life), Byron eventually gained some special knowledge. He is not unacquainted with certain documents of great significance in poetical theory. He translated and adapted the *Ars Poetica* of Horace, and can speak jocularly of the treatises of Aristotle and Longinus. At the same time, he regards the theory of literature as a set of arbitrary rules and precepts, not as a body of living principles; and his own critical estimates and predictions in *English Bards and Scotch Reviewers* turned out to be mainly wrong—as Aristophanes' criticism of Æschylus and Euripides did not. Nevertheless, Byron is in vital contact with literary tradition in many important ways; and in respect to his satiric vein particularly he merits special study.

Such study has been accorded him by Dr. Claude M. Fuess, whose work, entitled *Lord Byron as a Satirist in Verse*, is an outgrowth of certain investigations pursued at Columbia University in the field of English satire, especially that of the eighteenth century. His book appears in the series of Columbia Studies in English and Comparative Literature.

In his collection of facts relating to the activity of Byron as a satirist Dr. Fuess has shown commendable industry; nothing of great importance seems to be omitted. Moreover, the material has been arranged in good order; and the style of the monograph, if it betrays no unusual distinction, is clear and straightforward, and is pleasant to read. Direct references to Byron and his works are adequately supplied in the footnotes. One could wish that all references to other matters of fact, and to various authorities consulted, were given as fully. The allusion to Professor Tucker on page 2 is insufficient; the attribution of *The Simpliciad* to

Richard Mant, on page 62, needs substantiation from a recent article on the subject; if there is a reference to that article elsewhere in the monograph, I have missed and cannot find it, for the Index is inadequate; and there are other small defects of a like nature. The Bibliography 'includes only the more important sources of information' for the treatise. It does not include *La Légende de Don Juan* by Georges Gendarme de Bévotte, which ought to have been consulted. Chapter 11 of that work is indispensable to every student of Byron, and bears directly upon the subject of investigation selected by Dr. Fuess. Nor does the list include the *Studien über Byron und Wordsworth* of F. H. Pughe, which contains something to the purpose. In the main, however, this number of the Columbia Studies may be characterized as honest, painstaking, and substantial.

When we come to the more philosophical aspects of the subject, Dr. Fuess leaves something to be desired. They who wish to understand Byron as a satirist must possess a first-rate acquaintance with Latin satire, above all with that of Juvenal, if not with Greek satirical poetry and Lucian; and they who, in particular, would like to set a value on the satiric literary criticism of Lord Byron, or any other modern poet, had best begin by studying Aristophanes, especially in the *Frogs*. In the work of Dr. Fuess there is no indication that he has properly considered Byron with reference to a classical background. Two or three allusions to the Roman poet are not enough to put the modern in a due perspective. And there is no mention of Aristophanes. Now Byron may or may not have undergone much influence from the Greek, though he personally knew two translators, Frere and Mitchell, of 'a certain comic poet,' regarded the version of Mitchell as 'excellent,' and at least on one occasion borrows from the *Clouds;* there is some evidence, too, of his interest in Lucian. If we divided all the English poets according to their tendencies and likings into Greeks and Romans (and it is no bad division for the comparative study of literature), Byron, of course, would be labeled a Roman. But whatever his bias, and whether he has read Greek or Latin, or both, or neither, in the observation and comparison of literary types we are bound to examine him primarily with reference to ultimate rather than proximate standards. Dr. Fuess has carefully followed out the indebtedness of Byron to the mock-heroic verse of Pulci and the rest of the Italians—a task well worth doing in detail, although the French work on Don Juan, noted above, sketches the topic in a masterly fashion. Yet this is not enough. We must have a standard for Berni and Pulci, too. And, not to trench upon the disputed question of the Greek or Latin origin of satire, we must draw our standard in the main from classical writers, and, of these, in the main from Juvenal; not because he was 'conventional,' or had followers who were uninspired, but because he marked out certain lines which satire must take, so long as human nature remains the same.

In Roman satire, these lines are unmistakable, and hence we find in Juvenal the topics, treated with some regard to unity and coherence, to which Byron continually returns; since it is his misfortune never to have done with a given phrase or subject. But more than this, we find in Roman satire that the nature of the type is not alone what Dr. Fuess seems to think it. The essence of satire is not alone to be destructive. The proper effect of it is also partly indicated by the familiar Latin term, *satura lanx,* suggesting the full platter of various comestibles, including things tart, and savory, and even sweet—and not all bitter. Such are the sights and sounds of a monstrous city, though we must confess there is little that is savory in Juvenal's description of Rome. Yet one may compare Byron's representation of London in Canto 11 of *Don Juan* with the third satire of Juvenal, or indeed with one or other of the modern imitations of that famous dish—Johnson's *London,* for example, or perhaps Book Seventh of Wordsworth's *Prelude.* If Canto 11 of *Don Juan* shows Byron at or near his best as a satirist (and Dr. Fuess thinks well of this and the following cantos), it must be confessed that he is far behind both Johnson and Wordsworth not only in power of construction but also in wealth and choice of detail.

Turning to one or two minor points, we may say, first of all, that Dr. Fuess clearly underrates the mock-heroic *King Arthur and his Round Table* of Hookham Frere—as Byron did not underrate it. In point of time, we must remember, it lies between

the brilliant work of Frere for *The Anti-Jacobin* and his even
more brilliant translation of Aristophanes. Nor does there seem
to be any good reason for going behind Byron's own opinion that
his reading of 'the ingenious Whistlecraft' (*i.e.,* Frere) led him
to write in the vein of Berni and Pulci. In fact, to the present
writer it would seem that the supple spirit of Frere has better
adapted itself to the mock-heroic *ottava rima* of the Italians than
either Merivale or Byron. Even so, if one had not read Whistlecraft, one might credit the following stanza to Byron himself,
except that the style is more correct than is usual with him. Incidentally it helps to illustrate the theory of satire:

> We must take care in our poetic cruise,
>   And never hold a single tack too long;
> Therefore my versatile ingenious Muse
>   Takes leave of this illiterate, low-bred throng,
> Intending to present superior views,
>   Which to genteeler company belong,
> And show the higher orders of society
> Behaving with politeness and propriety.

Compare also the delicate irony at the beginning of Canto 3:

> I've a proposal here from Mr. Murray—

which has quite the tone of Byron's communications to the same
publisher.

Again, Dr. Fuess is unable to see why Byron continued to at-
tach so much importance to his *Hints from Horace;* but to me,
at all events, this adaptation constitutes one of the permanent
gifts of Byron to English literature.

Finally, I cannot help believing that Dr. Fuess on the whole
has rated Byron's satire too high, partly because of a conventional
attitude to the poet which has arisen on the Continent. There,
Byron has been overpraised, simply because very good critics
who speak and think in another language cannot have a sure feeling for the niceties of English, and are unaffected by such a manner as would disgust them in their own tongue. As for his substance, or what underlies it, his standards of judgment, Byron,
after all, as Dr. Fuess remarks, is negative. He whips hypocrisy

and vice, but does not by implication magnify virtue. His *saeva indignatio* is not, like that of Juvenal, supported by a basic love of rectitude and decency. One could not say of Juvenal what Praed makes Byron say of himself—properly enough in the very stanza which Byron took from Whistlecraft and the Italians:

> But I have moved too long in cold society,
>   Where it's the fashion not to care a rush;
> Where girls are always thinking of propriety,
>   And men are laughed at if they chance to blush;
> And thus I've caught the sickness of sobriety,
>   Forbidden sighs to sound, and tears to gush;
> Become a great philosopher, and curled
> Around my heart the poisons of the world.
>
> And I have learnt at last the hideous trick
>   Of laughing at whate'er is great or holy;
> At horrid tales that turn a soldier sick,
>   At griefs that make a Cynic melancholy;
> At Mr. Lawless, and at Mr. Bric,
>   At Mr. Milman, and at Mr. Croly;
> At Talma and at Young, Macbeth and Cinna—
> Even at you, adorable Corinna!
>
> To me all light is darkness;—love is lust,
>   Painting soiled canvas, poetry soiled paper;
> The fairest loveliness a pinch of dust,
>   The proudest majesty a breath of vapor;
> I have no sympathy, no tear, no trust,
>   No morning musing and no midnight taper
> For daring manhood, or for dreaming youth,
> Or maiden purity, or matron truth.

Patch, 'The Tradition

of Boethius'[1]

HERE are 123 pages of text proper; the rest is apparatus. Mr. Patch, who does not confine his study to the Middle Ages, has done a useful book on a subject that needed treatment. His references are full or adequate, and his Index is ample. His style is not as interesting as his theme or his factual information, or his seven pictures, a frontispiece and six plates from the twelfth (one plate) and (all but one) fifteenth centuries. Of superlative interest are the quoted translations of Boethius' Metra, but I had forgotten that the rendering of Queen Elizabeth was so poor. A very helpful section of the book is the clear account of the manuscripts and editions of the translation from Boethius by King Alfred; or so a graduate student in Ithaca has just reported.

The most notable omission is the want of reference to Guy Bayley Dolson, who in 1926 finished a Cornell doctoral dissertation of 658 typewritten pages, *The Consolation of Philosophy of Boethius in English Literature;* this work was duly noted at the proper time (as complete) in the Bulletin (No. 5, p. 48) of the late Professor Willard, and a copy of it once took a trip from Ithaca to Harvard College Library. It is therefore not utterly unknown. Further, Mr. Dolson's published articles on Boethius, for example in the *American Journal of Philology* for 1922 and 1926, are quite ignored by Mr. Patch, who has indeed found a

---

[1] *A Study of His Importance in Medieval Culture,* pp. xiv, 220; New York, Oxford University Press, 1935. Reviewed in *Modern Language Notes,* March, 1938, pp. 222–4. Reprinted by permission.

good many marks of the influence of Boethius that Mr. Dolson did not know of; but Mr. Dolson has materials that should have been of use to Mr. Patch.

As for what is offered in the present book, one should be more sympathetic than its author seems to be (p. 4, yet see p. 88 as well) with the fertile suggestion ('the idea of Usener and others') that the *Consolation* is related to the satire of Varro; the concept will link this dialogue with the *New Life* of Dante. And we may add that there is still much left to do in tracing out the influence of Boethius upon Dante; the subject has not been properly explored by Mr. Patch, and the neglect must mean a serious blemish in a volume purporting to deal with the significance of Boethius in the Middle Ages. Like others, again, Mr. Patch has failed to see the relation of Boethius to tragedy; in the *Consolation* the reference to Euripides, and a view of the Metra as choral interludes, are worth remarking.

This volume naturally invites comparison with the well-known Essay (1891) of H. F. Stewart. Mr. Patch, of course, can be abreast of recent scholarly opinion about Boethius. Even the 'reprinted' edition by Stewart and Rand is now over ten years old, though, by the way, they did not fail to pay respect to Mr. Dolson. Apart from scholarly opinion, however, Patch shows a distinct inferiority to Stewart in his treatment of Boethius in relation to Scholasticism, and, above all else, in the organization of his thought and the resulting style.

The style of this book is not of the merit we have a right to expect from a teacher of 'English.' Sometimes dull, in other parts, not all, it is pretentious, and there are in the writing far too many infelicities of usage: (p. 1) 'What name . . . has suffered such wane?' Does Boethius here suffer wax? (P. 32) 'the sympathy of the Middle Ages was primarily in that direction.' Read 'lay' perhaps for 'was'; but 'in that direction' we banish to the limbo where sit other semi-mathematical and wholly fumbling tags not used by Mr. Patch—'along those lines' and 'from this angle' (suffering from strabismus). 'Factor' he uses. And (p. 82) thither banish also 'case' in the use deplored by Quiller-Couch. (P. 79) Elizabeth's rendering, 'O framar of starry circle,' says the pro-

fessor of English, 'sounds hurried, something of a stunt.' On p. 81
see how an age 'took its Boethius.' Delete the Gallic and pro-
vincial 'its'; and away with all similar misappropriations to the
limbo mentioned above but situate below. For the 'motifs' which
the 'artists' take (p. 122) from the *Consolatio,* say 'themes.' These
locutions are mentioned less on account of Mr. Patch, and more
for the general good. The kind of sentence our English cousins
say the American scholars write is this (p. 119): 'The famous definition of personality which Boethius gave to the philosophers
shows his evaluation of the importance of that factor.'

A few miscellaneous notes follow. For something more important
than the relation of Thomas Usk to *Pearl* (p. 106), see Schofield in
PMLA. 19 (1904). 175–9 on the likeness of the speakers in *Pearl,*
dreamer and maiden, to the speakers in Boethius' dialogue. (P. 3)
'he completed a translation of the *De Interpretatione.*' Omit 'the'
or say 'the treatise *De.*' On p. 4 the work of Boethius is rightly called
Consolatio, but also *De Consolatione,* a use which is not preferred,
since the substance of the book *is* the comfort given by the Lady
Wisdom; as a Platonic writing the dialogue might have a subtitle 'On
Fortune,' 'On Free Will,' or the like. The best tradition favors *Con-
solatio,* and so as a rule does Patch. On p. 17 for 'earier' read 'easier,'
and print *gentilesse* on p. 66 in italic letters. More use might have
been made by Patch of Laistner's fine book, *Thought and Letters in
Western Europe, A.D. 500 to 900,* which is mentioned on p. 181. And
A. J. MacDonald's Hulsean Lectures, *Authority and Reason in the
Early Middle Ages,* Oxford, 1933, should be noted. (P. 135) 'the
Beowulf.' Why 'the'? Are we to say 'the *Julius Caesar*'? (P. 170)
Gröber's *Grundriss* 2.2 (1897). 104; the author of the article, Alfred
Morel-Fatio, should be named. The Cooper mentioned on p. 175 as
'W.F.' is W. V. And just before that entry should there not be one for
a Concordance of Boethius that was made by somebody in Ithaca,
New York?

Milton's name does not anywhere appear, nor Ben Jonson's. A
dozen years ago Mr. Dolson and I kept asking ourselves whether
Milton must not certainly have read the *Consolation of Philosophy.* My cautious pupil would draw no conclusion for which he
lacked external evidence. As for me, I seemed to catch the flavor
of Boethius in the lines (*Paradise Lost* 2.557–69) where some of

the demons, having leisure on their hands while Satan is gone upon his exploration, retire to a convenient hill and discuss the problem of free will and fate:

> Of Providence, Foreknowledge, Will, and Fate,
> Fixt Fate, free will, foreknowledge absolute.

The episode is in Milton's best vein of irony.

Let us not end on a note of censure. What Mr. Patch has brought together is of great value. His work displays the care and pains and hard research for which some of our friends across the water occasionally upbraid us, with injustice. These qualities are good, nay indispensable, and serve as a ground for higher achievement, as the higher virtues generally thrive in a soil composed of the humbler.

XXI

Anna Robeson Burr,

'The Autobiography'[1]

THE author of this work had a golden opportunity, yet a path beset with danger, especially at the beginning. Despite the ostensible modern interest in types of literature, very few of the recognized kinds have ever been methodically described, and the autobiography is not one of the few. Such tentative efforts as McNicoll's study (in *Essays on English Literature*, London, 1861 —not cited by Mrs. Burr) are hardly worth mentioning; nor does Professor James' *Varieties of Religious Experience,* though it brings together not a few examples of at least one form of confession, and has been a source of inspiration to Mrs. Burr, contain precisely an investigation into the nature of a literary species. In any case, the wide field of autobiography was as open to an original application of the scientific method as the field of tragedy was before Aristotle wrote the *Poetics,* or the field of the dialogue before the significant treatise by Hirzel.

It may seem unfair to appraise a recent work by standards such as those that underlie the *Poetics,* but on reflection this sort of comparison becomes inevitable; for the Aristotelian method, if we choose to call it so, is essentially the only possible one in the strict examination of a literary type. Indeed, we may ascribe the actual poverty in this branch of modern criticism to the fact that, however much attention has been given since the Italian renaissance to the results of Aristotle's procedure in relation to the

[1] Boston, Houghton Mifflin Company, 1909. Reviewed in *The Philosophical Review* 19 (1910). 344–8. Reprinted by permission.

drama and the epic, the essentials of the procedure have not often been clearly apprehended. So far as we now can discover, his fashion of investigating must have been somewhat as follows.

Starting with the Platonic assumption that a literary form, an oration, for example, or a tragedy, has the qualities of a living organism, Aristotle advanced to the position that each distinct kind of literature must have a definite and characteristic activity or function, and that this specific function or determinant principle must be equivalent to the effect which the form produces upon a competent observer; that is, form and function being as it were interchangeable terms, the organism *is* what it does to the person who is capable of judging what it does or ought to do. Then further, beginning again with the general literary estimates, in a measure naïve, but in a measure also learned (see *Poetics* 15. 9), that had become more or less crystallized during the interval between the acme of the Attic drama and his own time, and that enabled him to assign tentative values to one play and another, the great critic found a way to select out of a large extant literature a small number of tragedies which must necessarily conform more nearly than the rest to the ideal type. As in the *Politics,* which is based upon researches among a great number of municipal constitutions, yet with emphasis on a few, so in the *Poetics* his inductions for tragedy must repose upon a collection of instances as complete as he knew how to make it without injury to his perspective; that is, his observation was inclusive so that he might not pass unnoticed what since the days of Bacon we have been accustomed to think of as 'crucial instances.' By a penetrating scrutiny of these crucial instances in tragedy, he still more narrowly defined what ought to be the proper effect of this kind of literature upon the ideal spectator, namely, the effect which he terms the 'katharsis' of pity and fear, and such like disturbing emotions. Then, reasoning from function back to form, and form again to function, he would test each select tragedy, and every part of it, by the way in which the part and the whole conduced to this emotional relief. In this manner he arrived at the conception of an ideal structure for tragedy, a pattern which, though never fully realized in any existing Greek drama, must yet con-

stitute the standard for all of its kind. He proceeded, in fact, as
the sculptor does, who by an imaginative synthesis combines the
elements which he has observed in the finest specimens of humanity into a form more perfect than nature ever succeeds in
producing; or as the anatomist, whose representation of the normal bones and muscles is likewise an act of the imagination, ascending from the actual to an ideal truth, and is never quite
realized in any individual, though partially realized in what one
would consider a 'normal' man.

In the case of a literary type, then, the form is, or is determined
by, its essential quality or function; so that an adequate knowledge of the function, though it is the crowning fruit in the study
of a type, must be implicit in the beginning of the study. The investigations made by the author of this book into the nature of
autobiography do not betray such a knowledge at the outset, or
cause it to emerge in the process of her work. Her ill-defined notion that the purpose of the subjective memoir is to provide Tom,
Dick, and Harry with a faithful friend is scarcely scientific. If the
notion of friendship were analyzed in the light, say, of the Platonic, Aristotelian, and Ciceronian conceptions, and the friendly
relations to be established by the autobiographer were thought
of as designed, not for Tom, Dick, or Harry, but for Aristotle's
ideal spectator, or Hamlet's one judicious person out of a theatre
full, or one of the fit though few in the audience desired by Milton, more might be made of her suggestion. However, the reviewer will not hazard a statement of what the true function of
this kind of literature may be; nor if, as is likely, under the term
autobiography are to be included several distinct sorts of composition, is it his hope to differentiate these according to their
specific aims. This is what should have been attempted in the
book which we are examining; and it should have been done
with the assistance of a trained psychologist.

Mrs. Burr does, it is true, distinguish between the objective
memoir, the writer of which, like Xenophon or Cæsar, relates
external history as an impartial witness—if that be the case—and
the subjective memoir, in which the author professes to lay bare
his own intimate experiences. The objective memoir she quickly

dismisses as not being within the province of her research; she dismisses it without a suggestion that even under this head there may be as many different kinds as there are purposes in the minds of the witnesses, and emotional effects naturally arising from the contemplation of tragic, comic, and pathetic, or humorous, or shocking events in history. Among subjective autobiographies she arbitrarily considers those to be typical in which the author as candidly and rationally as possible gives, so to say, a photographic representation of his own inner development. And thus, strangely enough, neglecting the traditional verdict, as Aristotle would not have done, she lays inadequate emphasis or none upon the autobiographical writings of Augustine, Dante, Bunyan, and Rousseau, and comes to regard the not very well-known *Vita Propria* of Cardanus as the most suitable of all memoirs for the centre of her study. She goes on to say that Cardanus 'is among the first manifestations of what we term the scientific spirit'— which probably is nonsense to those who are familiar with the *Animalia* or *De Anima* of Aristotle, as it certainly is nonsense to any one acquainted with Dante's treatise *On the Vernacular Language*. Her failure to take account of Dante is surprising. Two or three glib allusions to the *Divine Comedy,* and the total absence of remark upon the *New Life*—the work is not even mentioned in her long, and on the whole valuable, bibliography— indicate the obvious limits of Mrs. Burr's literary and historical perspective. The evolution of the type, or types, which she has chosen to dissect is evidently connected with the change which has taken place in the value set upon the individual life by modern as against ancient times; and this change may have been so gradual as to prevent us from saying that here or there is the critical moment when classical objectivity passes over into modern romantic subjectivity, but if there is any such turning-point, is it not to be found in the thirteenth century rather than the sixteenth, and in the writings of Dante rather than Cardanus?

The objection to assuming that the photographically scientific memoir ought to be taken as the centre of a study like Mrs. Burr's, rather than the poetical or imaginative, may, however, be set forth in another way, which is suggested by what has been said above concerning function as the determinant principle of a type. The assumption implies that the material or substance of a memoir or autobiography, whether literally or imaginatively true, is of greater importance than the end for which it is collected, sifted, and organically arranged. But it is obvious that the purpose of the author, and the function of the type which he has chosen, determine the material or means which he uses, and not the reverse. If he deliberately lies, as Chateaubriand seems to have done, and tries to palm off as a photographic record what is demonstrably false, he will be at cross-purposes with himself, and the censure of his effort by the historian will not be long delayed. But suppose that, like Dante, and the host of those whom the *New Life* has animated, the author, being a poet, and—to adapt the observation of Sir Philip Sidney—neither affirming nor denying the truth of the photographic record, should deal with his experiences as poets are wont to deal with all other experience; suppose that, obeying the highest law of his nature, he should, out of the plastic elements of his own life, construct an ideal, not of what he has been, or is, but of what he ought and is to be; are we to judge of the result by the inch-worm measure of an ephemeral pseudo-science, or of meticulous fidelity to a standard of literalness with which the poet has but a secondary concern? Are we not rather to judge it by the feeling of exaltation, and of admiration for a lofty ideal of humanity, which he arouses in the soul of the qualified reader? Misled by an over-confidence in the present attainments of modern experimental psychology which its most able followers do not share, and deriving more nutriment from a bygone tribe of necessitarian and physiological critics in France—Taine and his clan—than the coming generation can afford to accept, Mrs. Burr has failed to base her study upon the solid foundations for literary investigation that were laid by the Greeks, confuses means and ends in observing the materials that she has industriously collected, and sets a premium on scientific prose, as against imaginative literature, that the cultivator of belles-lettres will not readily allow.

The main value of her work arises from her industry in collecting materials, above all in the bibliographical lists. Her Bibliography of Autobiographical Writings is, of course, incomplete, for no one person is able to cope with so extensive a range. However, some of the omissions are odd—beginning with Dante. If her lists are ever reconstructed, the following entries may be useful. For the sake of brevity, only the names of the authors are given:

Amiel, Blaine, Sir Thomas Browne, Catherine of Sienna, Clemens, Dante, Ulysses S. Grant, Sir Henry Holland, Charles Lamb, Max Müller, Occleve, Silvio Pellico, Rockefeller, Baroness Sutton, George Francis Train, Gideon Welles, Andrew D. White, Oscar Wilde.

The text and Index might be searched for titles not included in the Bibliography, as for example, Ashmole, Evelyn, Wesley.

A word must be added on her style, which is generally diffuse, at times muddy, and often pretentious; and on her Index, which is untrustworthy: see, for example, the second, eleventh, and twelfth references to Augustine.

XXII

Eliza Gregory Wilkins,

'The Delphic Maxims

in Literature'[1]

MISS WILKINS, now [1929] teaching at Hood College, in 1917 completed at Chicago a doctoral dissertation from which her present book is an interesting outgrowth. The book, after a general Introduction, treats of the Ἐγγύα, πάρα δ᾽ ἄτη, as a theme and in literary allusion (ch. 2), takes up similarly the better-known maxim, 'Nothing in Excess' (ch. 3), and then devotes eight chapters to the best-known Delphic maxim, 'Know Thyself,' in Greek and Latin Literature, in the Middle Ages, the Renaissance, the Eighteenth Century, and (for four of the eight chapters) in the period since 1775. Her dissertation was partly anticipated by Varisco's *Conosci se stesso* (Milan, 1912), which was translated into English by Salvadori (*Know Thyself*, London, 1915).

Miss Wilkins has spared herself no pains, and has produced a valuable collection of saws and instances. Out of fairness to her, I hesitate to dwell upon the omissions I have noted, but perhaps some should be mentioned. Her Index contains no reference to Plato's *Apology*, but surely the quest of Socrates after Chærephon came back to him from Delphi needs attention in a work dealing with the maxim on self-knowledge.

Again, according to Miss Wilkins, Sophocles alludes to but one of her chosen maxims—that is, twice (in *Antigone* and *Œdipus*

---

[1] Chicago, University of Chicago Press, 1929. Reviewed in *The Philosophical Review* 41 (1932). 220–21. Reprinted by permission.

Coloneus) to the one on the avoidance of excess. But the whole
story of Oedipus turns on the question of self-knowledge; on his
visit to Delphi he must have seen the maxim Γνῶθι σεαυτόν; even
the riddle of the Sphinx turns on it. Œdipus himself is the man
who, more than most, went on four legs (with a spike through his
infant feet) in the morning, stood proudly erect on two at the
noon of his power, and, self-blinded, groped with the help of a
third at night. In one version of the story, Œdipus on hearing
the riddle puts his finger to his forehead as he tries to think;
whereupon the Sphinx, supposing that he points at himself for
the answer, throws herself down from the crag to destruction.

Aquinas also is missing from the Index; nor, from the reference on page 186 to Varisco's book, would one understand
Varisco's allusion to Aquinas' words, 'Intelligendo se, intelligit
omnia alia'; this instance should have been included, for the
words apply to God. They might be contrasted with the sentiment of Goethe (p. 150) that, for man, self-knowledge comes from
knowing other men. And thus we are reminded of the quest of
Socrates. When the Delphic oracle calls him the wisest of men,
he tests the statement by inquiring into the self-ignorance of
others. The imperfect Index was leading me to say that the worst
omission of the book concerned Wordsworth. I find one or two
references to him in the Notes (pp. 248, 251), but no indication
how important *The Prelude,* with its subtitle, *Growth of a Poet's
Mind,* must be as a document on self-knowledge. More use of
concordances would have shown Miss Wilkins how rich and interesting Wordsworth's diction is in combinations with 'self-';
and would have taken her to other instances of her maxims. The
Greek Anthology also would furnish some references that are
missing from this book. But the book may be recommended both
to laity and specialist for what it does contain.

And hence we must regret that the style of the writer and the
proof-reading of the book are not all that they should be when
we consider the origin of the work and the auspices under which
it appears. On page 22 there is a very queer translation of a passage in Aristotle's *Rhetoric;* see Rhys Roberts' translation for the
right meaning. The account of Hervieu's play, *Connais-toi,* is,

on page 207, very dark. Or take this (p. 212) on the maxim, 'Know Thyself'; 'It came to be colored increasingly by the modern objective and social point of view.' How can a maxim be colored by a point? What is a 'social' point? A sign of the bad thinking by writers who cultivate current pseudo-sciences is the fumbling use of metaphors drawn from geometry.

The worst misprint seems to be *Adagio* for Erasmus' *Adagia;* yet that is hardly a misprint, for so the title is misspelled in the Index and all five occurrences in the text. Bernard of Clairvaux on p. 76 becomes 'of Clairevaux.' The late Professor Ladd (p. 186) is called George 'Trumbell' Ladd (instead of Trumbull); and the University of St. Andrews now belongs (p. 258) to the apostle himself ('of St. Andrew'). Other small matters (but of such is the kingdom of style) are these: p. 15, 'proven' (for *proved*); p. 23, 'of how' (for *how*); p. 76, bottom, an ugly split infinitive; p. 80, line 16, for 'worst' read 'worse'; p. 82, for *'Person's Tale'* (of Chaucer) read *Parson's Tale.* There are oversights in the Greek on p. 21 (line 10, wrong accent), p. 265, first column, and p. 269, second column.

XXIII

Santayana,

'Three Philosophical Poets:

Lucretius, Dante, and Goethe' [1]

THIS volume, the first in the series of Harvard Studies in Comparative Literature, contains the substance of six lectures which were delivered by Professor Santayana a year ago at Columbia University, and later at the University of Wisconsin, but which trace their origin to one of the regular courses in Harvard University. The circumstances of its growth may explain, if not excuse, an occasional lapse from the purity and elevation of style that one might look for in the opening number of such a series —as when the author (p. 12) *broaches an idea by which he sets some store*—'that poetry is essentially short-winded'; or when he speaks (p. 50) of Lucretius, with his usual 'smack of reality,' 'painting death to the life,' and of the 'brave arguments' which Lucretius offers us if we 'still fear death instinctively, like a stuck pig'; or when he says (p. 140) that the *thought* of Goethe, who 'was the wisest of mankind,' '*voiced* the genius and learning of his age.'

We also wonder a little at the kind of apology which we read in the Preface of a work that is to usher in a scholarly series. Though the phrase 'comparative literature' has no precise meaning, and does not seem to be good English (as *littérature comparée* may be good French), such a title nevertheless would lead

[1] Cambridge, Harvard University, 1910. Reviewed in *The Philosophical Review* 20 (1911). 443–4. Reprinted by permission.

us to expect a form of literary criticism based upon the method of observation and comparison of details both small and great which has been followed by every critic of importance from Aristotle and Longinus to Sainte-Beuve. Professor Santayana, however, calls himself 'an amateur,' disclaims the function of a learned investigator, and indeed seems to imply that scholarship and pedantry are the same thing—an amateurish but often ruinous mistake. When one is familiar with the writings of Munro and Bailey, for example, on Lucretius, it is painful to be told that an American book dealing with this poet 'is no learned investigation,' but 'only a piece of literary criticism'—as if literary criticism could be founded upon something short of a first-hand knowledge.

As a matter of fact, however, Professor Santayana's obligation to scholarship, for instance in the case of Dante, is not inconsiderable, or without discrimination. And his exposition of all three poets is more luminous than would be possible had he not turned to account the 'facts' and 'hypotheses about these men' which are 'at hand in their familiar works, or in well-known commentaries upon them.' He is, to tell the truth, more successful as an interpreter than as a critic, yielding himself up in turn to each of his chosen authors, until the students who attended his attractive lectures must have been successively convinced that each of these three poets 'was the wisest of mankind.'

As a critic, since he recognizes no permanent and decisive standards (p. 203), and has been willing not to carry his private researches to the point of making himself 'a specialist in the study of Lucretius,' or 'a Dante scholar,' or 'a Goethe scholar,' he is less convincing. 'T is a noble Lepidus, who loves Goethe as the Jupiter of men, yet he loves Dante, too, and finally leaves us with a hazy notion that he has an instinctive, though no rational, preference for the Arabian bird of the Divine Comedy. To mention but one promising avenue of research, it might be that a systematic inquiry into Goethe's Neoplatonism, and his affinity in classical literature for Euripides rather than Sophocles,[2] would

[2] See the references in Goethe's *Gespräche* (e.g., *Gespräche*, ed. by von Biedermann, 8.114); if these references show a theoretical preference for

stamp him as an Alexandrian rather than the exponent of the loftiest Hellenism which so many Germans take him to be. Such a procedure might enable us to place him rightly in that scale of better and worse which the sentiment of humanity is bound to demand of the critic, and which the regulated impulse of the true critic is bound to furnish. Professor Santayana has a number of suggestive remarks upon the subject of Goethe's demonology, which is Neoplatonic; but Professor Goebel's study in *The Journal of English and Germanic Philology* (8.1 ff.) is more to the point.

I am convinced that the class of students for which these lectures were designed is more in need of clear distinctions and rational standards of judgment than of anything else which a teacher can directly impart; that the late Arthur John Butler, a specialist on the subject of Dante, but a universal scholar and writer of well-nigh infallible taste, was justified in affirming of the *Divine Comedy:* 'It is not too much to say that there is no one work of human genius which can equal it as an instrument of education, intellectual and moral'; and that, in spite of many fascinating passages by Professor Santayana in all his lectures (such as that on the *Vita Nuova* in the middle of page 92), it is desirable to refer an immature reader to other essays upon the three poets here considered, in order that there may be no doubt in such a reader's mind as to the essential superiority of the great mediæval Christian poet over the melancholy bard of Rome, or the belated pagan of Germany. From the mass of interpretative literature, one may venture to single out the Introduction to the rendering of Lucretius by Cyril Bailey; the appreciation of Dante by Dean Church; and the remarkable essay on Goethe and his influence by Richard Holt Hutton.

Sophocles, we must nevertheless remember that Goethe actually translated and imitated Euripides to a much greater extent.

More, 'Hellenistic Philosophies'[1]

THE author of this solid and brilliant volume, on the later pagan philosophies before and during the early Christian era, began life as a teacher of Sanskrit at Harvard; then taught Sanskrit and Classics at Bryn Mawr; subsequently edited the *New York Evening Post* and then the *Nation;* and has to his credit a dozen volumes of *Shelburne Essays* on diverse literary subjects, in which he has shown the practised hand of a lucid, thoughtful, and stimulating writer. Of late, as a private citizen in an academic town, he seems mainly to have devoted himself to Greek philosophy; his present book follows one called *The Religion of Plato,* in a sequence entitled *The Greek Tradition.*

It has been the fashion to put Dr. More in a group with Professors Stuart P. Sherman and Irving Babbitt, two gentlemen who, with far less training than he has in the ancient Classics, are supposed to recommend the study of them as a cure for our ailing literary education; and who certainly have decried the investigation of the Middle Ages, which they have not investigated, as a pursuit injurious to prospective teachers of literature and torch-bearers of culture. If I am not mistaken, all three have had their fling at condemning 'German' doctoral dissertations, and have shown a tendency to depreciate Continental scholarship by calling it 'German.' Apparently they have wished to write in America the kind of literary interpretation produced by the great French critic Sainte-Beuve, without, however, subjecting themselves to the fearful drudgery of research that under-

[1] By Paul Elmer More, Princeton University Press, 1923. Reviewed in the *New York Herald Tribune,* May 4, 1924, p. 24. Reprinted by permission.

lay each one of the *Causeries du Lundi*. They have shared the limitations of his general interest, which was confined to the writers of antiquity and the great personalities of Europe since the time of the classical Renaissance; they do not share in his method of exhaustive study. Sainte-Beuve was an investigator, never impatient of detail, always going back to original sources, unresting till he had secured and arranged every bit of available information on the subject in hand. As a result, he had the complete sympathy of a scholar with everything human that he touched. Had he come a generation later, it is impossible to believe that he would have been out of sympathy with that third or more of European culture, the Christian Middle Ages. He was not, of course, the greatest scholar of recent times; if to any one, that title belongs to Gaston Paris, a Mediævalist.

Dr. More is no Sainte-Beuve; nor in his special field of ancient philosophy is he a Zeller or a Diels, two Germans who have succeeded, almost as well as the best French scholars, in uniting the indispensable basis—'dry-as-dust' research—with literary skill and the ability to popularize while writing for a learned public. But his early training was sound, and he latterly has struck deeper notes, including a religious one. The next step for him to take, we should think, would be a very natural advance, through Boethius and *The Consolation of Philosophy,* from the last of the ancient systems of thought into the philosophical writers of the Middle Ages proper. Professor Maurice De Wulf and the lamented Hastings Rashdall have shown us how full of light, of life and interest, these writers prove to be when a good method of scholarship is taken with them; modern Protestants are beginning to see that what they call the 'Dark Ages' seem such because of our modern darkness concerning them. A good student and skilful expositor like Dr. More, with a large following of readers in this country, might here do much to enlighten our darkness; but it seems that the forthcoming volumes of *The Greek Tradition* will be concerned with the Church Fathers up to A.D. 451.

In *Hellenistic Philosophies* he has produced a competent book, founded upon a first-hand study of sources, rich in illuminating quotations, interesting in its narrative. The reviewer has noted many a fine passage, which there is here no room to quote, and has not observed a single ill-formed or indistinct sentence in the volume. Some of the best passages are translations, the most notable, however, coming from the hand, not of Dr. More, but of James Adam; it is a rendering of Cleanthes' *Hymn to Zeus*—'a hymn to the Supreme Being,' said Cardinal Newman, 'which is one of the noblest effusions of the kind in classical poetry.'

This appears in the section on Epictetus. He and other Stoics are treated at length, and an equal measure of attention is given to Plotinus among the Neoplatonists. The volume begins with Aristippus, forerunner of the Epicureans. From Epicurus it passes to Cynics and Stoics. The latter part is devoted to Diogenes, the Cynic, and Pyrrho, the Sceptic. Last of all comes Sextus Empiricus, whose works Dr. More is almost inclined to reckon, 'after the Dialogues of Plato and the New Testament, the most significant document in our possession for the Greek Tradition as we are dealing with it in these volumes.'

The final chapter, on the Sceptics, is perhaps the least readable, or at all events less suited than the others for popular consumption. But here, as in the rest of the book, one great value of the treatment lies in the constant reference of later or divergent philosophies to ideas found in Plato and the other companions of Socrates. Less frequent are the references to parallels in modern philosophy; a striking exception is the parallel drawn between the scepticism of Sextus and that of Kant. Most useful to the general reader is the account of Neoplatonism, which, unrecognized, remains a popular philosophy of our own day, often disguised as a weak substitute for Christian belief. The difference between Platonism and Neoplatonism is well brought out by Dr. More.

It is said that every one is either Aristotelian or Platonist. Our author in all his sympathies is a Platonist and a dualist. He has no liking for what he calls the 'desiccating winds of Aristotelian scholasticism,' and hence he is, as we have implied, rather blind to some of the great philosophies of the later Middle Ages. In the followers of Aristotle he says there is 'no true marriage of the intellect and the will.' But the union of Plato and Aristotle was effected in Boethius, who is the father of Scholasticism. If we trace the Aristotelian doctrines from him through Aquinas to Dante, we find the truest marriage of the intellect and the will one can imagine. The synthesis of Platonic and Aristotelian philosophy with Christian doctrine, which characterizes the *Commedia* of Dante is really characteristic of the Middle Ages at their best, and represents the one essential advance the world has made upon the thought of ancient Greece, though it is implicit in Christianity from the beginning. In the tradition studied by Dr. More, as he shows, there is little that is new outside of Neoplatonism; here an Oriental element enters in. And I trust it will not seem heretical to affirm that in modern philosophy new ideas do not appear; possibly an exception may be asked for Leibnitz, who has an originality something like that of the pre-Socratics. Otherwise, new combinations and divergent individual perspectives may be observed, but that there is nothing properly new in itself one may generally see in a reading of *Hellenistic Philosophies*. Thus when, in popular phrase, we call a person 'philosophical' we mean that he is stoical. Or, again, 'the new thought' which furnishes the stock-in-trade of various modern pseudo-religions is a debased Neoplatonism. So the supposedly novel things in modern verse—in the earlier poems of Wordsworth, say—are Neoplatonic; the *Ode, Intimations of Immortality,* is of this description, and not a direct heritage from Plato.

One might naturally compare Dr. More's volume with works which he cites—and to which he is indebted—with the writings, for example, of Benn and MacColl; for he has made good use of English as well as of French and German authorities. But a better comparison may be made with the less scholarly, yet excellent, *Five Great Philosophies of Life,* by the late president of Bowdoin College, Dr. Hyde. This was formerly called *From Epicurus to Christ;* it takes up in order 'The Epicurean Pursuit of Pleasure,' 'Stoic Self-Control by Law,' 'The Platonic Subordination of Lower to Higher,' 'The Aristotelian Sense of Proportion' and 'The Christian Spirit of Love.' Hyde's book, admirably constructed for its purpose, is rich in modern illustrations; that of

Dr. More occupies a middle position between it and the scholarly investigations of specialists. One might urge the reader to study these two volumes together, for the combined result would be worth more than double that of taking either alone.

The Princeton University Press has made an effort to issue *Hellenistic Philosophies* in good form. But the printer has not always done his spacing well, and the effect of the page, though fairly pleasing at a first glance, is huddled at a second. The lack of an index is deplorable. The proofs have been read faultlessly.

Shorey, 'Platonism Ancient and Modern'[1]

WHILE the now lamented Paul Shorey was alive it was hard to be fair to him, because he was not fair to other students of Plato. When men as competent as he took issue with him, he tried in answer to play the merciless and superior critic; and when he found something he could agree with in the work of another, he seemed to think that it must needs have been borrowed from Shorey. It is a pleasure to say that here, in a last and posthumous publication, his more amiable qualities appear at their best; the old petulance is largely absent; his abiding interest in the work of his pupils is obvious; and the book is of such a nature that his amazing capacity for excerpt, allusion, and telling parallel does the utmost service for readers both learned and lay. It may be added that the editors of the volume have done their part with care.

In the first chapter, Plato and Antiquity, our author rightly says (p. 1): 'If we knew the life of the fourth century and the age that followed, we should perceive traces of the effects of Plato's educational and social ideas as set forth in the *Republic* and *Laws*.' He notes the influence of Plato upon Xenophon, upon Aristophanic comedy and the middle comedy in general, and upon Aristotle. A welcome bit in this chapter is Shorey's spirited translation from a play of Epicrates. Unfortunately, no indica-

[1] *Sather Classical Lectures*, Volume 14, Berkeley, The University of California Press, 1938. Reviewed in *The Philosophical Review* 50 (1941). 233–6. Reprinted by permission.

tion is given that the passage is divided between two speakers. In six lines, A asks what Plato and his school are doing; in the rest, the reply of B is our evidence that the Academy, at least in Plato's later years, was engaged in studying botany and the like, and saw such studies in relation to the unity of science; compare Friedrich Solmsen on Plato and the Unity of Science, in the *Philosophical Review* for September, 1940. The interest of Aristotle and Theophrastus in natural history may therefore be said to have originated, at least in part, in the Academy. The interest of the comic poets in such matters, of course, is anterior to the Academy; what their sources of 'natural knowledge' were is now hidden from us. Aristophanes' marvelous knowledge of birds was no doubt partly based upon his own observation; but could he have known all the detail without recourse to books? The works of Plato also are rich in a natural knowledge that antedates the founding of his school, and implies a wider use of books by him than anything in Shorey's volume would suggest. Of Plato's skill in composition it is said that 'Plato does know the rules as no other writer has ever known them.' I submit that the rules were studied before him and by him, that Dante knew them as well as did Plato, and that Aristotle in various ways knew them better. Shorey has some very good things to say on the relations between Aristotle and Plato. It is not true, however, that (p. 6) 'Aristotle studied with Plato twenty years.' Plato was absent when Aristotle entered the Academy, and at other times thereafter; towards the end, when Aristotle was thirty-six years old or more, he must have reached a high degree of independence as a fellow in research, and even as a teacher. It is also inexact to say (p. 5) that Isocrates 'persists in employing Plato's word philosophy for his own ideal of education and culture.' The word and ideal came to Plato's generation from Pythagoras and his school.

I pass over the chapter on Neoplatonism, not because it is weak, for the treatment there of this hard subject has a very real value, in particular for parallels, reminiscences, and instructive allusions, garnered from Shorey's well-stored memory.

Chapter 3, entitled Plato and Christianity, 'is at most an outline of the relation of Platonism and Christianity.' Here is a sample

(p. 71): 'Plato did not, as those who read him in Jowett are led to believe, quite invent the Golden Rule. . . . But the spirit of the Golden Rule pervades Plato's teaching. He is the first Greek to repudiate the generally accepted Greek formula, "Help your friends and harm your enemies." ' And here is a sample of Shorey's worse style (p. 76): 'The λόγος question also demands either a treatise or a paragraph.' Finally, here is one of many sure pronouncements that seem very doubtful (p. 84): 'The number of people interested in the cultural history of Byzantium to-day is very limited.' The number of such persons was rapidly increasing in Shorey's own time. How, then, did he come to say that? For lack of interest in pictorial art? The experts are now turning to Byzantine painting and mosaics, and to the Syrian art before them, for an explanation of motives and treatment in the subsequent art of Italy. As connected with Plato, we observe five references in the Index to Michaelangelo as a writer only, and no reference to Raphael at all.

The remaining chapters, 4, 5, 6, and 7, discuss Platonism in the Middle Ages, Platonism and the Renaissance, Platonism and French Literature, and Platonism and English Literature. For the Middle Ages, we have the statement (p. 89) that 'in general the condition of the mediæval mind in relation to the history and philosophy of the past was that of hopeless befuddlement.' Here again, Shorey seems to be unaware of the work of very important scholars in our time; for example, that of Étienne Gilson; otherwise he could not so express himself in a fashion common enough among Protestant scholars a few decades ago, but now utterly belated.

For the Renaissance, he properly values the work of Ficino; and for French literature, the place of Montaigne (p. 152): 'Montaigne regards himself as rather an Epicurean than a Platonist. But he adores the Socrates of Plato, and quotes Plato a hundred and fifty or two hundred times. . . . He apparently read Plato in the Latin translation of Ficino, as did Rousseau and all Europe for two hundred years.' On p. 125 we learned that 'Hardly anybody reads Plato's Laws now. But Montaigne has literally scores and perhaps hundreds of quotations from it.' Shorey should have kept a better count; and 'literally' betrays him, as it has betrayed many a fumbling writer. He does not specially mention Montaigne's essay *Of Conference,* which offers a good point from which to study the relation of Montaigne and his essays to the Platonic dialogue.

The final chapter on English literature offers much of interest, as the influence of Plato on Chaucer by way of Boethius; but the chapter generally seems huddled, an impression one receives from the book as a whole. The volume contains too many things gathered together rather than converging on a point. A better book could be made by developing the theme of any one chapter. A survey of the influence of Plato throughout the ages is indeed something to be desired, and this volume to some extent satisfies the desire. Yet perhaps the seemingly pedantic view is right; what is needed first may be individual studies of Platonism by ages and by countries, the kind of research that has recently been done by Agard and Miss Samuel. Then would come the crowning synthesis of all the net results of the individual students. Shorey's method gives rise to many palpable mistakes in detail. Thus, on p. 227, he says: 'Wordsworth was not, like Shelley and Coleridge, a student of Plato's text, or indeed a student of any books.' But the truth is that Wordsworth, when he got up a subject, read far more methodically than ever Coleridge or Shelley did. As for Plato, there is evidence that Wordsworth underwent an influence from the dialogues when he was a boy in school at Hawkshead; there is reason to believe that he read Plato there in Greek; and I may speak as one who has paid more attention than most to Wordsworth's reading and the impress of it on his writings, and affirm that, after the Bible and writings that are under obligation to it, Wordsworth owes a heavier debt to Plato than to any other writer or poet.

There is no room to comment at length on Shorey's style. Though generally effective, and always clear, it is not fine, but often cheap. On p. 19 he talks of 'rigid ideals,' where the proper epithet is 'rigorous.' On p. 7 he makes Aristotle say: 'As for the eternal Platonic ideas, they are just piffle and hot air.'

A word must be added on the make-up of the posthumous

book. The title *Platonism Ancient and Modern* is needlessly used for the running left-hand page-heads throughout the volume. Instead, the chapter-head should have been used with the number 1, 2, 3, 4, 5, 6, or 7. Before writing this review I inserted those numbers, in order to turn back and forth to the Notes at the end of the book, pp. 239–45; as matters stand, the reference from page to note is very hard to make. With proper left-hand page-heads, the right-hand page-head could then have been used to indicate the subjects dealt with on that page or on the two pages open before the reader at any given time.[2] The Index, pp. 253–9, is adequate. From it we discover that Shorey does not mention Thomas à Kempis, the *Imitation of Christ,* or Gerson, nor Andersen of the fairy tales, Jacob Boehme, or Galileo. Galileo, at first an Aristotelian, turned Platonist, and wrote Platonic dialogues. The book is singularly free from printer's errors.

[2] Nemesis has caught me at this point in 1952, despite my earnest effort to escape her. The page-head above should read LATE HARVEST. XXV; and similarly throughout the book.

XXVI

Prosser Hall Frye, 'Plato'[1]

IT IS natural to compare this posthumous volume with the posthumous volume of Shorey, also on Plato, issued in the same year. In each case the editors have done their work with care and piety. Frye was a more scrupulous thinker and writer than Shorey, and so far as he goes has given us the better book, save that he talks more of himself than does Shorey, who talks in that vein too much. Frye writes well of the Dialogues, and in sympathy with their author, his methods, and his aims. Long study and affection gave him a singular insight into the mind and activity, and the times, of Plato. It is a mistake, however, to say (p. 10): 'There is no evidence . . . of any genuine Socratic dialogues precedent to Plato's.' There is evidence that Alexamenos of Teos wrote some. Again, Frye mentions Socrates' 'chilly dismissal' of Xanthippe in *Phædo*. Burnet cautions us against any such notion as the two words imply, reminding us that in *Phædo* she returns on that last day, and is with Socrates for a time before he drinks the poison. But there is so much good in the book of Frye that one may highly commend it. The section, No. 5, on Plato's Political Ideas had appeared before, and also a part of No. 2, The Dialogues. No. 1, the Introduction, No. 3, The Ideas, and No. 4, The Sophists, are new. It is pleasant to think that America in our day has had more than one first-rate Platonist. I have marked dozens of good passages that might well be quoted in a longer review. On p. 54, line 8, the word 'as' seems to be omitted.

[1] *University of Nebraska Studies,* Volume 38, Nos. 1–2, Lincoln, Nebraska, 1938. Reviewed in *The Philosophical Review* 50 (1941). 339–40. Reprinted by permission.

'Classical Essays Presented

to James A. Kleist, S.J.'[1]

THIS is an unusual book of its kind in that the contributors are not many (seven), and the contributions are almost all very significant, and maintain a very high level of excellence.

Besides a winning portrait of Father Kleist (at work), the contents include Latin verses to him by Father Francis A. Preuss, S.J.; eleven illustrations for Charles Christopher Mierow's new text, along with a translation and variant readings, of Saint Jerome's *Life of the Captive Monk Malchus* (pp. 31–60, the longest contribution); a brief introductory Life of Father Kleist (pp. ix–xvii) and an incomplete list of his published writings (pp. xvii–xx), by the editor; The Greek Happy Warrior (i. e., Heracles), by Walter R. Agard (pp. 1–11); *Honor, Fides,* and *Fortuna* in Horace, by William Hardy Alexander (pp. 13–17); The Peaceful Conquest of Gaul (i. e., Cæsar's), by Norman J. DeWitt (pp. 19–30); The Didactic Significance of Erotic Figures in Plato, by Clyde Murley (pp. 61–73); The Church's Debt to Homer, by John A. Scott (pp. 75–91); and Virgil's Mezentius, by Francis A. Sullivan, S.J. (pp. 93–112). The notes to all the articles follow the essays (pp. 113–20); and the reader must not be allowed to miss the fine Epilogue on 'the sheer joy of the search,' as evinced by the scholarly Father Kleist and his kind. The author of the Epilogue is William Charles Korfmacher, Director of the Department of Classical Languages at St. Louis University. I

[1] Edited with Introduction by Richard E. Arnold, S.J. St. Louis, Missouri: *The Classical Bulletin,* St. Louis University, 1946. Reprinted by permission.

especially recommend it to deans and educational directors throughout the country, a not altogether scholarly flock, most of whom fancy you can expose young America to the humanities without help from the languages in which things human are primarily found.

In dealing with the contents of this book, I shall dwell rather upon matters on which, so to speak, I may have some right to an opinion; and not, for example, try to pass judgment upon what seems to me a fine piece of work on Jerome which occupies about half the printed pages. And first, as a retired teacher of English I note the following infelicities: *Foreword* for *Preface; sense* (p. 11) for *perceive; pretention* (p. 6); *literature* (p. 13) for books and other writings on a subject that are not literature at all, being but dictionaries and textual notes; *disassociate* (p. 66) for *dissociate; urge* (p. 67) for *impulse.* This last, *urge,* disfigures Robert Bridges' *Testament of Beauty,* and, like *claim* for *contend* or *assert,* has made headway in the London *Times Literary Supplement. Urge* and *claim* are no better than the expression *data is;* however tolerable this may seem to Merriam's Dictionary, *data is* will not be swallowed by the *Classical Bulletin!*

Let us go on now finding fault, so that ample, merited praise may come later, and thus be the more emphatic.

John Adams Scott is always good to read on Homer. The debt of the Church to Homer strikes one offhand as a paradoxical subject; indeed, Scott's article is sounder on the debt of the Church and all of us to the Greeks as that debt is revealed in the Biblical Acts (p. 77):

Nothing in the book of Acts is more remarkable than the quiet manner in which the conversion of the Greeks is taken as something for granted; we only know it took place, but we know little else; and we are never told how, when, or where such an important figure as Luke became a convert.

Good! But is there anything of Homer in the process, or in Luke? According to Paul, the Athenians were over-religious, or timid and facile in their rites; at all events, so far as Homer was concerned, they might well be ready for something better than

the theology of the Odyssey and Iliad. Note also, what I never
have read, that the two poems deal with legends of the gods as
Aristotle says Homer rightly did in the Odyssey with the tales
of Odysseus; the poet took such stories as he could weave into one
whole, and omitted those that did not serve this purpose. So he
takes such stories of the gods as befit the Iliad, and similarly again
such others as befit the other poem. For example, since the Odyssey is in the main, and altogether with respect to Penelope, and
women in general, a tale of fidelity to home and domestic morals,
and since Homer depresses the level of the gods in order to ele-
vate the human agents, therefore the poet introduces into the
Odyssey the naughty tale of Aphrodite and Ares as fit for his
artistic unity, a tale worse than, and a foil to, the tale of a faithful Penelope and the homing Odysseus. The legends of the gods
are subordinate to the needs of the Homeric plots.

Again (p. 79):

Herodotus wrote that it was Homer and Hesiod who created the
Greek conception of divinity. . . . As the poetry of Hesiod is so
limited and so dependent on Homer, the words of Herodotus really
mean that it was Homer who gave the Greeks their theology, a theology which remained almost unchanged until the coming of Christianity.

But of course the far fuller *Theogony* of Hesiod has a different aim from the ends that Homer has in view. Hesiod doubtless
omits details for the sake of condensation; but from much the
same sources as Homer had—doubtless a large stock from which
Homer took a little—Hesiod took more, though not all, namely,
what appertained to his subject, the Birth of the Gods; and he
introduced much else that had a natural, not necessary, connection with that subject. Further, if the popular theology of the
Greeks remained almost unchanged until near the beginning of
our era, it did not go unchallenged until then or near it. Would
Pythagoras accept it? Xenophanes, Socrates, and Plato challenged
it; and Aristotle is well aware of its defects. To Socrates and Plato,
it seems that the poetry of Homer and Æschylus is most vulner-
able in the picture these poets draw of the gods. And so it is. The

Apollo of Æschylus is slippery. The Zeus of the Iliad is not a model husband. Compare Homer with Dante and Milton, and see how right the Socrates of Plato is in his view of theology in the two great Greek epic poems.

Here is something better (p. 78):

> The common words connected with worship, such as *church, cathedral, Bible, angel, deacon, bishop, hymn, anthem, music, evangel, epistle, eucharist, dogma, doxology, apocalypse, psalm, prophet, apostle,* and many more, are simple Greek words, which in most languages are not translated but simply adopted, and they show how much the Greeks contributed to the Church in its early plastic period.

Yes, indeed, John Adams Scott, my good friend! But most of these words, and especially when they are ranged in a list, do not sound like Homer at all.

I have slipped into praise, and would go on quoting laudable passages from Scott, if the *Classical Bulletin* allowed it.

Instead, let us turn to the most valuable item in the book, The Didactic Significance of Erotic Figures in Plato, by Clyde Murley. In effect, all I have to say of the article is: Read it! Read the evidence, passage by passage, on the meaning of 'love' and 'lover' to Plato. Let those especially read it who think with Warner Fite that the *Dialogues* of Plato have (p. 63) 'as their background an unhealthy set (as of Oscar Wilde), representing moral standards lower than those in Athens generally.' Murley undertakes the inspection of every reference to *love* and *lover* in the *Dialogues,* and has tried, with full success, to show (p. 73) that if 'something in his Greek setting disposed Plato to be, or seem, more complacent about it [unnatural vice] than we would wish,' yet 'words capable of gross meaning did not necessarily and always bear such meaning, and such words were used by Plato, for the most part, in quite another sense.'

The worst villains I know of, among Platonic scholars, for turning decent words of Plato to indecency are Aldus and Jowett. Taylor (see his page 223) rightly translates a passage on p. 836 of the *Laws* as follows:

But what of the passion of love in the young of either sex, or love of grown woman or man for the other? We know its untold effects in the life of private persons and whole societies.

Plato doubtless knew the good effect of good love, and the bad effect of bad, in the life of man, as well as any writer in pagan antiquity. What did Aldus do with the passage? Without manuscript authority he inserted the word *evils* (κακά) so as to make Plato say, not that love 'has had a myriad consequences for mankind in private life and for whole commonwealths,' but 'a myriad *evil* consequences.' What does Jowett do with the passage? Neglecting the plain text (Jowett 5.218), he makes the first of Plato's sentences refer to homosexual relations, doubtless in part because of the *evils* introduced into the second by Aldus. For a fuller discussion of the passage of Plato and its context, and of the subject, I venture to refer to pp. xliii-xlviii of my translation of *Phaedrus, Ion, Gorgias,* and *Symposium, with passages from the Republic and Laws,* New York, Oxford University Press, 1938.

This volume in honor of Father Kleist honors one who has devoted his life to promoting the good love, of Christian scholarship and fellowship. Born in Silesia, Germany, on April 4, 1873, he still actively devotes himself to the good works which he was trained to do.[2] Such men as he are the true leaders of education in this country, and throughout the world.

> Let us now praise famous men—
> Men of little showing—
> For their work continueth
> And their work continueth
> Broad and deep continueth
> Greater than their knowing!

The teaching and scholarship of the religious order to which Father Kleist belongs, and of other like orders, especially the Benedictine, will continue when the names of deans and the like who are now devising Greekless courses and Latinless courses in the 'humanities,' godless humanities and Christless, are all for-

[2] Alas, he has since died.

gotten along with their courses; as completely forgotten as most of the past courses, mostly poor, some few good, about which Latinless deans and Greekless directors have not informed themselves. For there is a thing which experimenters in education, interested only in the fleeting present, are not concerned with, namely the recorded history, from the beginnings down, of those few experiments, one leading to the next, in which successful teachers taught successful students in the most important matters.

What the Benedictine monks did to save and promote teaching, scholarship, and publication has not been and will not be forgotten; for there is a cumulative human memory through which, under God, the fittest things human survive. What the religious orders are now doing and preparing in this country for humane education, for letters—that is, for grammar in the most particular and also most inclusive sense—will in due time be properly known. When many so-called universities shall have utterly forgotten what they are here for, and have become simply self-perpetuating money-machines, it doubtless will appear that the said religious orders have, like the Benedictines in their prime, again saved Western culture.

On the Study of English[1]

TO what end shall we study English? In part for the sake of the individual; in part for the good of our land. In an age like this when the so called useful arts are mastering rather than serving human life, and in a country like ours where luxury and crude ambition are choking men's finer instincts and an easy religion unnerves their sterner virtues, we must take what comfort we can in the thought that our schools and universities maintain at least an academic interest in literature and her sister fine arts— enough, it may be, to make possible some ennoblement in the spirit of a coming generation. For the present, the idea of beauty, we must admit, beats with a feeble pulse in our family life and the body politic, and is ready to fly away after our vanished an- cestral piety, leaving our national soul, if we have yet attained one, expressionless and unmeaning. What, then, can a university like Cornell accomplish toward bringing culture, above all the culture of letters, into the home, and thereby restoring the soul of the State?

Upon so broad and vital a topic any brief discussion must needs appear somewhat dogmatic and saltatory. Let us leap into the middle of things. The examples of Greece and Palestine, the dominant influence that those countries have exerted upon sub- sequent civilization, and the chief causes of that influence, namely Greek and Hebrew education, admonish us that the centre and core of a liberal culture for the youth of any race must be the language and the literature of that race—to use an in- clusive term, its poetry. As the tireless Nazarene, his early life

[1] Published in *The Cornell Era* 38 (1906). 139–45.

'private, . . . calm, contemplative,' but not 'unactive,' nourished his inward light upon the Law and the Prophets—upon
legal maxims in imaginative garb and the apocalyptic visions of
poetic seers, upon the history of a nation (his own) whose barest
chronicle is a moral epic, upon the denunciations and consola-
tions of the Psalms—in a word, upon the best and deepest in
Hebrew tradition and literature, so the broad-shouldered young
gymnast of Athens throve from the first upon the manna of his
national poetry and music—one art in ancient Greece—and from
the divine atmosphere of the Iliad and the Odyssey drew the half
of his inspiration, not merely as a scientist and legislator, but also
as himself a poet. Consciously or unconsciously, both Greek and
Hebrew education went on the principle that the development
of each individual ought to follow lines indicated by the evolution of the race, and hence must commence and continue with a
native poetry.

In the training of the Hebrew as well as the Greek there was
a union of beauty, simplicity, and severity, such as we moderns,
save at rarest intervals, have sadly failed to achieve. Our technical
studies to-day are severe, often too complex for successful teaching, not often beautiful or harmoniously adapted to the true ends
of life; our liberal studies, however engaging, are not seldom
perilous for want of moral rigor. We Americans are not prone to
recognize that culture has anything to do, not merely with religion, with a cult, so to speak, but even with industry. We have
not yet discovered that it is in many ways analogous to agriculture; that it implies the systematic, the laborious, tilling of some
field of art, more particularly the field of literature, and, more
definitely still, that portion of literature which is ours by direct
inheritance, the sacred and secular poetry of our mother tongue.
When shall we as a people by wise and loving toil within the
family, for example by the careful memorizing of Shakespeare,
Milton, and the Bible, begin to reclaim our racial birthright?
How soon will the mothers and fathers of our land discern the
pitiful fraud they now unwittingly practice on their children,
starving our youth with the sand and gravel of the Sunday press,

and denying them the bread of Chaucer, Spenser, Shakespeare, Milton, Wordsworth, and the English Bible?

The university can help teach the parents of the next generation to give their future children bread instead of stones. In a period when general education is defeating itself by confusion of aims and an inability to act upon the belief that a firm, even though limited, knowledge of one thing makes its owner more free than does a smattering of many things—nature study, physics, and what not, as taught in the schools—I plead for the recognition of truths which seem to have been neglected because of their obviousness and simplicity: that to the English-speaking peoples the vital heart of an emancipating culture can be nothing else than a careful and systematic attention to what is most enduring and uplifting in the poetry of our English tongue; that for us a course in liberal arts must necessarily have that poetry as its beginning and centre; that in such a course all other disciplines, amongst them music and athletics—athletics as a fine art, not a useful or self-seeking—must be subsidiary to this as chief. In the space at my disposal, I can not, unfortunately, go on to hint how still other disciplines, such as mathematics, history, alien languages and literatures, must in a system of popular education, as opposed to technical or special, generously grant the superior claims of our literary birthright; or how, on the other hand, an intensive study of literature gives meaning, impetus, and coherence to any cluster of subjects pursued in orderly connection with it; how, for example, the interpretation of an author like Tennyson involves and illuminates as much knowledge of the main trends of thought in the nineteenth century and of specific details in geography and its ancillary sciences—geology, zoölogy, etc.—not to speak of history and the Classics, as is needful for the happiness of a private individual or for the performance of his ordinary duty toward the State; and more knowledge of a permanent sort than the average student now brings away from uncorrelated experience in similar subjects.

Instead, let me outline briefly a few considerations which seem to bear upon the proper function of our university here and, to a

greater or less extent, of other high schools and colleges throughout our country.

First:—As teachers and as pupils we ought to realize, and to
act upon the conviction, that, with exceptions too few in the
gross to be regarded, the American household makes no pretense
of paying its debt to the State by familiarizing our children with
the best of our traditions. Consequently, the teaching and learning of English in school and college, grievously crippled through
that very condition in family life, must be shaped to supply as
far as possible the defect, even though the pupil's mind has begun
to lose the needful plasticity, and his memory has no longer the
keenness of childhood, and his heart-beat has never been at-
tuned to the melody of pure and simple verse. We can accomplish the more with him if we keep steadily in mind and make
evident now and then to him that we are teaching him poetry,
at a disadvantage, in order that he may teach his children, better.

Accordingly, second:—Even university instruction in English
ought with all but special students to be of an extraordinarily
simple sort. An introductory course, for Freshmen, say, might
well include not more than four or five authors, the best; and its
primary aim should be to introduce those authors, their exact
words and sentiments, into the student's soul. To this desider-
atum there is no road but the method of the Greeks: repeated
study of the same masterpieces, and accurate, permanent memorizing. Can we not in the matter of simplicity take a hint from
Wordsworth? 'When I began to give myself up to the profession
of a poet for life,' he said, 'I was impressed with the conviction
that there were four English poets whom I must have continually
before me as examples—Chaucer, Shakespeare, Spenser, and Milton. These I must study and equal *if I could;* and I need not
think of the rest.' And can we not in the matter of memory and
accuracy take a hint from Ruskin?

Walter Scott and Pope's Homer were reading of my own selection,
but my mother forced me, by steady daily toil, to learn long chapters
of the Bible by heart; as well as to read it every syllable through,
aloud, hard names and all, from Genesis to the Apocalypse, about
once a year; and to that discipline—patient, accurate, and resolute—

171

I owe, not only a knowledge of the book, which I find occasionally serviceable, but much of my general power of taking pains, and the best part of my taste in literature. From Walter Scott's novels I might easily, as I grew older, have fallen to other people's novels; and Pope might, perhaps, have led me to take to Johnson's English, or Gibbon's, as types of language; but, once knowing the 32nd of Deuteronomy, the 119th Psalm, the 15th of 1st Corinthians, the Sermon on the Mount, and most of the Apocalypse, every syllable by heart, and having always a way of thinking with myself what words meant, it was not possible for me, even in the foolishest times of youth, to write entirely superficial or formal English.

With Ruskin, then, dame Memory is still the mother of the Muses. The principles of excluding what is secondary and remote, of delay upon what is primary and repetition of what is essential, of unwearied accuracy in such details as really have importance, are, indeed, very old in education, far older than Ruskin and Wordsworth. But then, callow young America lacks reverence for age, and our schoolma'ams know little and care less about the pedigree of Melpomene and Thalia. They seem more concerned about 'covering' a certain amount of ground than about anything else, more about staking out a large amount than about cultivating any; with the result that the heroic Margites who profits by their 'methods' knows a great many things and all very badly. Does any one in this generation thirst for a knowledge of English literature? Let him seek first the kingdom of Chaucer, Spenser, Shakespeare, Milton, the English Bible, and, I believe, Wordsworth, and the rest shall be added unto him. Let him read these, and when he has read them let him read them again. When he has gone through them as many times as the neophyte medicus is expected to go through his text-book of anatomy, we will talk to him of Beowulf and Byron. If he read them with attention only once, he will have done something that ought to make the rank and file of the teachers of English in this country feel ashamed.

Third:—The appreciation of literature is inseparable from the study of language. The greatest difficulty in the study of language is the matter of vocabulary. The one potent help in that difficulty is the cultivation of Mnemosyne, whom the school-ma'ams have abjured. Even with Chaucer the diction offers no serious hindrance, if the glossary be used faithfully and a few select passages be gotten by heart at the outset.

Fourth:—At present our schools and colleges pay, to speak mildly, too much attention to English composition for composition's sake—as if there could be such a thing. Give me a bright Freshman who by any chance has spent as much time in committing to memory choice sections of the Bible as many a young hopeful under our college entrance-requirements has devoted to the expression of his 'original' thoughts on Macaulay's *Milton* and the rest, and I will match his English on some homely subject concerning which he has actual knowledge, born of his own experience, against the English of a dozen teachers in normal schools, all loaded to kill with rules for the paragraph and culled illustrations of faulty grammar. Not that paragraph structure and disconnected examples of good usage are not right when in their place; only their place is far down in the scale of incidentals to the study of literary expression.

Having cited the opinions of Wordsworth and Ruskin on a previous topic, I may be permitted to call in no lesser authority than Milton himself on this. I quote him as he is quoted in a most able article on The Teaching of English, found in the *Atlantic Monthly* for May, 1901, an article that at least every teacher of English ought to read:

On the premature practice of composition he [Milton] has to observe: 'And that which casts our proficiency therein so much behind' —he is speaking of Latin and Greek, but he would have held the same respecting English—'is our time lost, . . . partly in a preposterous exaction, forcing the empty wits of children to compose themes, verses, and orations, which are the acts of ripest judgment, and the final work of a head filled by long reading and observing, with elegant maxims and copious invention. These are not matters to be wrung from poor striplings, like blood out of the nose, or the plucking of untimely fruit.'

Fortunately at Cornell we are beginning to react somewhat against the unblest tendency of American colleges to demand from unformed minds inordinate quantities of words without knowledge.

Fifth:—The aim of the cultivation of literature can not be any approach to idleness or passive enjoyment. Apart from the prosaic desirability of having hours of university credit always represent hours of industrious application, and of stimulating intelligent self-activity on the part of each student in this as in all other branches of study, it is sheer nonsense to suppose that any one can duly appreciate good poetry without gladly undergoing some such labor as the poet underwent, gladly, in order to produce it. Culture, we must remember, is connected, deep down in the roots of language, with the Latin word meaning *plow*. Culture presupposes plowing, methodically working the soil, the labor, the joyful labor, of healthy men. Foolish children sometimes plant little gardens of cut flowers, sticking the severed stems here and there in the undisturbed earth. They have their reward: their miniature polity is cheered, if they go away before the sun is strong. The lives of men and women are embellished after another fashion.

Joachim Wach, 'Das Verstehen'[1]

THE method of scholarly interpretation and criticism is a study that is little cultivated in America, perhaps less in England, more (at least with respect to history) in France, and most in Germany. This solid work of Wach should do much good if it were properly introduced to our literary and linguistic, and historical, scholars; but I suppose most of these persons in America and England will continue to muddle along at their tasks, in a 'practical' fashion, without much care for the ultimate nature of what they are doing. Our 'philologists' are content with proximate ends, and the obvious means thereto. It is significant that Wach finds but one important English treatise to mention, Farrar's *History of Interpretation,* 1886, which he says is little known in Germany, and which certainly has been neglected in America. Wach might, it seems, have paid more attention to the French Encyclopædists, and to their forerunners in Italy, and so have taken us back through the Middle Ages and the Fathers to Alexandrian scholarship, and thence to Aristotle and Plato.

But he is not unjustified in limiting himself to the methodologists of central Europe. The main course of methodology in recent times lies through German writers; the great body of writings on the subject is in German or the Latin of Germans. We had been taught that the greatest systematic treatise in its field, Boeckh's *Encyklopädie und Methodologie der philologischen Wissenschaften,* was produced by Boeckh partly through

[1] *Grundzüge einer Geschichte der hermeneutischen Theorie im 19 Jahrhundert; 1 Die grossen Systeme,* Tübingen, Mohr (Siebeck), 1926. Reviewed in *The Philosophical Review* 38 (1929). 282–4. Reprinted by permission.

the stimulus of Goethe. Wach, after duly stressing the importance of Biblical hermeneutics from the time of the Reformation down, shows the preponderant effect of Schleiermacher in the philosophical development of a theory of interpretation, and the powerful influence of Schleiermacher upon Boeckh himself. The immediate forerunners of Schleiermacher were Ast and Wolf. Ast, a Platonist, now too little remembered, had a better philosophical head than Wolf, whose comprehensive scheme of studies for an understanding of the life of Greece and Rome was somewhat chaotic. Wach devotes some 30 pages to Ast; 20 to Wolf; 85 to Schleiermacher; 60 to Boeckh; and 40 to a reconstruction of the theory of Wilhelm von Humboldt, who constantly reverted to the problems of interpretation, but published no systematic work on the subject.

Wach thinks Boeckh less inclusive in his view than Schleiermacher, because Boeckh confined his *Encyklopädie* to the interpretation of Classical Antiquity. That is hardly fair. Boeckh's thought is absolutely generalized, and becomes the more vital through its specific application, while attaining clarity and distinctness through its logical division. His system is better balanced than any of the others, including that of Wach himself, because of Boeckh's distinction between the process of interpretation (the understanding of a thing in and for itself) and the process of criticism (the understanding of a thing in relation to other things, and to a standard derived from all of them). And his fourfold distinction of Grammatical, Historical, Individual, and Generic Interpretation (repeated for Criticism) will always remain valid; we must, for example, understand a poem, first with respect to the words and syntax of it, then with respect to its historical setting, then with respect to the individuality of the poet, and finally—so to speak, finally, since the fourfold activities are conjoint and endlessly interpenetrating—with respect to the kind of poem it is, whether lyric, epic, or dramatic; and we must criticize or judge the poem in the same fourfold way.

Boeckh is not general enough for Wach (p. 25); he is too general for some more recent systematizers like Paul in the *Grundriss der germanischen Philologie*. Yet Wach is enthusiastic when he comes to his section on Boeckh. And that is well. How much fog would be dispersed if writers such as Matthew Arnold and Croce, and yet more the followers of Croce, had made the *Encyklopädie* an intrinsic part of their mental furniture! [2] How soon the study of Boeckh would quiet the debates over the means and ends of 'appreciation' and 'criticism'; the debates arise because the difference between *interpretation* and *criticism* is neither affirmed nor understood. But the first task of understanding would seem to be the Platonic effort to define our general terms.

Professor Gildersleeve used to remark that, when his head needed clearing, he got down the volume of his old teacher, and a few minutes' reading brought his mind into order again. Toward the close of his life he wrote (*Hellas and Hesperia,* p. 42): 'Boeckh was a great master, the greatest living master of Hellenic studies, and if I became after a fashion a Hellenist, it was due not merely to the catalytic effect of his presence, but to the orbed completeness of the ideal he evoked.'

[2] In a recent work of some value on method in the study of literature, *Theory of Literature* (New York, 1942) by René Wellek and Austin Warren, the *Encyklopädie* of Boeckh is underated and disregarded, and his name misspelled as 'Boekh.'

Wach, 'Das Verstehen,' Vol. 3[1]

TWO volumes of this thoroughgoing work have already been noticed by the *Philosophical Review*. With the present volume, which is dedicated to the memory of Wilhelm Dilthey, Wach concludes his helpful labor, presenting materials which it is hoped many historians and philologists will read. What I have said before will bear repeating, that methodology is too much neglected in America. The layman will find this volume of more interest than the second, which presents a mass of detail concerning the methods of interpretation and criticism of a great age in German theology. Now we hark back to an interest like that of the first volume, following it in Chladenius, Gatterer, Wegelin, Rüss, Wachsmuth, Gervinus, Ranke, Droysen, and Sybel, and, turning from the historians, still pursue the philological interest in Steinthal, Bernhardy, Reichardt, Ritschl, Haase, Curtius, and, on the archæological side, Levezow and Preller. The work is characterized by the same fulness of detail and absence of error as before, including absence of oversights in the printing. The number of words with space between the letters is excessive, or certainly the corresponding use of italic words in an English book would be so.

It is perhaps unfortunate that Wach should end his sketch of the philological method with Preller. There are, of course, writers like Paul in his *Grundriss* who have given us a view of the later development of the method of Boeckh. Still it is disappoint-

---

[1] *Das Verstehen in der Historik von Ranke bis zum Positivismus*, Tübingen, 1933. Reviewed in *The Philosophical Review* 44 (1935). 88. Reprinted by permission.

ing not to see in a historical perspective the method of interpretation that latterly has been associated with the name of Sievers, and depends upon the study of metre, melody, and cadence, a method which was announced by Sievers in the first number of Ostwald's *Annalen der Naturwissenschaft* some thirty-three years ago. However, it is seldom fair to raise serious objection to a man who has done his task as well as Wach has done it for not doing what he never undertook to do. And if he had done more than this, the upshot would not be greatly different. To me his monumental work demonstrates the supreme value of Boeckh as a writer on methodology in studies of the past, as one in whom theory and practice are justly and effectively harmonized. Boeckh is permanent, yet fresh and modern. Not long ago I had occasion to return to Schleiermacher on Plato's *Phædrus*. Schleiermacher is right, but now seems naïve. With a mighty effort he sweeps away the cobwebs of a false tradition concerning the lack of unity in this dialogue, and demonstrates the unity of it, reaching a correct view which probably can be found in the Italian Platonists, and is easy enough for any one trained in the method of Boeckh to find for himself.

A Letter on the

Recognition of Scholarship[1]

YOU ask on behalf of your committee for suggestions as to ways and means of improving the scholarship of the University. Before applying remedies it would be well to determine the exact nature, and the special seat, of the disease, lest we squander time in trying to palliate the symptoms, and strike but feebly at the root of the evil. This, however, is a mere piece of advice, for I must not enter into a long discussion, and will merely say that the following suggestions are based upon long consideration of the trouble. I put them down in no special order, but as they now occur to me.

1. To begin with, as it seems to me, far too much of our instruction, so-called, is given in the form of lectures; there is too little self-activity on the part of the student, who does not like to be passive (though he is willing to be entertained), and naturally turns to the student 'activities' in order to find something to do that he deems worthy of a man with a backbone. Furthermore, the larger the audience, the more must the lecturer descend to their level if he wishes to gain attention. This is a cheap kind of teaching, measured in dollars and cents at the Treasurer's office; but it saps the energy of a good teacher (who is not bent on amusing), and is of slight permanent value to the student who

---

[1] This letter was sent to the Chairman of a Committee of the University Faculty on an Inquiry by the Cornell Alumni regarding the Recognition of Scholarship; the letter was published in the *Cornell Alumni News* 19 (1917). 376–7.

desires first-hand knowledge of his own. Because of my own interest in literature, I think it may interest your committee to know that the poet Wordsworth expressed himself with vigor on this topic:

As to teaching belles-lettres, languages, law, political economy, morals, etc., by lectures, it is absurd. Lectures may be very useful in experimental philosophy [= physics], geology, and natural history, or any art or science capable of illustration by experiments, operations, and specimens; but in other departments of knowledge they are, in most cases, worse than superfluous. Of course I do not include in the above censure 'college lectures,' as they are called, when the business consists, not of haranguing the pupils, but in ascertaining the progress they have made.

And at Cornell we may well give heed to the opinion of Goldwin Smith, who said of the University, in 1869:

I try to keep [the President] from spending more money in flashy public lectures (of which we have far too many already) and other unsubstantial things, and to get him to turn all his resources, limited as they are, to the provision of means for hard work. . . .

Curtis and Lowell come to lecture next term. I regard their arrival socially with unmixed pleasure; academically with mixed feelings. They will both be most brilliant I have no doubt; and the more brilliant they are, the less inclined our boys will be after hearing them to go back to the hard work by which alone any solid results can be attained. . . . The lesson of thorough hard study is the one which these people have to learn. They will listen to Curtis, Lowell, and Dwight generalizing on their respective subjects, without knowing any of the facts on which the generalizations are based, and go away fancying themselves on a level with the most advanced thought of the age.

2. The methods employed in recruiting the faculty are not the best. So far as I have observed, the choice of a new professor depends upon the ability to give a popular lecture more than upon anything else. But there is no established procedure—and there should be one, clearly understood and always followed. Here we should do well to follow the plan of the German universities, now in operation at Yale, if not elsewhere in this country.

The record of a candidate for a professorship is fully investigated —every line he has written, I am told, is read by a competent committee.

Particularly vicious is our way of adding to the staff at the bottom of the list. I recall the haphazard fashion in which I myself found a position as instructor at Cornell—and where I can observe it, the fashion now is worse. If the University is the Faculty, a more or less permanent body, rather than the students, who continually change, nothing can be of greater importance than the training of the men who are to be instructors, and the selection of the fit. In these days of enlightenment, God no longer winks at the appointment of a university instructor, overnight, who does not possess the doctoral degree, and does not bid fair to become a productive scholar.

I suggest the desirability of a committee to consider the best methods of securing new members of the staff as a whole, when vacancies are to be filled. The same committee might well consider the principles to observe in promoting men who are here. If the University is really bent upon improving scholarship, the first necessity is to foster scholarship in the Faculty: no instructor or assistant professor should be promoted until he has shown by his publications that he is not sterile as a scholar; and the merits of his scholarly productions should be appraised by productive scholars, including one or more professors from departments other than his own.

All I have said reposes upon a belief that there is an essential relation between adequate training and successful teaching; we must disabuse ourselves of any belief to the contrary. There is little hope so long as people deceive themselves, and pretend that in the long run the best scholars are not the best teachers—an error not borne out by the facts.

3. I fear it is true that we have allowed the desire for numbers and external superiority to result in something very undesirable, and that a large proportion of the actual teaching is done by underpaid and inexperienced men, who will never rise to eminence in this profession. Many of them do not remain long enough in it to learn the art, so that far too many classes are like

cadavers undergoing dissection at the hands of neophyte surgeons. With a large actual income, the University is, so to speak, *student-poor,* and *instructor-poor*—as we call a man 'land-poor' when he has thousands of acres, and can barely pay the taxes. If we are to have better scholarship, something drastic must be done to make our relatively small means relatively great. We must either secure (not hope for) more money, or we must have fewer students.

I hope you will excuse me if I end what was meant to be an informal letter with another quotation, from Burke. I have often thought of this passage in connection with American universities:

It may be new to his grace [the Duke of Bedford], but I beg leave to tell him that mere parsimony is not economy. It is separable in theory from it; and in fact it may, or it may not, be a *part* of economy, according to circumstances. Expense, and great expense, may be an essential part in true economy. If parsimony were to be considered as one of the kinds of that virtue, there is, however, another and a higher economy. Economy is a distributive virtue, and consists, not in saving, but in selection. Parsimony requires no providence, no sagacity, no powers of combination, no comparison, no judgment. Mere instinct, and that not an instinct of the noblest kind, may produce this false economy in perfection. The other economy has larger views. It requires a discriminating judgment, and a firm, sagacious mind. It shuts one door to impudent importunity, only to open another, and a wider, to unassuming merit.

The University President[1]

AT THE moment, it is said that no fewer than seventeen presidents of American colleges and universities have resigned or announced their intention of resigning. With so many important positions soon to be filled again—the presidency of Yale, of Cornell, of the University of Minnesota, and so on—the question of the right man for leader in education, and the proper functions of such a man, calls for thoughtful discussion. It is not often discussed on the basis of principle alone, and it should be discussed on no other. Personality, tact, qualities that defy analysis, pertain to the individual case; they do not enter into a general consideration of the topic.

First of all, should the position of college or university president exist at all? Certainly not, with the indiscriminate functions now attached to it. Strive as he may to save himself as a leader of scholars and a promoter of scholarship, the American college president—at the beck and call of the undergraduate, the parent, the impecunious instructor clamoring for an increase in his stipend, the world clamoring for tangible 'results,' and expecting vast external growth in the 'plant'—finds himself unable to keep up more than a show of the contemplative life, and sooner or later—insensibly and slowly, or promptly and with open eye—makes his compromise with the crowd and with Mammon; if indeed he has not fully compromised himself beforehand in order to win the position. The position as it now exists is truly anomalous. It originated in the small colonial institution that was modeled after the English college, and, by

[1] Published in *The Review*, New York, 2 (1920). 410, 412.

accident as it were, has been transferred to institutions that have grown, at least in externals, to resemble the populous and many-sided university of Continental Europe, with a polytechnic school superadded. The president of an American university combines the functions of the head of a small college with those of the Vice-chancellor of an English university and those of the Rector of a German, though not with those of the head of the Collège de France. But the term of the Vice-chancellor of Oxford is four years, ordinarily enough to spoil his best energies for the rest of his life, as was the case with Jowett. And the tenure of office for the Rector of a German university is one year. The post has often been refused by eminent men, such as the geographer Ratzel, who preferred not to interrupt their usefulness in research and publication even for so brief an interval. No man can adequately perform the duties of an American university president as they are now generally conceived, having come to be what they are by force of circumstances, through the numerical growth and ever-increasing complexity of institutions, and through the process of uncritical imitation, each man deeming that he must undertake all the activities of his predecessor and of his fellows who are similarly placed.

The first thing to suffer is his scholarship. The rare individual like Pepper of Pennsylvania, or Harper of Chicago, working nineteen hours a day, and able to tire out three stenographers, may succeed in preserving an active interest in the specialty for which he was trained. As a rule, however, an elevation to the presidency of a large institution has ended the participation of the new incumbent in systematic research, and therewith his complete understanding of the men who form the true kernel of the university.

There is much to be said for abolishing the position; for university administration by some form of commission government, with a changing committee and a rotating chairman. But since we are not likely to see it generally abolished in the near future, the question of what is expedient under present conditions becomes more pressing. How can the position be transformed from one that no productive scholar dare accept into one the incumbent of which will not lose his scholarly soul?

In two ways. First, by limiting the tenure of office to four or six years. Secondly, by relieving the president of every function (save his duty to scholarship) of which he can easily be relieved. The budget of the university, for example, though subject to his approval—yet not to his alone, nor even his in the main—should not be his production. He should not in effect have the financial responsibility of the organization; and, above all, it should not be considered his duty to secure funds for the institution. And again, the responsibility for the relations of the institution with all sorts of individuals—students, their parents, and the like—should not be his. Three-fourths of the duties now performed by him should be the affair of a secretary of the university and a secretarial staff. At a Continental university there is a clerical force that the average person sees but twice a year who render most of the services with which the time of our university leaders is squandered; that force is not a part of the administration proper.

By relieving the president of unnecessary burdens, we should make it possible for him to know his faculty. A man in his position may commonly be fairly well acquainted with one thousand persons; but the thousand or five hundred members of a university faculty are not usually the persons whom the president knows well, or desires to know best. The present nature of his position leads him to wish for an influential acquaintance outside the institution. He is likely to know all the trustees better than he knows all the faculty. He usually knows but a few of his faculty well. He ought to know every one of them, down to the newest assistant, before knowing any one else in the world. As it is, instructors come and go, meeting the head or chairman of a department often after the barest contact with the president, sometimes with none whatever.

By relieving him of all needless burdens, we should also render him free for a certain amount of intensive study in the field that was his before he became president; such freedom is even more necessary than that he should try to teach. In this way he would retain his ability to estimate the promise of candidates for positions on the faculty, and especially of those at the bottom of the ladder, from whose ranks are to be drawn the professors of the future.

Meanwhile, if the duties of the university president are to be reconstructed, a much better system should be introduced for the selection of faculties, and the advancement of the men already composing them; that is, if there can be said to be any system at present. Promotion should in some sense be an affair of the academic community, not a departmental one. This, as well as the selection of new professors who are called from other institutions, should be arranged at least by a committee of the faculty concerned, with the advice and consent of the president. His should be the veto power, but his vote in favor of a candidate should not be worth more than the vote of a member of the committee who understands the subject to be taught. As an executive, he should see to it that competent men examine every line the candidate has written, in order to determine, in the first place, whether the man is at bottom a scholar, and, in the second, whether he has the ability to communicate that sound learning which is a part of character.

Our country has run too far in the direction of what is called 'administration.' Everywhere we have developed a kind of genius for rendering administration complex and difficult. That the national tendency has invaded the realm of education hardly needs remark; there the mechanism of administration has become so involved as almost to throttle independent scholarship. Given the real scholar and teacher, the mechanism of teaching is simple. And whatever 'administration' may signify at Washington, or in the collection of an income-tax, in the university it means, not government, but service.

The chief function of the university president is to be the intellectual leader of the institution—of its faculty, who are the intellectual leaders of the students. His first duty is to create a current of ideas in the organism of which he is the *head*. In choosing our university leaders, let us go to Europe in order to learn what sort of men are taken on the Continent for the heads of educational institutions, and what they do after they have been raised to places of eminence. And having chosen real scholars, let us make it possible for them to retain their scholarly leadership while they occupy the posts to which they have been advanced. Make the pay in money less, and the pay in honor more.

The president of an American university is, or should be, the intellectual leader of what is at once an aristocracy and a democracy of intellect and spirit. A true democracy is possible among scholars. How strange that, in this American commonwealth, the one place where true democracy might hope to flourish so frequently tends to become a pure bureaucracy, or an affable tyranny in the guise thereof.

Should the Teacher of English

be a Scholar?[1]

IF YOU give a farmer in one of the Central Atlantic States some bit of novel information, he will exclaim: 'I want to know!' The response of our man of culture—agriculture—is typical. 'All men,' says Aristotle, 'by nature desire to know.' Elsewhere he adds that, among human pleasures, the greatest is the pleasure of learning. Dante calls Aristotle 'the master of them that know,' and speaks of Aristotle's doctrine as 'the first philosophy.' The culturists of the Central Atlantic States, one of which is my own native state, might well take the opening maxim of the *Metaphysics* as their motto: All men desire to know.

The second maxim, that of all human pleasures the greatest is our pleasure in learning, conveys a truth that will readily be accepted by those who till the fields of learning in these states. The sentiment is taken, in fact, from that work of Aristotle which has the most significance for teachers of literature, the culturists proper—for us. As such teachers doubtless have all driven a furrow or two through the Aristotelian *Poetics,* I need not pause long to remind you that there is no culture without plowing; that you can not gather your own rosebuds until you have cultivated, fertilized, and irrigated the soil; and that, as plowing and planting are hard work, so is drawing water. Paul and Apollos— you and I—plant and water, and God gives the increase.

[1] An address delivered before the College Conference on English in the Central Atlantic States, at George Washington University, Washington, D.C., November 29, 1924. Published in *School and Society* 21 (1925). 188–92. Reprinted by permission.

Well, have I told you enough of this labor? Shall I meddle or make any further? 'He that will have a cake out of the wheat must tarry the grinding.' Troilus: 'Have I not tarried?' 'Ay, the grinding; but you must tarry the bolting.' 'Have I not tarried?' 'Ay, the bolting; but you must tarry the leavening.' 'Still have I tarried.' 'Ay, to the leavening; but here's yet in the word "hereafter" the kneading, the making of the cake, the heating of the oven and the baking; nay, you must stay the cooling too, or you may chance to burn your lips.'

As you observe, we are still talking of literary enjoyment; and I return to Aristotle's famous treatise on the art of poetry. He goes on to say that the pleasure of learning is great, not merely in mankind as a whole, but in those of limited capacity, or limited opportunity, for scholarly things. This additional particular, you will see, if you think for a moment, puts your speaker in a less embarrassing situation. Let us boldly attack our problem.

The question is: Should the teacher of English be a scholar?

The answer is: He or she can not help being one in some measure. We are all, teachers and pupils alike, engaged in that process which Bacon calls the advancement of learning. Now there is no sharp dividing line between one kind of learning and another, unless it be the line that separates good learning from bad; and bad learning, properly considered, is not learning at all. The human mind has its own ways of working. If it works rightly according to its own nature, that is all we can ask of it. When the subject is the English language and literature (one subject), or any organic part of that subject, if the mind of the student advances by the correct method, that mind is the mind of a scholar. It makes no difference whether by 'student' we mean one who at the moment leads others in the advance, or one of those who at the moment happen to be led; in the advance of learning the positions of leader and led are constantly shifting. One mark of a good teacher is the capacity he shows to learn from his good pupils. And since the all-important thing is a correct method, it follows that there is no great difference between learning what we did not know before, and learning what we had completely forgotten; no great difference between learning something new and learning something that a generation or two may have lost from the collective human memory. The transition from ignorance to knowledge is discovery; now a discovery never is effective until it is thoroughly assimilated, and hence has the qualities of a recognition.

I lay some stress on this point of *re-cognition,* because the office of the teacher of English so largely consists in helping the best of human life to live again, or to live more abundantly than before. Present life is constantly growing out of the past, every day out of a preceding day, and thus out of many, or rather all, preceding days. That is the natural process; the artificial—the artistic— process is ours. If we are teachers of English, it is our function to make the new life draw into itself the best life we can lay hold on in the past, whether near or more remote. The artistic process is selective. We choose the best authors; we betake ourselves to the best sources of a rich, full, expansive life. We go to Chaucer, Spenser, Shakespeare, Milton, and the English Bible, and endeavor to reknow, to relive, those forms of life. This is better than trying to build up the life of to-day in the main out of yesterday's newspaper; though yesterday's journal likewise represents part of a life that is already past. Accordingly, we select the kind of life we are to induce our pupils to relive.

Should the teacher of English be a scholar? I repeat, he can not help being one in some measure. The desire for learning is innate in every one of us, and the pleasure of learning is the greatest of pleasures even in those whose capacity for pleasure— human, not bestial—is not vast, or whose opportunities for it are limited through adverse conditions; I mean, for example, through having more pupils in a class than one person can teach, or more hours of drudgery than are good for the mind. Under adverse conditions the instructor in English may tarry and tarry, and at length hardly taste of the cake.

The teacher of English can not help being a scholar to some extent. But he may argue that he need not be one; and that is very bad both for him and his pupils, partly because the fear of scholarship, in the last analysis, always proceeds from the fear of work. The old Adam, who does not like to hurt himself, can argue so subtly for his cheerful indolence that he will deceive himself along with his children. The baleful argument, the evil communication, is contagious, and may almost corrupt the manners of an entire age or nation. Indeed, it is one of the bad possibilities of rhetoric that you may argue on either side of this question; and I am afraid it is a sign of degeneration that the question ever should be put with an air of seriousness. But one does, in fact, hear people arguing that teachers of English need not be scholars; very likely every one of us has met some one who contends that great scholars are not good teachers. The charge seems to fly in the face of all reason. There may be, here and there, a useful pedant, or even a scholar in some limited way, who can not teach to advantage; that is, there may be exceptional cases. If so, the exceptional case has received more attention from our lazy old Adam than it deserves. So far as my own experience goes, let me say, please, that for years I have looked for the really excellent scholar who can not teach, yet have not found a single specimen. There are, indeed, not a few men with the reputation of scholars who do not advance learning in their pupils; but reputation is not character. Surely the possession of sound, first-hand, well-digested, growing knowledge, and the possession of a sympathetic imagination capable of reliving the life of a poet—Chaucer or Milton—and his age are the first requisites in a teacher of English.

How, indeed, can you be sure that a man *has* scholarship, if he is unable to impart it? If there really is some sort of scholarship that does not make for the advancement of life and learning, then the less we have of it the better. I trust it is plain that by scholarship in English we mean something that contributes to that higher life of the intellect and spirit which is usually termed the life of contemplation. This is nothing but the life of the student and teacher in whatever grade or capacity.

The teacher of English, then, will be a scholar, since he can not avoid the pleasure of learning. Further, he should admit that he is what he is, since to deny it will do more harm than any natural lack of capacity, or any outward circumstance that may limit his opportunities for study. The more sincerely he admits this truth, the better will his native talent thrive; the more time will he find for study and reflection—in the minutes or ten minutes he has heretofore squandered; and the more will the difficulties of an untoward environment tend to vanish.

The teacher of English should be a scholar because the history of scholarship in England is well-nigh identical with the history of our literature. He will be a scholar because our poetry and prose have grown out of scholarship, and our great poets and prose-writers have either been scholars or obviously sympathetic with the scholarly life. Shall I, like the author of the Epistle to the Hebrews, make a list of these men of vision, beginning with the Venerable Bede? See what Wordsworth says of Bede, in a notable sonnet:

> The saint, the scholar, from a circle freed
> Of toil stupendous, in a hallowed seat
> Of learning, where thou heard'st the billows beat
> On a wild coast, rough monitors to feed
> Perpetual industry.

The first great poet we can certainly name in our language is Cynewulf, a scholar. The founder of English prose, King Alfred, was a scholar. So much for the earliest period.

In Middle English, Chaucer is a scholar—not to mention Wyclif, Rolle, and the author of *Pearl*.

In the period of the Renaissance, Spenser and Sidney are scholars. Shakespeare, who ridiculed pedantry, which he did not confuse with scholarship, is invariably respectful when he refers to the scholarly life. My friend Professor Adams persuades us that Shakespeare was a teacher, in some one of the good outlying schools like that in Stratford, before he went to London to become a dramatist. As for Milton, he is not so much characterized by the writing of 'easie, unpremeditated verse,' as by what he calls 'labor and intent study'—intensive study, we now call it—which, he says, 'I take to be my portion in this life.' For a time he was a schoolmaster, wise and effective; his tractate *Of Education* should be laid to heart by every teacher of English.

And what shall we say of Pope and Dryden? Were not both of them scholars? Was not Pope the first Englishman to plan a history of the native literature? Or what of Gray at the end of the eighteenth century, or of Wordsworth at the beginning of the nineteenth? The last was a better scholar than Coleridge, who passes for a great one.

And what of our prose-writers?—beginning again with Alfred, the father of them, and coming down through Wyclif to Hooker and Jeremy Taylor, and to the scholars who produced the Authorized Version of the Bible. What of Bacon and Burke and Johnson, of Ruskin, Newman, and Goldwin Smith?

How can we sympathize with any of these poets and prose-writers if we do not share in that which was their chief interest from day to day—scholarly labor, intensive study? Wordsworth's library contained a surprising number of dictionaries. It was not likely, he thought, that the ordinary reader of poetry would know as much as the poet about the history of words. The teacher of English, who is not an ordinary reader, should know much. With the Oxford Dictionary now complete, any one of us can know more about the history of English words than did Spenser, Gray, or Wordsworth.

I speak of diction because we teachers of English have to revive the spirit of a noble past mainly through the study of words and their relations. Literature, the chief record of the past, consists of proper words in proper places. I speak of dictionaries, too, because the makers of them are human beings like you and me, persons with an interest in life and literature and engaged in the advancement of learning. Learning spreads through the use of proper words in proper places. I dwell upon this point because one of the things an American teacher of English may do for the general good, harassed though he be by unfavorable conditions, is to make a special lexicon of some favorite poet. There is nothing else that will teach the maker so much about the chosen author; and the published work will remain helpful to students as long as that author shall be studied. The teacher in a German secondary school who in spare moments made an invaluable lexicon of Shakespeare used his time to better advantage than most or all editors of single plays.

The doing of such work, or of any true scholarly work, promotes one's self-respect, clears one's mind of cobwebs, gives one a sense of proportion, brings one into the fellowship of good men in all nations and all ages. It increases one's vitality. I mean just that: your step becomes more elastic, as body and mind take the pace.

The teacher must give scholarship—above all, the habit of study—to his pupils. How can he give what he does not possess? 'Ah,' some one says, 'you tell us to be good. It is easy to tell any one to be good; being good is hard.' The Platonic Socrates goes further. He says, in effect, that it is impossible to be good; but he has a long argument showing that it is possible to become better. Goodness, scholarship, is not a state of being, but a process of becoming. It is the pursuit of an ever-advancing ideal, and the joy lies in the pursuit. We have thus come round full-circle to the point where we began: All men take pleasure in the advancement of learning.

No doubt I should now close with a character-sketch, done after the fashion of Theophrastus in 'The Surly Man,' or perhaps rather in the spirit of one of the English imitators of Theophrastus, as Earle, or Hall, or Overbury. This sketch should be called 'The character of a scholar.' When it was done you would see that it was also the character of a teacher of English. Should we call it 'The joyous man,' 'L'Allegro,' or 'The contemplative man,' 'Il Penseroso'—or both in one?

The College Graduate in the World of Learning[1]

MR. TOASTMASTER, Assembled Guests, and Brethren of the Alumni of Rutgers: Let me thank you heartily for your welcome. To your Toastmaster [Mr. Haley Fiske] I am indeed grateful for the allusion to my honored father, whose spirit doubtless is with us at this moment. Would that a portion of his eloquence were mine, that I might fitly say what you should willingly hear about 'The College Graduate in the World of Learning,'—since this topic has been assigned to me.

Does the title need explanation? We graduates all remember something of the process of learning; and, whether in the simpler or the more complex forms, every one recognizes the products of learning in the results of scholarship and science. Perhaps one term, 'the world,' may give us pause. Are we to think of the scholar as abiding in his own world, apart from the rest of human life? Are we not rather to think of the scholar and the scientist as living in that world which is composed of all men, sharing their interests, their sorrows, and their joys? Yet we must not forget the usage of the New Testament with respect to the word in question, the 'world.' Is the scholar actually to be part and parcel of that world which is transient, dark, and deceived—that world which finally will be overcome? It may be that he now far more than previously conceives of himself as a man among men,

[1] Published in *Rutgers College, the Celebration of the One Hundred and Fiftieth Anniversary of its Founding as Queen's College,* New Brunswick, New Jersey, 1917, pp. 148–53.

but he dare not regard himself as conformed to a world which is not yet saved. My topic will not appear too remote from the subject announced when I call it: 'The Rutgers Scholar and Scientist, in the World, but not of It.'

Seven generations of scholars has Rutgers College sent out from her halls of contemplation into the life of America. What sort of persons have they been? Possibly the classes of a recent vintage differ in more than one respect from the students I knew some twenty years ago. Possibly when they leave this place they find themselves at home a little more quickly in large cities and great and involved undertakings, or in other and larger institutions of learning. And yet I am ready to believe that in essentials they now are, and always have been, what they then were, and that the following description might fit the Rutgers scholar of any period.

He is not sophisticated; he is at first unfamiliar with numerous things one has to learn in the world, some of them better learned late than too early. He has to acquire by conscious effort many items of knowledge that a man in a populous university unconsciously absorbs from the very atmosphere. But he knows a few things well; and, above all, he is, in comparison with the machine-made product of more than one large and unwieldy institution, truly an individual. The men who have gone out from Rutgers may have been, in their time, somewhat ignorant of worldly affairs, but they have been men of essential power; men, one may aver, of unspoiled powers. From the number of those who have learned to observe, compare, and infer for themselves has ever come the race of scholars and scientists.

How many fair names there are in the long roll of Rutgers scholars! Our fellow-alumnus, Dr. Augustus H. Shearer, is compiling a bibliography of the books and articles produced by men who have been connected with the College, and hence I am free from the embarrassment of trying to enumerate the many learned individuals who should receive notice in such a list. If we began to count, where should we stop? I have, indeed, made a selection of three score that I should like to discuss particularly; but, con-

197

sidering the limits of time, I can mention only a few, and these very cursorily.

Among the foremost have been: Jeremiah Smith, of the class of 1780, a man of great erudition; John Romeyn Brodhead; Talbot W. Chambers; David D. Demarest, the noble father of our President; John De Witt, of the class of 1838; Philip J. Hoedemaker, a man of wide learning in theology, writing entirely in the Dutch language; Dr. Edward G. Janeway, of the class of 1860, in America the leading physician of his generation; Edward A. Bowser, of the class of 1868, who produced highly useful textbooks of mathematics; Professor Louis Bevier, at home alike in ancient and modern languages; Edward B. Voorhees, well known for his writings on agriculture; Professor John C. Van Dyke, interpreter of painting and of external nature; and, among more recent graduates, Dr. Henry H. Janeway, Professor J. L. R. Morgan, of Columbia University, Professor James Westfall Thompson, of the University of Chicago, Professor Richard S. Lull, of Yale University, Professor Jacob G. Lipman, of our own College of Agriculture.

But I must not prolong the enumeration. Not all our scholars and scientists have been productive in the sense of publishing many books. The characteristic of the Rutgers scholar and scientist, as it seems to me, has been his power of transmitting his own living thought directly to students, in an intellectual current which has gone from man to man, and from the teacher of one generation to him who was to be a teacher of the next. And that, after all, is the best form of expression—where one man writes in the heart of another. At the same time we have had no lack of men productive in the stricter sense as well. Some have already been mentioned. But I make bold to single out the late George W. Hill, of the class of 1859, an authority on celestial mechanics, and Professor Albert S. Cook, of the class of 1872, now of Yale University, a master in the field of the English language and literature, as preëminent for their published researches, respectively, in pure science and humane learning. These two, in their several provinces, have achieved as much as any others of their time in this or any other country—as much as any others be they who they may, and come they from what institutions they may come.

'Man looks before and after,' say the philosopher and the poet. Upon an anniversary occasion like this, retrospect is not more fascinating than anticipation. What of the future?

The scholar is often pitied, I believe, because he does not know the world. Is the world ever pitied because it does not understand the scholar? The time is coming, I trust, when this country will better appreciate the needs of pure scholarship and pure science, and will cease to measure their value in terms of lower utility and immediate application. The present tendency in American education may seem to be utilitarian; the superficial current may actually be so. But the eternal current of the human spirit sweeps on beneath resistlessly, and the permanent interest of mankind remains in the world of ideas. In our colleges, at all events, let there be no mistake. If after-life must often be 'practical,' education is necessarily 'theoretical.' Institutions of learning are precisely what they are called, and they will continue to be institutions of learning primarily, and not primarily of application. Whatever the tendency of the moment in the country at large may be, the permanent function of a college like ours is to send out men of learning into a world that without them will sink into brutal apathy.

Would that it were in our power to see, as in a magic glass, the long line of Rutgers scholars in the future, so that we might characterize the type. I dare not attempt a characterization at any length. No doubt it is safe to say that our scholars will always be trained in the fundamentals. They will know a few things well, rather than many things (and some of them unimportant) badly. And their studies will lead them to a knowledge of humanity. Now a knowledge of the humanity about us is not easily gained without an acquaintance with the civilizations upon which our civilization is based; so that the scholarship of Rutgers will never neglect the civilizations of Greece and Rome and Italy and England. Nor will it ever neglect the civilizing force of the Bible.

Education, indeed, whether it be called scholarly, or however it be called, is of little avail if it does not give the scholar an understanding of his own people; if it does not lead them to trust him; if it does not enable him to give them what they need rather than what they happen to crave; if it does not enable him to withhold what they wrongly desire. Such being the objects of a scholarly education, we may ask how they are to be obtained. No end is secured without means, and the means are either spiritual or material; it may be said that nothing is accomplished in this world save by the interaction of the two kinds. Yet it is very difficult to make the American see the relation between money and scholarship, between money and pure science. It does not seem very difficult to secure funds for the advancement of applied science; it is relatively easy to find money for college buildings, for brick, for stone, for libraries and laboratories—for the apparatus that one may see and touch. It is not so easy to set a pecuniary value upon the trained soul of the learned man; but that the disciplined mind of the scholar and scientist is beyond all value does not warrant the American people in trying to secure its services for little or nothing. In scholarship the relation between means and ends is the same as in any other realm of life. There is, we must say most emphatically, a pecuniary basis for the life of the scholar. A scholar must be free from anxiety. A scholar must have means for the prosecution of long and expensive researches. I desire to record my plea for the scholarly function of the College, and to urge upon the alumni of Rutgers not to let the scholarly and scientific activities of the institution suffer, through lack of support, in comparison with any other activity here fostered, or in comparison with the scholarship and science of any other institution in this country. I beg the alumni to enable the College to give to the country, in greater measure than ever before, what the country needs—the vision of the scientist, the scholar, the poet, and the divine. Where there is no vision, the people perish.

XXXV

War not Inevitable

TO THE editor of the *Cornell Daily Sun,* Nov. 2, 1926: Your editorial pronouncement on the responsibility for the late war in Europe [1914–18] ends: 'It [the war] was inevitable.'

It is a sign of grace to admit that Germany was not altogether responsible for the war—that the responsibility must be shared by other nations. It has been a sign of grace in England to be more prompt than some other nations on the winning side to admit it.

On the other hand, if Germany had not, more than other nations, desired the war, the war would not have occurred. Had she tried as hard as England to avoid the war, it would not have occurred. Had she not confidently expected to win the war, it would not have occurred. Had she not grown more pagan, less Christian, it would not have occurred. Had not many of her leaders of opinion thought, like the *Cornell Daily Sun,* that 'it was inevitable'—and yet that the inevitable might be anticipated —it would not have occurred. Some of her unamiable qualities, shared in a measure by other nations before the war, may well be studied as a warning in their recent development outside Germany since.

Nothing will more readily plunge a nation into war than the supposition that war is inevitable.

But it is not inevitable that a thinking person should hold this supposition. It is perhaps inevitable that a number of thoughtless people should hold, or at all events occasionally utter, it. Of the leaders, who should be first thoughtful, and then restrained in expression, we expect better things. And educational leaders, including all who mould opinion in the students, are they who should teach thoughtfulness and restraint. There is ground for believing that the seeds of the last great war were sown in the Balkan schools and universities, and nourished in the words and acts of students.

The two main causes of war are the notion that it is inevitable, and talk.

'Behold how great a forest a little fire kindleth. And the tongue is a fire; . . . which setteth on fire the course of nature; and is set on fire by hell.'

XXXVI

The Worldly Wisdom

of Polonius[1]

IN MY windfall of calendars for the new year there is one, a
'Shakespeare Calendar,' representing the king of dramatists in a
singularly vacant mood, and having for its motto this precious
bit of counsel:

> Give every man thine ear, but few thy voice;
> Take each man's censure, but reserve thy judgment.

Admirable sentiments, are they not? Yet I marvel that the artist
who made this calendar did not choose for its legend the beati-
tude, so much more popular, at the end of the same passage. The
passage, as every one knows, continues and closes thus:

> Costly thy habit as thy purse can buy,
> But not expressed in fancy; rich, not gaudy;
> For the apparel oft proclaims the man,
> And they in France of the best rank and station
> Are most select and generous in that.
> Neither a borrower nor a lender be;
> For loan oft loses both itself and friend,
> And borrowing dulls the edge of husbandry.
>   This above all: to thine own self be true,
> And it must follow, as the night the day,
> Thou canst not then be false to any man.

'To thine own self be true, Laertes!' How excellent! There is
nothing like it in Scripture. It is a new and improved Golden

[1] Published in *The Cornell Era* 39 (1907). 292–5.

Rule, so applicable to the conditions of modern life that it is quoted by many writers as if it were an utterance of Shakespeare himself.

Fortunately, it is not. It is a pronouncement made by one of Shakespeare's characters, and a very despicable character at that. It is the final and most bombastic utterance of the shuffling Polonius in his discourse to Laertes on respectable self-seeking. Listen (but reserve thy judgment) to Professor Dowden's opinion of this discourse:

The advice of Polonius is a cento of quotations from Lyly's *Euphues*. Its significance must be looked for less in the matter than in the sententious manner. Polonius has been wise with the little wisdom of worldly prudence. He has been a master of indirect means of getting at the truth, 'windlaces and assays of bias.' In the shallow lore of life he has been learned. Of true wisdom he has never had a gleam. And what Shakespeare wishes to signify in this speech is that wisdom of Polonius' kind consists of a set of maxims; all such wisdom might be set down for the headlines of copy-books. That is to say, his wisdom is not the outflow of a rich or deep nature, but the little, accumulated hoard of a long and superficial experience. This is what the sententious manner signifies. And very rightly Shakespeare has put into Polonius' mouth the noble lines,

> To thine own self be true,
> And it must follow, as the night the day,
> Thou canst not then be false to any man.

Yes; Polonius has got one great truth among his copy-book maxims, but it comes in as a little bit of hard, unvital wisdom like the rest. *'Dress well, don't lend or borrow money; to thine own self be true.'*

Apparently, the artist has not chosen well when he offers us as vital wisdom the foolish phrase, 'Give every man thine ear.' But would Dowden's choice be any better? *Is* this a great truth? If so, why should the great dramatist keep it, among all these windy mouthings, for the very climax of the speech? Because, as Dowden suggests, coming from the lips of shallow senility the expression is all the more empty for its intrinsic worth? No. To me at least, this climax is unconditionally ignoble, the final sentiment essentially more hollow than any of the maxims that lead up to it.

It is not degraded by rubbing shoulders with the flatulent assemblage from *Euphues;* it is inconsequential in itself. As I have hinted, it is directly antagonistic to the spirit of unselfishness; an altruist would say immediately that Polonius had the cart before the horse; that ideal fidelity to others comes from entire denial of self.

Shallow and inconsequential, without doubt, is the reasoning in these lines, as in those that precede them. Towards the middle of the harangue we learn that 'the apparel *oft* proclaims the man'; an argument for putting all the money you can possibly spare into your clothing. In the whole speech there is not a single word about charity, even for the sake of appearances. But just as *oft* the apparel does *not* proclaim the man; in fact,

> The man of independent mind,
> He looks and laughs at a' that.

Similarly, the argument for *never* lending is that 'loan *oft* loses both itself and friend.' Equally cogent is the formula at the end: being true to yourself is the cause of your being true to others, as the day is the cause of the night. The night and the day are, I believe, a stock illustration in logic of a *post hoc non propter hoc*. At all events, since the time of Corin in *As You Like It,* philosophy has taught us to believe 'that a great cause of the night is the absence of the sun.' There is likewise good Scriptural authority for the belief that if you want to be true to your fellows, you had better not think very much about yourself.

Such, at any rate, seems to be the point in the following dialogue, for the abruptness of whose introduction here I suppose I must apologize, though the modern writer serves my purpose well. Lovers of Robert Louis Stevenson will remember a scene in *The Merry Men* where the hero, Charley, is urging his sweetheart to leave the desolate island of Aros, giving her father up to his own evil devices:

'Well, Mary, you may be sure of this: you had better be anywhere but here.'

'I'll be sure of one thing,' she returned: 'I'll be where my duty is.'

'You forget, you have a duty to yourself,' I said.

'Ay, man?' she replied; 'will you have found that in the Bible, now?'

He might have found it in the Summary of the Law by Polonius:

> This above all: to thine own self be true.

I would not inflict my Scottish sermon on the *Era*, or talk about an interpretation of Shakespeare that is doubtless a commonplace in the class-room, but for one consideration: outside the class-room this swollen sentiment of Polonius is too often ascribed, without qualification, to the mind that created Polonius. Now it is obviously the stupidest of errors to impute to a creative dramatist, about whose personal history we actually know so little, the exact opinions even of his better characters; not to speak of such characters as he might himself be the first to condemn. This also seems like an academic commonplace, in the sanctum of the literary critic a mere truism. Yet it needs to be published, now and then, from the housetop and in the forum.

Accordingly, when you feel tempted to credit 'Shakespeare' with the maxim,

> To thine own self be true,

or

> Give every man thine ear,

or to accept either as the Shakespearian philosophy of life, please recall that neither is Shakespeare's dictum; but remember that both are the unsubstantial bombast of a rash, intruding fool whom the poet, meting out justice to each personage in his drama as each deserves, makes die like a rat behind the arras, as the price of eavesdropping.

What Is a Poet?[1]

IN THE beginning God creates each man in His Own image. He blows the breath of life into the nostrils, and the man becomes a living soul. Creation is not a thing that ended long ago; it is a ceaseless work. Each day is one of light and darkness, a morning and an evening as at first. But it is individual; unique in the works that are done upon it; neither more familiar nor less wonderful than the first day. So, each appearing man, compact of clay, bears in his forehead and between his eyes the new yet changeless mark of the Potter, that the first man bore. Is not the work of every artist in the artist's own likeness? By his fruits we shall know him. Also, it is the heritage of all the children of the King, His creatures, wrought cunningly and very well, to shadow forth their Imperial Artist's self.

But must not he that is made in the similitude of a Creator himself be a creator? Yet as creation is done with a word, when it is said, 'Let there be light and a firmament, and herbs and fishes, fowls and beasts and creepers, and lastly the erect one,' and these all are and continue, so we may look upon the power of man to produce, to see if this has not its most perfect measurement and expression in language. Therefore it was that the Greeks, the race of old that even played its games artistically, dignified the one who used the medium of words to body forth his brooding idea, as *par excellence* the maker among men, ὁ ποιήτης, or, as we have it from their quickening, not dead, tongue, the poet.

[1] Master's Oration given at Rutgers College, June 20, 1899; published in the *Reformed Quarterly Review* 4 (1900). 213–18. Reprinted by permission.

To the question, then, 'What is a poet?' we answer, 'First of all he is a creator.' See how he takes the formless material that lies about him, the crude passions of commonplace men and women, to refine, to harmonize, and to blend in the admirable characters of his heroes. 'Let us' we might hear Homer say, be he one blind bard, or a band of bards imbued with one idea—'Let us' we might hear him say communing, 'make men in our own image.' Accordingly, there come down the avenues of time those mirrors of the childlike Grecian mind and genius, wrathful Achilles, and subtle Odysseus, and heedful Penelope—all wrought out of their maker's mind, as alive to-day as on the yesterday on which the timeless poet formed them; far more alive than those of us who have with shallow joy received the seed and word of life, yet do not choose to be participant in the work of giving life. In these children Homer still survives. He has added to the measure of power entrusted him; he has given his soul a new and manifold expression. Into his art and his labor he breathed his life, and they, being in the likeness of their creator, are themselves creative and a source of inspiration unto us.

Are we not conscious of a more abundant being in us when we read the Odyssey? Surely the Homeric mantle falls upon us and we have a double portion of spirit; the day on which we read becomes, as it were, a thousand days; wide vistas stride forward upon us; we see more clearly the excellence of the universe. There is also a bodily exhilaration: we would rejoice as an active man to run a race. In many senses of the phrase, we experience a new creation.

Such an influx and elevation of life and spirit we feel as we enter the various worlds that Shakespeare has brought to pass. Here are groups of men and women weaving out their destinies, some well, some ill; in the comedies, all harmoniously at last; in the tragedies, by a deep and mighty order, which allows what seem at first most frightful inconsistencies and contradictions, yet, at last, by the great reconciler and pacifier, death, all harmoniously. For the poet makes his survey from the standpoint of a creator, seeing in all things possibilities of strength and weakness, good and evil, and choosing the strong and the good; nevertheless, with a use for the feeble and a tolerance of the foolish and the harmful, until, at his pleasure, he shall reduce them too to order, power, and beauty. He retires behind the veil of time and space, gathering his materials, and consulting for a season. Suddenly he breaks forth and projects his organized idea upon this warp and woof of our imagination, and we behold a new creation, wonderfully fair and very good. We also, following him in his effort, feel a sharing in his agency, and he in us and we in him are recreated. It is a part and form of immortality.

It does, to be sure, make little difference what materials the artist uses. What shape he puts upon them, what order he puts in them, measure him. He may take a product already wrought; as Shakespeare took from Plutarch, with marvelous economy saving a divine energy for the difficult last touches; as Rubens took his pupils' canvases, and finished them, as he, and not his pupils could. He may mould his men, of dust, so to speak, and nothingness. Yet he will mould men, if he be a great poet. How Browning's spirit leaped to be embodied in a multitude of personalities, one after another, formed out of (almost) nothing that had previously existed! A hint or two from Samuel to give us in elaboration and concretely the character of 'Saul'; 'Rabbi ben Ezra' arising with his rich philosophy out of little more than a mediæval name. Browning saw nature as a whole, with civilized man its highest product. In the reverse lay the misconception of Rousseau, although he too was undoubtedly a poet. And if in the work of a writer of to-day the animals and the boy considered as an animal are better art than the men and women, this author cannot be held among the highest.

In other ways also it makes little difference what material the artist uses. After all he is not toiling with anything altogether crude or incapable of artistic moulding. What the Primary Imagination has furnished for the secondary, that is, what God has made, is not common or unclean in itself. That is foul and sinful for us which we as evil poets make so; we may turn a temple to a den of thieves. But the author of the Book of Job saw a poetic use for a back corrupt with scabby boils; and for Homer there is poetry in Nausicaa and her maids as they wash the dirty garments and spread them on the shore; yes, there is poetry for him in twelve full pig-sties. Toward the close of the Odyssey he pits a miserable beggar, as it seems, against a real mouthing abject, to fight at fisticuffs, and we find the glory of the former and the downfall of the latter alike enchanting. All the poetry of the Bible is centred in a manger. There the lowly is uplifted and the proud brought down to dust. Before the poet, sin and sorrow and suffering flee away, vanishing in love and joy and laughter, transformed by the power of a maker. His own peculiar griefs he makes beautiful and universal, and in them we see our own all purified, and suddenly reconciled and emulous for the crown for very joy we seize and bear our cross again. So Goethe gathers his pains and lost loves in his Werther, and later, with a better-balanced genius, in his Meister, and there they have an outlet and a use; since out of things once full of pangs, or even bad and ugly, he has, according to his power, made forms of beauty.

What God has made is essentially all very good. This we must believe. This the poets know; for they are most in His likeness; and they see with a measure of Divine sight, and put forth again what they have seen, with a measure of the Divine imagination. And they confess, as Shelley did, that there is a perfect poem-hymn of which their strains are only fragments; and they can conceive of an artistic scheme, with an aboriginal beginning, a middle of agony ineffable, and a triumphant trumpet-sounded ending—an artistic scheme, wherein, as in one grand unutterable theme, too lofty for the infirmities of human speech to cope with, all things, in a seeming state of incompleteness and inconsistency, are moving onward to perfection and a final glorious reconciliation; wherein, as we are lifted up and re-created by the sorrow and fear of a tragedy, or the passion of a fugue, or the exceeding humanity of a masterly portrait, so by the skill and anguish of the greatest Poet, who is also the Perfect Word or Poem, we shall be raised even from the very negation of life and given endless life.

We have chosen here, as the race has chosen, to call him poet who adapts the means of language to the ends of his creative impulse. But the painter also has the power of inbreathing life, and figures forth ideal men with their environments. And the sculptor is a poet: who compels the chilly stone to be alive; ascending toward the heavenly ideal, and drawing all men after him. And, in fact, whoever follows nature, the Divine art-product, in her continual effort to bring forth more complex and lively forms, and strives as a conscious part of her to evolve something better than could be without his aid—he is a poet.

Therefore it is clear that in some sense every man can be a poet —as also was seen, since every man is in the image of the Word, the Maker. Now, he who makes his fields to flourish has the artistic impulse; and whoso heals men's bodies and gives them longer, fuller lives, displays it; consciously or unconsciously doing the Creator's own work of replenishing life. So, also, he who labors on men's souls, with agony and ardor moulding them to fairer forms. Thus the teacher is a poet, fashioning a material as plastic as language, yet more subtle; aiding the Divine Parent and the earthly in producing a symbol and an image of the Original; forming what Dante says all art is, a grandchild of God.

Not all of us by any means can become poet-prophets like Isaiah and Ezekiel, men for whom the distinctions of time are abolished, who see not paltry signs of happenings to come, but everlasting truths to be spoken forth, and powerfully justify the ways of the Eternal to time-considering men.

Nor can all we be poet-priests like Taylor and Charles Wesley, with majestic ejaculations on our lips, or songs upon them; with blessed full-toned tongues of charity for all to stir and make abounding the spiritual life of men. Albeit we as they draw inspiration by no laying on of hands, nor by any ceremony bolstered up with the false dignity of time, that shadow of smoke, but by direct receiving of the breath of the Creator.

Nor can all we be poet-conquerors like David and King Alfred, men of hearts and voices powerful to fill a host with courage, yet to suffer no diminishing by the outlay; making and keeping realms in decorative order by our good cunning and wise activity.

We must be, most of us, of the mighty numbers that only stand and wait, our lot to hold a golden silence. We may be but hewers and drawers for a masterbuilder.

And yet, in another fuller sense, according to the message that

211

all literature contains, if rightly read, we may be prophets, priests, and kings, and masterbuilders, too, and withal poets. 'Life,' says Goethe, 'lies before each one of us, as a great quarry lies before the architect. He little deserves the name of architect who elaborates therefrom no structure corresponding to his own good and preconceived idea.' The poet is a maker: we are poets when, having assured ourselves what poetry is, we make our lives abiding-places for it, or, to gather from the most sublime and artistic of all books, when we make ourselves habitable for the Word, the Λόγος; when also we shall be lovers of it, too, and in the finest sense, φιλόλογοι, philologists. Then, indeed, we shall have built a new temple, a mansion for a Prophet, Priest, and King, and the Spirit of a Prophet, Priest, and King will be in us. And the conquering, vivifying Word shall also be the standard and the critic of the perfectness of each life; and to the poet He shall say in commendation, as once in agony He said of His own life and labor: 'It is finished.'

Grace, Truth—and Peace[1]

OF OUR boys in the fox-holes and trenches the late Father Cummings said: There are no atheists in those holes and trenches. Godless men no doubt have been just as rare on our battleships in action. No atheists, either, in our airplanes; no atheists in our fighters and bombers face to face with eternity. A favorite pupil of mine was flying over the trees and the sea, early in the war, above and about New Guinea, with room aboard for one book. It was a volume of Plato, a writer full of grace and truth; in fact, among pagan writers that author who comes nearest in such qualities as grace and truth to what we call the Authorized Version of the Bible. That young friend of mine had the book of Plato with him, not for the chance protection of the heart that pumps his blood, against a piece of shrapnel, though it is good for a man to have that species of protection. My young friend carried his book about with him for the sake of his spiritual heart. Having room aboard for but one volume, he did not take the Bible, for he knew already enough of the Bible by heart to keep his heart intact, his spirit safe, that well out of which are the issues of life. Of course he owns a copy of the Bible, the best seller. How many know it is that? The Bible is always the best seller. In Germany it has outsold *Mein Kampf,* and in America it outsells whatever at the moment may be reckoned the publication that is advertised the most—'A Stinkweed Grows in Brook-

[1] Adapted from a Commencement address delivered at Wesleyan University, October 21, 1944. I have not aimed to quote the words of the saintly chaplain, Father Cummings, exactly.

Privately Published. Printed at the Cayuga Press, Ithaca, New York, March, 1946.

lyn,' let us say, if that is accounted the temporary favorite piece of reading in the world. On duty, you had better have the Bible in your breast-pocket, over your heart, to ward off shrapnel and Satan.

But there is this trouble about the Bible and the reading of it. Safe at home, young men and women too often read at it, and not in it, as they should. Having been exposed to the book in childhood, it may be, they now slide over what they read, because they never learned to read as a good driver drives a car. The Bible is full of signs, Stop, Look, and Listen—Amen and Selah, if you like; but the bad driver, the hasty reader, does not stop, so how can he listen and look? Listen, please! We are going to stop before two words, which were announced but a little while ago, when the hasting herd, not a few perhaps, passed over them without knowing that the syllables carry freight. In the Bible, many of an older generation went over those two glistening words at high speed when we were at the age of graduation from a university or college. It is a great good to begin reading the best book early; even nowadays many little children somehow gain a measure of familiarity with the Bible. If it was not so with some of you, make up for it when you have children of your own. But in the Bible children meet ideas that a child can hardly grasp; and hence as we grow older we must strip the film from our eyes, indeed must learn to grasp the words with all our senses. Stop, look, and listen. Thus we come to grips with ideas of the utmost import for a world that fumbles with ugly terms like 'ideologies.' I never met a man who knew precisely what he meant by 'ideology'; it really is no English word, but a malformation, or an unassessed import from abroad. There is something to be said for returning in our time to a better literary training than most of our recent graduates from colleges have had, and to a strict discipline in the use of words. Do you say *ration* with an *a* as in *hash*, or do you follow Lewis Carroll, Browning, and the best of English dictionaries, and properly rhyme *ration* with *nation?* All these courses in 'English' for the past forty years and more, yet the taste and usage of our writers—novelists, journalists, and the very teachers of 'English' themselves—have gone

214

from bad to worse. Such is the result of literary studies divorced from a painstaking attention to grammar and *belles lettres;* I mean just that, the study of letters and syllables as the elements of literary grace and truth.

Did you hear them? Grace and Truth! Those are the two main words we used in describing Plato. But they come from the Bible. O listen! for the vale profound is overflowing with the sound.

Stop and look at the word 'grace.' We all know what grace is in a young woman, and in older women too, when they are good. Think of your mother. Or think of some one whose first name, or last, is Grace; Wordsworth's heroine, Grace Darling, for example; I was going to mention the beautiful and powerful name, Eugene Grace of Bethlehem, but am turning to the men for illustrations rather of truth. Every one knows what truth is in a brave young man, or in an elderly man, for that matter. Take Mr. Churchill, for example. He has had a singular habit, and so has Mr. Grace, of seeing and telling the truth. He happens to have done research in history, as did Theodore Roosevelt, real research. He has gone to the sources, the wells, as a good graduate student does, or a good undergraduate at times, and has come to grips with facts. That practice got Mr. Churchill into the habit of looking for the truth everywhere, so that he has seen the truth with his own eyes, by the Grace of God, before trying to tell it in public. Would that England and America had had the grace to listen to Winston Churchill when he told them, and told Stanley Baldwin, the truth about Germany before Attila Hitler started to upset the world.

Here, then, let us say a word about writing and speaking. Hitler has told us, and Churchill and Montgomery [2] have shown us, how utterly important to the State is a command of eloquence in the leaders. Every one, of course, would like to write and speak much better than he does; would like to tell the truth so as to awaken and hold his listener or correspondent, and to tell

[2] Now (August, 1952) add Eisenhower. Since I could watch, after beginning his *Crusade in Europe,* to my knowledge he has known when to hold his peace, and has not said or done a false or foolish thing.

it in words of beauty, with the rhythm and cadence of a noble
heart and pure speaking to a pure and noble heart. Now almost
everybody could write and speak better than he does. We may
dimly wish to do that, and yet never stiffen the will to carry out
the wishful thought. You can do it if you make up your mind
to pay the price; for the price is high. How high it is you can
discover if you hunt out the right sources of information, and
study how the authors every one admires have with infinite pains
gone about the task of preparing themselves to write. There is
no call to go into the subject fully here. Study the Classics; study
the Oxford English Dictionary; and learn much of the Bible, in
the 'Authorized Version,' by heart.

The main thing is to love the truth, and to believe that the
truth as a whole is beautiful. For some part of the truth, and
some part of beauty, you may trust to grace. And now by 'grace'
I simply mean a gift that comes from on high in response to
prayer. You have to go about the business in the proper way; you
must take the necessary pains, on your knees and in your chair,
as Montgomery and MacArthur do. You must take a portion of
the truth, and know it, as Theodore Roosevelt knew some part
of American history, from the sources. In that way you secure a
base-line and a scale with which to find out whether some one
else draws a sharp line between what he knows and what he does
not know. And here be warned by the example of Hitler that
playing politics successfully does not of necessity mean knowing
or telling the truth. A clever politician may feel out the minds
of multitudes of other shallow persons like himself, may get
their votes, and may get himself elected, and know nothing as
things should be known, from the bottom up. He may be a college professor, and come to be president of the United States,
and still not know where the island of Yap (Uap) is in the Pacific
Ocean, when it is his business to know just that. Theodore Roosevelt knew. Or the supposed leader might not know that in a
country he was going to call Czecho-Slovakia there would be two
million or more Germans. 'Two million Germans?' said Wood-
rovius to Bullitt on the way to France. 'They did not tell me
that!'

But we were to deal with grace before dealing with truth—so far, that is, as you can deal with either alone; for, rightly considered, they cannot exist apart. The two are like thinking and thanking; when we look in the Dictionary, we see that *thinking* and *thanking* spring from the same verbal root. A considerate person is thankful, and a person who does not think is inconsiderate. When you go out from your university or college, it is an unthinking, unforeseeing, thankless world that you go into.

Still we here lay emphasis first on grace; for here we come to our text, from the Apostle John, who says that He who now has conquered the disgraceful and untruthful Hitler came to dwell among us, 'full of grace and truth.' John adds: 'For the law was given by Moses, but grace and truth came by Jesus Christ.' For us, Isaiah calls him the Prince of Peace.

We have no occasion now for entering into technical theology. We take the word *grace* in its common English meaning of *beauty*. It is a gift, something in which we all have a share, yet specially bestowed on gifted individuals. It is a favor. And when some one does you a favor, you say 'Thanks.' At breakfast you say 'grace,' that is, thanks for the food that comes from the Universal Giver, and you go on with pleasant conversation, not sour talk about the quality of the food, but grateful, that is *graceful,* talk about good and ample food in Middletown, or wherever you happen to be. Later, when a beautiful girl, 'Grace Darling' as aforesaid, goes by you on the street, you do better than did the late Chief Justice Holmes, at the age of ninety-odd. When she had got by, he said to his aged colleague from our highest court: 'Don't you wish you could be seventy again?' True beauty, however, is ageless, and the appreciation of it is ageless too. Mr. Justice Holmes should simply have said, 'Thanks, Grace Darling,' and not have had another thought about himself at all; for there is a higher court than his, and that highest Law-giver, who is the Giver of grace and truth. Him Dante had in mind when he said, in effect, of his Beatrice: Only her ageless Creator can fully appreciate her beauty.—That is not meant to be an exact quotation.

So much for grace, beauty, favor, thanks. Do you 'favor' your mother, as they say; do you look like her? Say thanks. When your

friend or mother favors you with a smile, say thank you. At lunch
and dinner, too, say grace. When you look at a beautiful sunset,
say grace. When you note a beautiful tree in Prospect Park, for
there is many a beautiful tree in that part of Brooklyn, say thank
you to the Universal Gardener who helps all human gardeners
and foresters with their trees. He helped Luther Burbank too,
whom, alas, Joyce Kilmer notably forgot.

And now we turn briefly to things disgraceful. Thus, 'A Stinkweed Grows in Brooklyn,' for that is what we boys called the
Ailanthus-tree some fifty years ago in a small town in New Jersey
—'Stinkweed.' A book does not have to tell the smelly part of
truth in ugly words. Perhaps we cannot avoid observing some
ugly things apart and by themselves before we see them in relation to all things, in what, when you see it all, is a beautiful cos-
mos; and that cosmic vista is as far as mortal eye can see. But a
good writer does not lug in filth in order to sell a book. A good
writer like Robert Louis Stevenson can give you a telling picture,
almost Homeric, of pirates, men ferocious, without using one
vile word in all of *Treasure Island*. Kipling, at his best a writer
both graceful and true, as in *Puck of Pook's Hill,* does not do so
well in depicting drummer-boys; for him the bad ones talk as
bad boys do. The Bible uses better words and rhythms than any
other book. The writers in the Bible do not talk of filth because
they like it, or with the expectation that their readers will like it.
They talk of filth, when they need to, and seldom, because they
do not like what is filthy, and wish the reader to hate it. But the
Good Book does not hesitate to call a tree, or man or woman,
'stinkweed' if that happens to be the case.

And why will ladies, who can read good books, and hence
ought to be Graces, continue to think that the tree of the knowledge of good and evil bears fruit that is good to eat? Let the radio
announcer, or the printed advertisement, tell them why. With
respect to books some readers have the halitosis, and do not know
it. 'Poetry,' said Wordsworth, 'is the breath and finer spirit of all
knowledge'; he meant that the essence of good speech and writing is the breath and spirit of grace and truth. In reading, hold
your breath, and watch your step. When Eve, and Adam after

her, did eat of the tree of the knowledge of good and evil, what was the result? They found, when they had swallowed that 'Strange Fruit,' that now they had but the memory of a perfect good for ever lost, and the bitter experience of present evil. Their paradise, their Prospect Park, was locked against them; all they had left to them outside was stinkweed. Does literary taste seem only a light matter when we are at war, or hardly out of it? The ruling class in Germany gave up their standards of decency, of grace and truth, about the year 1900, if not before; thereafter came the deluge.

Must we say more of things disgraceful? However, let us emphasize a thing for which we may give thanks. Now more and more the girls of better taste do not paint their fingers and faces as the starving women of the street once did exclusively in order to look healthy when they were diseased. And thank goodness, let us all say grace for it, the better boys prefer the natural color of health in the cheeks and on the mouths of those who smile on them. And matrons who recall their own good mothers do not go about half-clad in bitter weather to catch and spread the influenza. Nor do they paint their toe-nails pink, as some few elderly Zinnias are said to do; who knows it among mankind but the elderly Zinnias, the spinsters in question? When the style of the day does no harm, follow it, not too keenly; in general, avoid the graceless spirit of the crowd. Watch your step; stop, look, and listen, and smell. A good nose is useful both when you eat and when you read; it helps one to detect the lie in the soul of an evil generation.

One more disgrace, as we come back to the radio announcer, and the 'singer' who wails intimately by wireless to the individual girl, so she thinks, but really to a million silly girls, in so-called music that has in it not one single note of gladness and joy. What an abuse of the greatest invention of man since the printing-press! They manage the radio better in Great Britain. In America, the popular music of my youth, and much more recently than that, was often far from being all it should be, but there was gladness in it.

As for the announcers, let Professor Harlow Shapley return

to his charge against them till the charge re-echoes beyond the columns of the *New York Times,* for his voice is more potent than the voice at the moment appearing. Yet here we may refer to the disgrace of mingling the news of the blood, sweat, and tears our boys and their parents and their Grace Darlings have shed, the tears they will go on shedding, with news of Kreml, Quink, and Super-suds. Have we really been fighting to make the world safe for cheap advertising and the sale of oil, or safe for Grace and Truth?

Grace and Truth are the formula of John. I was going to say more about truth, and now have only space to recall that she is in a well. Adolf Hitler did more than any other lad to put her there, and Winston Churchill more than any other lad to pull her out. Even a boy can help in the pulling if he has the necessary grace.

To Grace and Truth add Mercy. Shall we say that we have been fighting an endless battle for Grace, Mercy, and Truth? Or for Mercy, Grace, and Truth, and Peace? The formula of Paul, used over and over again, for what a man, under God, should give to his brother man, is Grace and Peace. In those dark days, as we awaited the dawn, how much we talked of Peace! Oh how we longed for it! How we still long for it! And will the Prince of Peace be sitting at the table where the peace of Europe, and the peace of the World, is to be decided? Blessed are the peacemakers when the Prince of Peace is with them. If He is not sitting there, look out for another war in future, as the boding owls predict. And in the Pacific Ocean too—mark the name—you cannot have peace without Mercy. Justice must indeed be dealt out to the sneaks and gangsters, to the gangsters of the islands and of Central and Southern Europe, of South Eastern Europe also. But there must be mercy too for the countless numbers of Central Europeans who had as little to do with putting in power the gang that came to rule them as half or more of the college men in America had to do with putting the well-meaning gang a dozen years ago into power at Washington. You can't do business with men, or rather beasts, like Hitler. But you can do business with Mercy, Grace, and Truth. And with them you can have Peace.

Grace, peace, and truth, were given to the world, but they are not characteristic of the world. By the world I mean the world of men alive at any time, the people now living in the flesh. For the history of the word consult the Dictionary—the Oxford English Dictionary, best of all such books. If you want to know what the thoughtless, thankless world is like, read the New Testament. No doubt you recall the other two parties the world, men say, habitually trots about with; you recall the triad, so shy even of the three pagan Graces, the triad of the World, the Flesh, and the Devil.

The best Commencement address I ever heard was given years ago at a little college in New Jersey by a clergyman who had looked up with a concordance all the references there are in the New Testament to the World. The gist of his address was a collection of choice passages from the Sacred Book, a lively set of uncomplimentary passages about the World. He read the passages aloud, in full, effectively. Then he said to the members of the graduating class: 'Young men, that is what you now are going into.' But to-day I say to all young men and women who are ready for the business: Go out with Grace and Truth, and make a better world of it.—Why? See John 3.16 (and compare 1.10): 'He was in the world, and the world was made by him; . . . for God so loved the world, that he gave his only begotten Son, that whosoever believeth in him should not perish, but have everlasting life.'

Index of Personal Names

Abba Thule, 42-6
Achilles, 118, 208
Adam, 218
Adam, James, 153
Adams, Helen Banks, 5
Adams, J. Q., Jr., viii, 5-12, 193
Adams, J. Q., Sr., 5
Adams, Mamie F. D., 5
Addison, 2, 40-1
Æschylus, 111, 115, 130, 164-5
Agard, 159, 162
Aldus, 165-6
Alexamenos, 161
Alexander, 162
Alfred, 19, 135, 193-4
Almain, 36
Alvarez, 61
Amiel, 144
Andersen, 160
Angot, 49-50
Aphrodite, 164
Apollo, 165
Apollos, 189
Aquinas, 146
Arbuthnot, 25-6, 28-9, 31-3, 35, 39, 40
Ares, 164
Argyle, 38, 40
Ariosto, 109
Aristogiton, 117, 118, 119
Aristophanes, 130-1, 133, 156-7
Aristotle, 2, 101, 126, 130, 139-42, 149, 153-4, 156-7, 159, 164, 175, 189-90, 195
Armstrong, 69
Arnold, M., 2, 177
Arnold, R. E., 162
Ashe, 72
Ashmole, 144
Ast, 176
Astyanax, 127

Attila, 215
Augustine, 17, 142, 144
Autenrieth, 72

Babbitt, 151
Bacon, 2, 74, 140, 190, 194
Bailey, C., 150
Bailey, N., 22-3
Bakewell, 126
Baldwin, 215
Bartram, 42, 46, 60
Bede, 19, 193
Bedford, 183
Beethoven, 129
Bell, J., 74, 76
Bell, Peter, 93-4
Benn, 154
Bentley, 6
Beowulf, 172
Bernard, 147
Bernhardy, 178
Berni, 129, 132-3
Bevier, 198
Biedermann, von, 149
Binet, 67, 75
Blaine, 144
Blumenbach, 70, 72
Boccaccio, 2, 123
Boddy, 20-3
Boeckh, 175-9
Boehme, 160
Boethius, 19, 135-8, 152, 154, 159
Boswell, 20, 23-4, 35-9, 41
Bowles, 42-4, 52, 89
Bowser, 198
Bowyer, *see* Boyer
Boyer, 16, 103
Brandes, 47, 50
Brandl, 8